LEST WE FORGET

Cover Photos

Front Cover—top: The National Life and Accident Insurance Company's new home office, dedicated February 19, 1924. The building in the background was the Young Men's Hebrew Association (YMHA) building, also dedicated in 1924. bottom left: The scoreboard at Sulphur Dell, the longtime home of the Nashville Vols. The photo, by Bob Grannis, was taken April 5, 1953, during an exhibition game between the Brooklyn Dodgers and the Milwaukee Braves. The Dodgers won 3–1. bottom right: The crowd assembled for the dedication of the Life & Casualty Tower at the southwest corner of Church Street and Fourth Avenue North in 1956. The photograph is courtesy of the Kermit C. Stengel Jr. Estate.

Back Cover—top: This photo taken circa 1954 by Bob Grannis shows, from left to right, the edge of the Maxwell House Hotel, on the northwest corner of Church Street and Fourth Avenue North; the Noel Hotel, on the northeast corner of Church Street and Fourth Avenue North; the Third National Bank building, on the southeast corner of the same street; and the excavation for the Life & Casualty Tower on the southwest corner of Church and Fourth Avenue North. bottom: This photo from the early 1980s shows, from left to right: J. C. Bradford Jr., senior partner of J. C. Bradford & Company; Luke Simons, managing partner; and Norris Nielsen, partner. They are standing in the company headquarters which were located at the southeast corner of Church Street and Fourth Avenue North. Photo courtesy of Mrs. James C. Bradford Jr.

LEST WE FORGET

Nashville's Lost Businesses and Their Stories

Ridley Wills II

Printed in the United States of America

17 16 15 14 13 1 2 3 4 5

Library of Congress Control Number: 2013941758

ISBN: 978-1-937824-12-9

Cover design by Joey McNair @ DefyCreative
Page design by Holly Jones

Every effort has been made to make the information presented here as complete and accurate as possible. Should readers discover errors or omissions, please notify the publisher so that corrections may be made in subsequent editions.

PLUMBLINE MEDIA, LLC
415 BRIDGE STREET
FRANKLIN, TENNESSEE 37064

This book is dedicated to my father, Jesse Ely Wills, who excelled as a Fugitive poet, an iris hybridizer, a horticulturist, a life insurance executive, a Bible student, an ornithologist, and a scholar particularly interested in American Indians and modern warships. Endowed with great ability and blessed with material success, he nevertheless always remained a gentle, unassuming person whom I've tried to emulate.

CONTENTS

Foreword

The freedom born of the United States was bred into its people and gave to them both energy and optimism. So endowed, the people undertook enterprises. Dozens of them, millions of them. As elsewhere to be sure, but surely in Nashville, did they bubble up. Born in hope, many, although not all, flourished. The businesses were nurtured by their founders and their families, and they, in turn, nurtured the towns. The successful companies provided the productive plenty and wealth that underlie the republic. This fundamental is often overlooked in our conventional histories.

Our local irreplaceable treasure Ridley Wills II has examined this phenomenon. He has reached back and plucked more than 220 companies that he has crystalized and preserved. As Ridley has done before in other venues, he has put together this valuable and unique collection for posterity. It is indispensable to an understanding of how Nashville came to be and continues to become.

We use the French word *entrepreneur* because its English equivalent *undertaker* has an entirely different and contradictory meaning in our vocabulary. There was, however, in Nashville one man who was both. Zema Hill, he of the polar bears at Twelfth and Edgehill. (Older Nashvillians will remember that Hill owned the polar bear statues that stood in front of his funeral home on South Street.) His fame as a funeral director was partially deserved by his memorable and irrefutable slogan, "Why walk around half dead when I can bury you for twenty-five dollars?"

For mnemonic purpose I have reduced some iconic enterprises of my lifetime to pairs.

Harveys/Cain-Sloan (department stores)
Banner/Tennessean (newspapers)
First/Third (banks)
Paramount/Loews (movie theaters)
Bennie Dillon/Doctors (medical buildings)
Wallace/Duncan (prep schools)
May Hosiery/Werthan Bag (industries)
Nashville, Chattanooga & St. Louis/Louisville & Nashville (railroads)
Cross Keys/Satsuma (restaurants)
Zibarts/Mills (bookstores)
Litton/West (high schools)
National Life/Life and Casualty (insurance companies)

These dyads among many seemed as permanent and immutable as the limestone upon which Rock City stands. Yet it is not so. I am old but life is short. In that short span all of the above have altered; most have disappeared. Their existence proved as evanescent as the morning mist on our soft surrounding hills or the once-dirty smog surrounding Union Station.

Thus it is fitting that we have gratitude to Ridley (who else) for his prodigious knowledge and careful scholarship. His practiced reportage has brought another gift to Nashville. Enjoy as he reaches back, chooses, captures, and crystalizes long-ago happenings. He makes them fresh. Without these memories it is not possible to appreciate today.

This is more than a reference book. It is a delight.

Joseph L. "Jack" May
Former CEO of May Hosiery Mills

Preface

In December 2011, my latest book, *Nashville Streets and Their Stories*, reached Nashville area bookstores. Despite missing nearly all of the pre-Christmas buying period, book sales were strong over the balance of the holidays, and after two or three months, I realized that many Nashvillians in all parts of town and all walks of life were enjoying the book. That gave me the incentive to write a comparable book on another aspect of Nashville's rich history.

A friend, Andy Miller, who has published more of my books than anyone else, suggested that I write about Nashville businesses that, while once here, are now gone. I thought that made sense and started working on the book in April 2012. The first abbreviated history I wrote was of the National Life and Accident Insurance Company, where my grandfather, father, and I collectively worked for over one hundred years. Remembering Nashville restaurants that I once enjoyed, I decided to write about some of them, drawing on my memories, the memories of others, and whatever material I could find in the State Library and Archives and the Metro Archives.

By August, I had written summaries of the histories of more than 220 Nashville businesses, from Becker's Bakery to Zanini's Restaurant. Doing so was great fun, particularly when I wrote about companies once managed by friends of mine or by families I know. In many of those cases, I asked for the input of former owners, presidents, or people associated with the companies and, after writing the histories, shared with them the drafts so that they could make final suggestions and corrections. Because members of my family and my wife's family have lived, worked, and shopped in Nashville for generations, I often mentioned their relationships with various business with which they were involved.

I realize that not long after this book hits the stores, friends will ask me, "Ridley, why didn't you write about my family's business?" or "Ridley, if I'd known that you were going to write about automobile dealers, I could have helped you." That is absolutely true, but the reality is that, even if I wrote about six hundred companies, I would have still left out many more that, in retrospect, I would have enjoyed researching and memorializing.

In addition to preserving the histories of these Nashville companies, I am including photographs of many of these companies that readers will never have seen. If you enjoy this book as much as I have enjoyed learning and writing about companies as varied as dime stores and race courses, I will feel good about having written *Lest We Forget: Nashville's Lost Businesses and Their Stories*.

Ridley Wills II
October 30, 2012

Acknowledgments

I am indebted to the following people who helped me, none more than William H. "Bill" Cammack, who wrote more of the history of Equitable Securities than I did.

Melville M. "Mel" Barnes Jr.
Robert E. Baulch Jr.
Roger Blackwood
Dennis C. Bottorff
Lillian "Tootie" (Mrs. J. C. Jr.) Bradford
Seawell J. Brandau
L. P. "Bill" Brittain
Marvin R. Bubis
Carolyn Weesner Callighan
William H. "Bill" Cammack
Bill Carey
Fred Cassetty
Picksley Cheek
James H. Cheek III
Robert L. "Bob" Chickey
Paul Clements
George H. Cole
Thomas W. "Wick" Comer
Charles W. Cook Jr.
Robert "Rob" Crichton
Annie Herbert (Mrs. Eslick) Daniel
Charlie Daugherty
Karen Davis
W. Lipscomb Davis Jr.
Matt H. Dobson IV
Harvill C. Eaton
Alfred C. Farris III
Carney (Mrs. Alfred C. III) Farris
Jean Dobson Farris
Ken Fieth
Ben S. Gambill Jr.
Leanne Garland
Robert "Bob" Gordon
Leila Grossman
Roupen Gulbenk
Ray Harness
Robert E. Harwell Jr.
L. O. "Buzz" Heidtke Jr.
Sam B. Herbert
Dottie (Mrs. George) Hetzel
Stanley E. Hime
Edwin Lee Holt
Ellen (Mrs. Thomas M.) Hudson
Thomas M. Hudson Jr.

Betty Jo Patten Jones
Lucy Keeble
Peter Keeble
Christine Kreyling
Fred W. "Ted" Lazenby
Chloe Fort Lenderman
Jean (Mrs. James R. III) Love
Thomas H. "Tom" Loventhal
Joe Marchetti
Joseph L. "Jack" May
Robert E. McAdams
Robert S. McAdams
Patricia McDonald
Robert E. McNeilly Jr.
Anita Corsini Monohan
Carol (Mrs. Edward G.) Nelson
Edward G. Nelson
Henry Neuhoff
Betty Chiles Nixon
Beth Odle
Jack A. Oman
John A. Oman Jr.
Frank Orr
Ophelia (Mrs. George) Paine
James W. Perkins Jr.
Richard "Dick" Philpot
James R. "Jimmy" Pickel Jr.
Dave Price
Harry Howe Ransom
Jim Reed IV
Dean (Mrs. Robert) Reeves
Ann Byrn (Mrs. Jack) Roberts
Kenneth L. Roberts
Elizabeth Moore Rodgers
John Alden Rodgers
Luke Simons
Daniel Smith
E. Gray Smith Jr.
Gayle (Mrs. Alden H. Jr.) Smith
Gary Smith
Jeanne (Mrs. Bob Dudley) Smith
Anderson Spickard Jr.
Betty (Mrs. James R.) Stadler
James R. "Jim" Stadler
Mark K. Stengel
Lemuel B. Stevens Jr.
Ogden Stokes
Whit Stokes
Bolin (Mrs. Lawrence B. Jr.) Stumb
Lawrence B. Stumb Jr.
Mary (Mrs. Paul R.) Stumb
Paul R. Stumb
Lee Ann Thornton
Tom Vickstrom
Lattie (Mrs. Hamilton) Wallace
Ann (Mrs. Fred) Webber
Meg Weesner
Ann (Mrs. Charles E.) Wells
Bernard Werthan Jr.
Dudley (Mrs. John) White
Linda T. Wynn
John "Jack" Zuccarello Jr.

Thanks also to my publisher Andrew Miller at Plumbline Media; Tammy Spurlock for her usual thoroughness in editing; Joey McNair at DefyCreative for his excellent cover design; and Holly Jones for keeping the project moving in her usual competent manner.

LEST WE FORGET

AIRLINES

CAPITOL AIRWAYS was a charter airline founded by former Army Air Corps pilots Richmond McGinnis, Francis Roach, and Nashvillian Jesse Stallings soon after World War II. Capitol Airways was active in the eastern United States and Europe. It had hubs at John F. Kennedy International Airport in New York City; Brussels, Belgium; and San Juan, Puerto Rico. The company was incorporated in Delaware but had its headquarters in Smyrna, Tennessee.

In June 1963, Capitol Airways received a $6,376,273.44 contract from the US Air Force for air transport of freight and passengers for Log Air Operations within the continental United States. An earlier contract of $4.211 million was for movement of troops and supplies overseas. That brought to more than $10.5 million the amount of government contracts Capitol had received that year.

The Capitol Airways fleet was primarily composed of McDonald Douglas DC-8 jets until about 1980, when Capitol supplemented its fleet with DC-10s. In the early 1980s, one of Capitol's DC-8s was hijacked and diverted to Cuba.

In the mid-1980s, new owner George Bachelor (who also owned International Air Leases in Miami) dismantled Capitol Airways to supply planes to his new venture, Arrow Air, another charter airline that was converting to become a scheduled airline. As a result, Capitol Airways declared bankruptcy.

AIRPORTS

CORNELIA FORT AIRPARK was a private airport on Airpark Drive built after the death of Cornelia Fort (1919–43), for whom it was named. She had grown up at Fortland, the home of her parents, Dr. and Mrs. Rufus E. Fort, on nearby Riverside Drive. After graduating from Sarah Lawrence College, she learned to fly and became Nashville's first female flying instructor. She was in the air over Pearl Harbor, giving flying instructions when the Japanese made their surprise attack on December 7, 1941. In 1942, Fort voluntarily joined the Army's WAFS (Women's Auxiliary Ferrying Squadron). On March 21, 1943, she was ferrying a BT-13 from Long Beach, California, to Love Field in Dallas, Texas, when an accidental collision with another plane caused her to crash near Merkel, Texas. Cornelia Fort became the first American woman in US history to die while in military service.

Cornelia Fort Airpark was on Cumberland River bottomland purchased from J. B. Henderson, president of the Southwestern Company, whose 508-acre farm, Wild Acres, was on the west side of the river. Sometime after World War II, Henderson leased half his farm to Bill Miller and Bill Coleman, each of whom had a flying service. After ten years, Henderson, also a pilot, sold them the 254 acres. The airport was used for many years by private planes, charter services, and as a servicing center for small planes, some from as far away as South America. After the flood in May 2010 destroyed many of the planes and inundated buildings, the property was sold to the Land Trust For Tennessee, who put a conservation easement on the land and, in 2011, deeded the property to the City of Nashville Park Board to be incorporated into Shelby Bottoms.

HAMPTON FIELD was the first flying field in Nashville. It was a two-thousand-foot grass strip that ran east to west in a pasture owned by E. L. Hampton along present-day Hampton Avenue. Transient airplanes, mostly Jennies or DH-4s, first began landing there in 1915 or 1916.

One day, a barnstormer in an open-cockpit plane landed on the grass strip that soon became Hampton Field. He offered to take two teenage girls on a fifteen-minute ride for fifteen dollars. Marie Kuhn accepted the offer. After her flight, she was so excited she encouraged her friend, fifteen-year-old Ellen Stokes, to do the same. Ellen didn't have fifteen dollars, but the pilot told her she could pay him later. After Marie agreed to watch Ellen's dog, "Hell," Ellen climbed aboard. An old country man, looking on, said, "She shore do look scared." Ellen heard him and said, "She shore is scared!" The pilot flew Ellen over her home, Breezemont, less than a mile away, and then as far east as the State Fairgrounds, where he circled the race track before returning to the landing strip. Hampton Field was abandoned in 1921 when Blackwood Field opened.

AMUSEMENT COMPANIES

Crescent Amusement Company was formed in 1911 by Henry Sudekum; his son, Tony Sudekum; and Wiley J. Williams. The company had its beginnings upstairs in the Dixie Theater building on Fifth Avenue North. The company grew quickly and soon began buying other Nashville theaters. Tony Sudekum became head of the company in 1916, leaving his father to run their bakery business.

The company's first theater outside Nashville was in Murfreesboro. At it's zenith, Crescent owned twenty-one theaters in Tennessee, Kentucky, and Alabama. The Tennessee theaters stretched all the way from Union City to Kingsport. The total included three drive-in theaters: Crescent Drive-In on Murfreesboro Road at Thompson Lane, Skyway Drive-In on Dickerson Road, and Bordeaux Drive-In in Bordeaux.

In 1929 Crescent Amusement Company owned and operated the Alhambra, Elite, Fifth Avenue, Knickerbocker, Orpheum, Rex, and Strand theaters in town. At that time, Tony Sudekum was president; R. T. Wilson was vice president; and Harry Sudekum was secretary. Their offices were at 531–33 Church Street.

After Tony Sudekum's death in 1946, Robert E. Baulch became president. Crescent Amusement Company sold all its Davidson County theaters to the Martin Theater chain in 1960.

AMUSEMENT PARKS

Opryland USA was WSM Incorporated's entertainment-recreational complex designed to surround the new home of the Grand Ole Opry. WSM was an affiliate of NLT Corporation, a holding company that also owned the National Life and Accident Insurance Company and NLT Computer Services. The theme park, connected to both I-65 and I-40 by the soon-to-be-completed Briley Parkway, was located on four hundred acres of gently rolling land in Pennington Bend, six miles from downtown Nashville.

With the help of two mules and a plow, ground was broken on June 30, 1970, on Opryland USA. Presiding over the ceremonies were Irving Waugh, president of WSM Inc.; G. Daniel Brooks, chairman of the board of National Life and WSM; and William C. Weaver Jr., president of National Life. The theme park opened on June 30, 1972, two years before the new Grand Ole Opry House opened next door. Called the "Home of American Music," Opryland featured a large number of musical shows, usually performed in the Showboat Theater. The most popular show, "I Hear America Singing," was staged like a Broadway musical and was the launching pad for numerous professional entertainers. The park's overall theme was American music, including country and western, jazz, bluegrass, gospel, pop, and rock and roll. The major thrill rides at the beginning included the "Rock 'n Roller Coaster" and the "Flume Zoom." Over the next twenty-three years, many new rides were added, including the Wabash Cannonball (1975), Grizzly River Rampage (1982), Screaming Delta Demon (1984), and the Hangman (1995). The park also attracted top country music stars, who performed nightly at the Chevrolet-Geo Celebrity Theater, built in 1992.

In 1982 NLT Corporation was acquired by American General Corporation, a Texas corporation (now a part of A.I.G.). Not interested in a theme park, American General sold the entire complex to Gaylord Broadcasting Company of Oklahoma City that same year. Gaylord also purchased WSM radio station; WSM's cable network, The Nashville Network; and its production affiliate, Opryland Productions. After the acquisition, Gaylord changed its name to Gaylord Entertainment Company.

During the late 1980s, nearly 2.5 million people visited the park annually. This was despite the fact that during the late 1980s and early 1990s, two new theme parks, Kentucky Kingdom and Dollywood, emerged as regional competitors. There were also geographical limitations in that Opryland USA had no room for expansion, and the Cumberland River, bordering the theme park on the west, was a potential flood threat. Because of Nashville's climate, year-round operations were nearly impossible and seasonal workers became increasingly difficult to find.

When attendance flattened in the nineties, Gaylord management made a business decision to close the theme park and convert it into a shopping mall called Opry Mills. The park closed permanently on December 31, 1997. All five roller coasters and many other attractions were sold; the park site was cleared and paved by July 1999. Opry Mills opened on May 12, 2000, under the ownership of the Mills Corporation. Gaylord would focus on its Grand Ole Opry House and its hospitality assets, including the ever-expanding Opryland Hotel.

ARCHITECTURAL FIRMS

Edwin A. Keeble Associates Inc. was established in 1946. When I think of Nashville's most important architects from the past, Edwin A. Keeble, Adolphus Heiman, Henry C. Hibbs, and Moses McKissack quickly come to mind.

The fact that I have been a member of the Monteagle Sunday School Assembly (MSSA) for nearly fifty years influenced me to write about Keeble to represent Nashville architectural firms in this book. When my wife and I purchased our first cottage in the MSSA in the 1970s, we were proud to learn that Edwin Keeble had designed the simple stairway to an upstairs loft. Keeble had been born in Monteagle, Tennessee, in 1905 in the Woodlawn cottage; had enjoyed sharing the Home Again cottage (that his father built in 1913) for forty-two years; and had later owned Morningside, the cottage given him and his wife, Alice, by her father, Peter Beasley, in 1950. Two of the MSSA's best and most-used buildings are the chapel and the dining hall, both of which Keeble designed.

Edwin A. Keeble was from a distinguished Tennessee family. His father, John Bell Keeble, was dean of the Vanderbilt Law School from 1915 until his death in 1929, and his great-grandfather, John Bell, ran for president of the United States in 1860.

Edwin Keeble attended Montgomery Bell Academy and Vanderbilt University, graduating from the latter in 1924 at age nineteen. He studied architecture at the University of Pennsylvania, where he graduated in 1928 at age twenty-three. He also studied architecture in the summer of 1926 at the École des Hautes Études Artistiques at Fontainebleau, France, and the following year under Georges Gromort at the École des Beaux-Arts in Paris.

From 1929 until 1944, Keeble practiced architecture in Nashville with Francis B. Warfield in the firm of Warfield and Keeble. During this time, he designed Westminster Presbyterian Church at 3900 West End Avenue. Completed in 1939, the church has Grecian columns, a non-Gothic tower influenced by Sir Christopher Wren, and a large sanctuary based on the Roman basilican plan.

Keeble designed or designed additions for approximately 150 private homes, including a stunning International style house at 5335 Stanford Drive that he designed in 1936. At the top of the hill, at 5405 Stanford Drive, is the home that Keeble designed for himself. Built in 1936, it is a classical and modern house with portico and columns, a two-story vaulted living room, and beautiful moldings.

After serving two years in the US Navy as a lieutenant, Keeble returned to Nashville in 1946 to establish his own private practice. Almost every day, I drive by Woodmont Christian Church at 3601 Hillsboro Pike, with its slender 220-foot-high steeple, pointing like a finger to heaven. Keeble designed the new building in which the first worship service was held on July 17, 1949. The building's unusually tall steeple was designed to overcome the church's low elevation. Some church officers called it "Keeble's Needle." It is a Nashville landmark. Keeble also designed Vine Street Christian Church at 4101 Harding Road, completed in 1958, and Immanuel Baptist Church at 222 Belle Meade Boulevard. He presented the Immanuel Baptist Church plans in August 1966, two years before the building was completed.

Keeble's most unusual design was that of Memorial Gymnasium at Vanderbilt University, built in 1952. Keeble's charge was to design a building that could be used as a gymnasium, theater, and auditorium. The gymnasium floor was built up above its surroundings so it could serve as a stage as well as a basketball court. The gym was also unusual in that the areas out-of-bounds along the sidelines were very wide. He also placed the benches for the contending teams at each end of the court, confounding

Life and Casualty Tower dedication, 1956.
Collection of Kermit C. Stengel Jr. Estate.

many visiting coaches. Memorial Gymnasium, the home of Vanderbilt's men's and women's basketball teams, originally only held about 8,000 seats. Today, it accommodates 14,316.

Edwin Keeble's crowning achievement came when he designed the thirty-one-story Life and Casualty Tower, when completed in 1956, the tallest building in the Southeastern United States. The first major building erected in Nashville following World War II, this distinctive structure reaffirmed confidence in the city's central business district.

A wonderful feature was the L&C sign on top of the building that was green when weather was forecasted to be fair and red when bad weather was expected. The sign is still there but no longer changes color with the weather. The observation tower on the thirty-first floor provided a spectacular view of the city, the hills surrounding the Nashville basin, and the nearby Cumberland River.

Keeble was proud of the building's solar energy efficiency. He sited the tower so that, in the summer time, no direct sun hits the building between 9:30 a.m. and 5:30 p.m. Another remarkable feature of the skyscraper is the absence of columns from the ninth floor up, substantially increasing office space and revenues.

In 1959, Keeble designed a block-long Veterans Administration Hospital later built at 1310 Twenty-Fourth Avenue South. The massive structure replaced the Veterans Hospital that had been on White Bridge Road since 1946.

One of Keeble's last major projects was to design the First Baptist Church at the southeast corner of Seventh Avenue South and Broadway. Built in 1970, Keeble designed a large, modern sanctuary to hold the congregation's growing numbers. The acoustics are remarkable. As a wonderful reminder of the church's long and rich heritage, Keeble kept the tower from the old church, built in 1887.

Edwin Keeble died in 1979 in Sewanee, Tennessee. He had designed a dormitory at the University of the South and two buildings for Sewanee Military Academy. It seems appropriate that he died within seven miles of where he was born. Keeble's impact on Nashville architecture was huge.

AUTOMOBILE DEALERS

GEORGE COLE MOTOR COMPANY was established by a native of McComb, Mississippi, who had trained as a mechanical engineer and came to Nashville with his wife in about 1913 to open an automobile dealership that sold Fords, Lincolns, Fordson tractors, and farm equipment. (Fordson was a brand name used for a range of mass-produced general-purpose tractors manufactured by the Ford Motor Company.) Cole had experience as an automobile dealer, having earlier owned a Ford dealership in San Antonio, Texas, and, before that, having worked at a Ford assembly plant in Dallas. Cole started his Nashville business in a building on Second Avenue North next door to the Broadway National Bank.

In 1925 the George Cole Motor Company was located at the corner of Ninth Avenue North and Commerce Street. It was one of three authorized Ford dealers in Nashville and offered "24-hour guaranteed service." The company slogan was "We Know We Know Fords."

Cole acquired an automobile dealership in Louisville, Kentucky, and began driving back and forth between the two cities. The Depression hit him and his motor company hard. Cole lost his grip on the company, then located at 117–123 Ninth Avenue North, and it filed for bankruptcy.

In the mid-1930s, Lemuel B. Stevens bought George Cole Motor Company from First American National Bank and became the company's vice president. In 1938, he became president with E. W. Cain as his general manager. In about 1940 Stevens moved the company to the Seventh Avenue Garage, a building he owned at 145 Seventh Avenue North. He kept the used cars department at 1311 and 1404 Broadway.

When George Cole died in 1946, Stevens changed the name of the business to Seventh Avenue Motors. Stevens closed Seventh Avenue Motors in about 1942 and formed Oak Motors at 915 Fifth Avenue North. The new company, an authorized Ford dealership, sold used cars and trucks until the end of World War II, when new models were available. Stevens sold Oak Motors to his general manager, Ernest P. Boyte, in about 1956, at which time Boyte became president. For many years Oak Motors sold company cars to the National Life and Accident Insurance Company, including one I drove in the 1970s.

DORRIS MOTOR CAR COMPANY was owned by Duncan R. Dorris. In 1897 he ran a bicycle, camera, and photographic supply business at 153 North Spruce Street. He advertised his bicycle repair shop as the best in the South. By 1905 Dorris was also selling automobiles. Two years later, he was affiliated with the Nashville Motor Car Company. While he was busy there, W. L. Hix managed his bicycle, camera, and photograph supplies store on Eighth Avenue North.

On October 22, 1907, Duncan Dorris was pleased that a number of his big Stanley Steamer automobiles were in the procession that took President Theodore Roosevelt to visit the Hermitage.

By 1909 the Nashville Motor Car Company had moved to a new brick building at Ninth Avenue and Church Street with its show windows facing Church Street. Dr. Charles Brown was president, Matt S. Pilcher was vice president, and Duncan Dorris was secretary.

That same year, Duncan's brother, George Preston Dorris, founded the Dorris Motor Car Company in St. Louis to produce a car Preston had designed in Duncan's bicycle shop in Nashville in 1897. Called the "Dorris," the car came in several colors and had an initial price of $2,250. Preston sold the car in St. Louis while Duncan sold it in Nashville.

Duncan Dorris had the distinction of being involved in one of Nashville's first traffic accidents. He struck two ladies at the corner of Twelfth and Broadway while going six miles per hour. Neither lady was seriously hurt, and he got a ticket for "fast and reckless driving" that was later dismissed.

From about 1919 until Dorris retired in 1943, he was sales manager of Cumberland Motor Company, dealers in Dodge Brothers Motor Cars and Trucks at 1533 Broadway. Duncan continued to drive until he was ninety-five years old and died in 1972 at the age of one hundred.

DRESSLAR-WHITE COMPANY was an early automobile company located at 201 Woodland Street, where it served the affluent East Nashville area. In 1925 Dresslar-White was one of three Nashville dealers for Ford, advertised as "the universal car." The company's president in 1928 was Otis W. Dresslar. He also sold Fordson tractors and had a service department. Dresslar was still president of the company in 1937. By then, Dresslar-White was a dealer of Chevrolet automobiles and trucks. With the economic decline of East Nashville and the advent of World War II and gasoline rationing, Dresslar-White closed in about 1942.

HIPPODROME MOTOR COMPANY was founded in 1916 and was located at 1212 Broadway for its long life that lasted ninety-one years. In the beginning, the building was a modest assembly plant owned by Ford Motor Company. There, Ford automobiles had windshields and other accessories added after the cars were unloaded at nearby Union Station. Workers made five dollars a day, far above the standard wage in Nashville. The Chamber of Commerce didn't encourage Ford to stay in Nashville, so the giant motor company sold the building to two brothers and built an automobile plant in Memphis. In the early 1920s, Hippodrome's president was Tony Sudekum, and William D. Narron was the general manager. The dealership, located next to a Western Auto store, sold Fords, Lincolns, and Fordson farm tractors, and was considered one of Nashville's top dealerships.

Robert E. McAdams, who got his start in the automobile business at Ralph Nichols Cadillac-Oldsmobile in 1946, bought Hippodrome Ford in 1953. Over the years he acquired considerable land on both sides of Broadway, putting his used cars lot on the north side of the street and keeping his new car sales on the south side. After Ralph Nichols's death in 1963, Hippodrome Ford acquired the Oldsmobile franchise the next year. By then, Hippodrome was also selling Fords, Falcons, and Thunderbirds, as well as providing a complete service department. For many years, during the 1950s and early 1960s, Hippodrome Ford was the number-one Ford dealership in the United States for service and parts sales.

By the 1960s, McAdams's son, Robert S. McAdams, was in business with his father. The younger McAdams would, in time, become president and his father would become board chairman. In 1970 the company, then known as Hippodrome Olds, added the Datsun franchise, becoming the first Datsun franchise in Middle Tennessee.

The inner loop (I-440) was built in the 1970s. Its construction impacted Hippodrome Olds adversely for two years.

In 1986 Nissan Motor company, which had owned the Datsun Motor Car Company since 1933, phased out the Datsun brand. Consequently, the next year, Hippodrome was selling Nissans instead of Datsuns, along with Oldsmobiles. Hippodrome Olds-Nissan won the President's Cup Award for excellence in sales and service as measured by the Customer Sales Index (CSI) three times.

In 2004, General Motors dropped its Oldsmobile line and the company became Hippodrome Nissan Inc. Four years later, the McAdams family sold their dealership, but not the name, to an automobile dealer from Florida named Terry Taylor. It had been a good run.

JIM REED CHEVROLET COMPANY INC. was an automobile dealership started by Jim Reed Jr. in 1930, the first full year of the Depression, and the year after Ford introduced Reed's biggest competitor, the Model A. The first few years, Reed only had a couple of models to sell. He could offer his customers a two-door or a four-door Chevrolet in a standard or deluxe model.

The Jim Reed Chevrolet dealership was located for its entire existence at 1512 Broadway. Three generations of the Reed family owned and operated the dealership: Jim Reed Jr., Jim Reed III, and Jim Reed IV. Jim Reed III joined the dealership in 1946 following his discharge from the US Air Force. When Jim Reed Jr. and Jim Reed III were running the dealership, customers, who knew them well, called Jim Reed Jr. "Old Jim" and Jim Reed III "Young Jim."

In 1952 a motor tune-up cost $5.10 and a front-end alignment cost $6.10. When Jim Reed Jr. retired in 1959, Jim Reed III was named president and general manager.

Jim Reed Chevrolet continued to grow and expand. In 1967 Jim Reed III was the winner of *Time* magazine's prestigious Quality Dealer Award, given annually in recognition of exceptional dealership performance and distinguished community service. Jim Reed III served as a member of the General Motors President's Advisory Council and was the first dealer in the United States to receive the Chevrolet Service Supremacy Award. He was also honored that two of his sons, James H. Reed IV and John Clay Reed, joined him in the family business and proud that Jim Reed Chevrolet had so many second-generation customers and employees.

By 1980 the company had established the Jim Reed Chevrolet Truck Center at Fifteenth and Hayes Streets. The dealership later changed its name to Jim Reed Hyundai-Subaru, as it no longer sold Chevrolets. When Jim Reed III died in 2010, he was still chairman of the board although his son, Jim Reed IV, was president. The dealership closed in 2011, purchased by a Bowling Green, Kentucky, group who, in 2012, opened Downtown Nashville Motors in the former Jim Reed Chevrolet facilities.

E. GRAY SMITH MOTOR COMPANY was established in 1923. When he was eighteen years old, E. Gray Smith sold his first car. The year was 1910, and he was still a student at Wallace University School. Smith sold the car to the city's engineering department for $3,000 "without the top and without the windshield."

From 1910 to 1922, Smith handled the Winton line of automobiles. In 1923, after Winton quit manufacturing cars, Smith acquired the prestigious Packard automobile franchise in Nashville.

In 1957 Smith reflected on the early days of automobiles in Nashville. He said, "We had auto shows a lot like the horse shows of today. We showed the cars in a ring at the state fair and at all the surrounding county fairs, too. Each car was graded on three points: the skill of the driver, the looks of the driver, and the car itself. We took special care to pick out a pretty gal who could drive well."

In about 1928 Smith employed Carlton Brush Architects of Nashville to design a handsome building in the 2400 block of West End Avenue, in the middle of an exclusive Nashville residential neighborhood. In addition to the showroom that faced West End, Smith had offices upstairs and a large parts department and a large service area in the back. A second showroom, with large glass windows, faced Elliston Place. It was for used cars. The new dealership's grand opening was on September 2, 1929. For the next two and one-half decades, Smith sold Packards from this location to many, perhaps most, of Nashville's wealthiest people.

E. Gray Smith Motor Company moved out of its 2400 West End Avenue building early in 1956 when Rich, Schwartz & Joseph relocated there. In October 1955 Smith said he would open a new Packard agency, but that he would not announce his plans at that time. Instead, he closed his Packard dealership in 1956 and became Nashville's Rolls Royce and Bentley dealer, with his showroom and service department on Broadway. After being in the business for sixty-nine years, the E. Gray Smith business closed in 1979.

After serving multiple uses, including that of a record store, the E. Gray Smith building on West End was torn down in 2012 to make way for a seven-story Homewood Suites hotel.

E. Gray Smith Motor Company showroom in 1939, showing Packard convertibles, coupes, and sedans.
Collection of E. Gray Smith Jr.

Russell Willis Inc. began when Willis got his start in the automobile business by opening a small car lot on Third Avenue. In the late 1930s, he moved to the old Waldorf Garage at 519 Broadway, which had a capacity of 250 cars and where, in 1948, he carried in stock an average of two hundred vehicles of all makes and models of automobiles, trucks, and tractors. Under Bill Willis's direct management, his retail and wholesale business grew to annual sales of about 5,000 cars. In February 1948 Russell Willis Inc. sold 400 automobiles.

Part of Willis's marketing strategy was to advertise on radio stations WSM, WLAC, and WSIX, as well as in both daily local newspapers. His advertising budget in 1948 often ran as high as five thousand dollars a month. Willis was assisted in his business by his wife, Margaret Willock Willis, who was secretary and treasurer of Russell Willis Inc.

In 1949 Russell Willis described his firm as the South's largest automobile dealer. The business sold all makes of new and used automobiles, including Fords, Chevrolets, Cadillacs, Pontiacs, and Buicks. By 1954, Capitol Chevrolet had acquired Russell Willis's Broadway property for its used cars operation. Russell Willis was then selling used cars at the corner of Lafayette Street and Sixth Avenue South. He retired around 1956.

AUTOMOBILE MANUFACTURERS

Marathon Motor Works began in 1910, when Nashville capitalists, headed by A. H. Robinson, vice president of both the American National Bank and the Belmont Land Company, acquired controlling interest in the Southern Motor Works of Jackson, Tennessee, a company that was founded in 1907. The Nashvillians moved the automobile manufacturing company to the corner of Clinton Street and Twelfth Avenue North and changed its name to Marathon Motor Works.

In a plant, built in 1881 for the Nashville Cotton Mills (that still stands), the company produced Marathon touring cars in four models from 1911 until 1914. The cars had either four or six cylinders, and thirty to thirty-five horsepower engines.

Marathon Motor Works closed its manufacturing operation in 1914 due to financial difficulties but continued to operate a parts and service business until 1918. In 1912 and 1913, A. H. Robinson was president of the company. He was succeeded by G. W. Killebrew, who became president in about 1914.

In 1991 Barry L. Walker converted the complex that had been Marathon Motor Works into studio space for artists and set up his commercial furniture business in the old administration building. Walker, who owned a 1911 Marathon automobile, spent the next few years looking for the nine remaining Marathons he thought existed. When asked why Marathon Motor Works failed, he said, "The company was ahead of its time as most people still depended on horses in the 1907–1914 period." It was also felt that the company made too many models.

BAKERS

AMERICAN BREAD COMPANY was founded by C. K. Evers in 1899. Located at 619–621 Church Street, the bakery advertised, in October 1899, "We ship bread to merchants in nearly every town within three hundred miles of Nashville." Later, the American Bread Company moved to a building on Fourth Avenue North. The company's final move came in 1951 when it moved to 702 Murfreesboro Road, where the Evers built a $1 million state-of-the-art bakery, capable of producing two hundred thousand units daily. In Nashville supermarkets, American Bread's Sunbeam and Roman Meal breads were well known and appreciated staples.

In 1981, American Bread Company, under the guidance of president Bernard Evers Jr., was baking seven thousand pounds of bread, twenty-five hundred pounds of buns and rolls, and eight hundred pounds of donuts an hour at its Murfreesboro Road plant, and only slightly lesser amounts at its Huntsville, Alabama, plant.

In 1993 the Evers family, realizing that their forty-two-year-old plant was no longer efficient, sold American Bread to Mobile, Alabama–based CooperSmith. Jimmy Phillips, American's vice president of industrial relations, explained the rationale for the sale. He said, "Rather than shut it down we sought a buyer who will maintain our business and provide as many jobs as possible for our employees."

CooperSmith didn't keep the bakery long. In 1994 their management reached a tentative agreement to sell the bakery to Lewis Brothers Bakers of Evansville, Indiana. At the time, CooperSmith was in the midst of negotiating with the Bakery, Confectionary and Tobacco Workers local union #128 on a three-year contract. The union representatives were shocked to learn about the sale. On October 27, 1994 the news got worse. The plant's 284 workers learned that the baker's new owners, Lewis Brothers Bakers, would shut down the bakery and consolidate bread-baking at its Murfreesboro bakery around December 30. The only symbol of American Bread left would be the Sunbeam and Roman Meal breads that Lewis Brothers would continue to sell.

Becker's Bakery opened in 1925 and served the Nashville community for seventy-nine years. In 1932 its formal name was George Becker Modern Bakeries Inc. Generations of Nashville ladies depended on Becker's Bakery for wedding and birthday cakes. When Granbery Jackson III was a little boy in the 1950s, he insisted that all his birthday cakes come from Becker's. This was despite the fact that his mother was an excellent cook who made wonderful cakes. Each Easter, Mrs. Jackson and many of her friends with small children would order from Becker's one of their delicious Easter-egg cakes. Granbery's older sister, Irene, remembers sitting in the back of Becker's watching cakes being decorated. Each time she or her brother came in the store, "Miss Mary" would give them a taste of cake. Located at 2600 Twelfth Avenue South, the Nashville institution closed in 2004.

The Becker's Bakery at 2543 Lebanon Road is a different company. It is owned by cousins of the owners of the Twelfth Avenue South Becker's Bakery.

BANKS

Bank of the United States established a branch in Nashville in 1827. On December 1, 1826, Tennessee Governor William Carroll wrote Nicholas Biddle, president of the Bank of the United States, asking that his firm establish a branch bank in Nashville because of the "incompetence of the state banks to pay specie and at the same time afford the facilities necessary to the trade and business of the country." Ninety-four prominent Nashville citizens followed up by sending a petition to Biddle requesting the same thing.

The letter from Governor Carroll and the petition had the desired effect, and the branch of the Bank of the United States was established in August 1827. It was initially located in a brick building on the northwest corner of the public square and College Street. Josiah Nichol (a friend of Andrew Jackson) and John Somerville were elected president and cashier, respectively.

Despite the fact that among the directors of the Nashville bank were "some of Jackson's oldest and well-tried friends," he remained adamantly opposed to the Bank of the United States and, in 1832, vetoed a bill to recharter it.

On June 17, 1835, the Bank of the United States in Philadelphia ordered the branch bank at Nashville to collect its old debts by the fourth of March 1836, and close its new business within six months from November 1, 1835, in order to enable the office to be closed by May 1, 1936. The Nashville branch stopped accepting new business on January 4, 1836, and closed soon thereafter.

COMMERCE UNION BANK was established by Edward "Ed" Potter Jr. When he was twenty years old, he talked to his father, A. E. Potter, about his prospects at his father's Broadway National Bank, where Ed had worked since 1913. Realizing that he would have to wait his turn there because Broadway National had its share of older officers, the ambitious young man decided to start his own bank.

At a meeting on May 11, 1916, it was announced that the bank charter had been filed with Tennessee's secretary of state. Edward's intent was to attract as customers the growing number of good, solid German-Americans who had prospered in North Nashville. The German-American Bank first opened its doors on July 3, 1916, in rented space at 312 Third Avenue North, with a capital of fifty thousand dollars. The first president was A. E. Potter, then president of Broadway National Bank. Everyone knew, however, that Edward Potter Jr., officially the cashier, was running the bank.

After the United States entered the Great War in April 1917, anything in Nashville labeled "German" was suspect. Accordingly, in November 1917, the bank's stockholders changed its name to Farmers & Merchants Bank.

By December 31, 1920, the bank's deposits were $1,110,000 and its loans amounted to $1,112,000. Because national banks could not have branches outside their own counties, Ed Potter Jr., the driving force at the bank for its first fifty years, made the first of many daring moves. He got his stockholders to approve establishing a holding company, making agreements with five Middle Tennessee banks under which control of those banks would go to individuals who were friends of Farmers & Merchants Bank. The "affiliate" banking relationship kept the stockholders in the five towns, and the officers of the same banks were retained. The national banks reacted by organizing holding companies, which were state-chartered institutions and which were empowered by their charters to purchase stock in banks in various counties.

The name changed to Commerce Union Bank in 1923. By 1925 Potter, who then had the title first vice president, had taken advantage of this breakthrough by acquiring branch banks in nine Middle Tennessee towns, as well as the Camden Bank in West Tennessee. By then, his father's bank was the Broadway branch of Commerce Union.

The opposition to branch banking in the early 1920s was fierce, as country banks were fearful of being bought by a city bank or of a city bank establishing a branch in their towns. They pressured the Tennessee State Legislature to prohibit a bank from establishing a branch in a county other than the one in which the bank's head office was located.

The law was not retroactive, so Potter had a leg up on the competition. He also had made some enemies. Until the anti-branch law was passed in 1925, some country bankers dreaded the idea of Commerce Union invading their territory. The heads of the largest banks in Nashville also didn't like thirty-year-old Ed Potter Jr. either, finding him brash, "too venturesome," and an "upstart."

During the 1920s, Commerce Union continued to increase its capital. In 1930, when A. E. Potter died, Edward Potter Jr. officially became president of the bank. In 1932, there were only six banks in town. Commerce Union, combined with Broadway, stood third with combined capital of $1.1 million behind American National and Nashville and American Trust Company. Progressive Commerce Union was the first bank in Nashville to establish a separate department for financing automobiles. Two years later, in 1938, Commerce Union became the first Nashville bank to establish a consumer loan department to help customers buy expensive appliances. By this time, Commerce Union needed a larger main banking building. Consequently, the bank bought the Nichol Building constructed in 1923 on the corner of Fourth and Union.

During World War II, Commerce Union had a contract with the US Army to pay soldiers who were on maneuvers in Middle Tennessee. One day, bank couriers, under armed army escorts, carried over $3 million to the Lebanon branch to pay soldiers. After the war, Commerce Union was the first Nashville bank to raise its savings deposits interest rate to 2 percent. Commerce Union was also the first Tennessee bank to issue a credit card. It was called "Supercard."

The 1950s saw Commerce Union dealing with overcrowding, parking, and traffic problems at its various branches. In 1955 the bank increased its interest rate on savings accounts from 2 percent to 2.5 percent. On January 1, 1957, the bank bumped the rate again, this time to 3 percent. The decade ended with Commerce Union being the largest state bank in Tennessee, with deposits of $116,640,000.

Having suffered a stroke in May 1960, Ed Potter Jr. asked his board not to reelect him president of the company in 1961. The board concurred and elected thirty-five-year-old William F. "Bill" Earthman as president, effective January 1, 1961. Potter remained chairman of the board, despite having to have a nurse accompany him to work.

Bill Earthman had been with the bank eight years and had demonstrated executive ability both as a branch manager and as the vice president of the main office. His first big accomplishment was to merge Broadway National Bank with Commerce Union. This took place on May 2, 1962.

The bank continued to grow. On January 1, 1965, with deposits of $229,882,000, Commerce Union was still the largest state bank in Tennessee, and 188th in size in the country. The same year, Commerce Union became the first Nashville bank to install automatic teller machines.

Edward G. "Ed" Nelson, president of Commerce Union from 1974 until 1981, succeeded Bill Earthman as chairman and chief executive officer and served in that capacity until year-end 1984, when he resigned to become chairman of Nelson Capital Corporation, a diversified merchant banking firm.

Dennis C. Bottorff, who had been with Commerce Union since 1968, was named bank president in 1981. When Nelson resigned, Bottorff followed him as chairman of the board. The stockholders of Commerce

Union realized substantial rewards between 1985 and the 1987 merger with Sovran, with the stock increasing from $123 million to over $705 million in value. When the merger materialized, Bottorff was elected president of Sovran and continued in that position when Sovran merged with C&S Bank of Atlanta to create C&S/Sovran, the nation's fifth largest bank.

First American National Bank was preceded by the American National Bank, that first opened its doors on September 1, 1883. The bank had capital of $600,000 and deposits of $369,240.88. E. W. Cole was president. In February 1884 American National merged with the old Third National Bank. This increased the capital to $1 million. By 1910, deposits had grown to $4,292,405.

On October 4, 1918, a group led by P. D. Houston Sr. and Paul M. Davis purchased control of the bank; they became president and vice president, respectively. By 1920, the bank moved to the first floor of the Stahlman Building, then Nashville's largest office building, and soon acquired the Cumberland Valley National Bank. Branch offices were established on Broadway and Church Streets in 1924. Three years later, Houston became chairman of the board and Davis became president.

After the stock market crash in the fall of 1929, Caldwell & Company began to have problems. When it failed a year or so later, the public thought that its demise might cause the Fourth & First National Bank, headed by Rogers Caldwell's father, James E. Caldwell, to go down as well. Customers were already withdrawing funds from the bank.

Eugene R. Black, governor of the Federal Reserve Bank in Atlanta, asked Paul Davis, president of the American National Bank, if his bank could take over the Fourth & First. Although Fourth & First was a little larger than American National, American took over Fourth & First and made it a branch, stopping the run. As a result, American National suffered losses of $5 million. It was worth it, however, as, had not American National taken such bold action, more banks in Middle Tennessee would have failed.

When P. D. Houston was bank chairman, he was the best known banker in Tennessee. Houston retained that position until 1948, when he became honorary chairman of the board, with Paul M. Davis becoming

Run on the Fourth National Bank on College Street, August 10, 1893.
Collection of Ridley Wills II.

board chairman, and Parkes Armistead being elected president. Two years later, the bank changed its name to the First American National Bank. The next two presidents were P. D. Houston Jr., in 1957, and Andrew Benedict Jr., in 1960.

In 1969 the stockholders approved a plan to form a one-bank holding company, First American National Corporation. That year, First American, under Benedict's leadership, was the nation's 105th largest bank, with twenty-two offices in Davidson County. The bank also had the distinction of becoming the first bank in Davidson County to report total resources in excess of half a billion dollars. Andrew Benedict Jr. was elected board chairman on August 1, 1969, with T. Scott Fillebrown succeeding him as president.

In 1973, under the watch of Benedict and Fillebrown, the amber-colored twenty-eight-story First American Center was completed with open spaces for plantings, walkways, and fountains. The building occupied an entire city block, bordered by Union Street, Fourth Avenue North, Dederick Street, and Third Avenue North.

Kenneth L. Roberts joined First American in 1976 as president and chief executive officer of the bank and the holding company. He held those positions until Benedict retired as chairman in 1979. At that point, Roberts became chief executive officer and chairman of both the bank and First American National Corporation. Benedict remained as senior chairman, a position he would hold with two successor banks, AmSouth and Regions. During the fourteen-year period between 1976 and 1990, the First American National Corporation grew from $1 billion to $10 billion in assets and became the largest bank holding company in the state.

In 1986 Robert E. McNeilly Jr. joined First American National Bank as president. His assignments were to represent the bank in the community and recruit new commercial customers. In 1993 McNeilly moved to the First American Trust Company as president before retiring in 1996.

Ken Roberts was replaced as chief executive officer and chairman in 1990 by Jim Smith, formerly vice chairman. Smith aggressively dealt with the bank's serious credit issues. When Dennis Bottorff arrived in 1991 as chief executive officer of First American National Corporation, Smith returned to Knoxville. Bottorff built on Smith's accomplishments and saw the bank's shareholder value climb dramatically. In 1998, First American acquired Deposit Guaranty Corporation of Jackson, Mississippi. Its integration into First American proved difficult, alienating customers and discouraging employees. After attempting to repair the damage, Bottorff decided that the sale of the bank was the best path to preserve shareholder value. Only AmSouth Bank of Birmingham, Alabama, was seriously interested. It acquired First American National Corporation late in 1999. Bottorff became chairman of AmSouth until his retirement in 2001. In 2006 AmSouth was acquired by Regions Bank.

Freedmen's Savings Bank and Trust Company was chartered by Congress in 1865 to benefit the newly freed black population in the former Confederate States of America. Four of the thirty-three branches were in Tennessee: Nashville (established 1865), Memphis (1865), Chattanooga (1868), and Columbia (1870). The Nashville branch had a primarily black staff. Its directors, some of whom were white, also included these African Americans: Chairman Nelson Walker, a businessman and barber; Frank Parish, a barber; Peter Lowery, a preacher and real estate businessman; Henry Harding, a hotel owner; Richard Harris, a preacher; William C. Napier, a hack operator; Daniel Watkins, a preacher and educator; Benjamin East, a businessman; and Nelson G. Merry, Nashville's first ordained black minister. Black businessman Alfred Menefee became the first cashier upon posting $5,000 bond.

Freedmen's Savings Bank and Trust Company required a very small minimum deposit and paid up to 7 percent interest, extremely helpful to people at the bottom of the economic order. The Nashville branch generated the most capital of all the thirty-three branches. However, a financial recession in 1873–74 and mismanagement by directors forced the Freedmen's Savings Bank and Trust Company to close. Black depositors, including abolitionist Frederick Douglass, who deposited $10,000 in 1874, lost hard-earned and badly needed money and were bitter, often unfairly blaming those local bank leaders who were black. White reaction to the bank failure was largely unsympathetic. The *Memphis Avalanche*, a white newspaper, mocked the dejected blacks, like Henry Harding (a prosperous furniture store owner whose wife had abeen a slave at Belle Meade), who lost thousands of dollars, with the following headline: "Whar's Dat Money." Naturally, Nashville's black population lost confidence in supposedly black-run financial institutions. It would be 1904 before the black-owned One-Cent Savings Bank and Trust Company would open in Nashville.

NASHVILLE BANK & TRUST COMPANY was born on July 6, 1889, when a charter was issued authorizing a group of five Nashvillians to organize a bank that would conduct ordinary banking business and engage in a safe deposit and trust business. Nashville Bank & Trust opened for the first time on September 9, 1889, on the ground floor of the Vanderbilt Building on Cherry Street. The men who obtained the charter were Dr. Walter M. Dake, Herman Justi, Charles Nelson, Joseph Phillips, and Gates P. Thurston. Their original capital was $250,000. The men decided to initially focus entirely on the trust business. Accordingly, they named their company The Nashville Trust Company. The directors named Charles Nelson as president, Joseph H. Thompson as vice president, and Herman Justi as general manager.

By 1890 the company had increased its capital stock to $350,000, had demand loans of $50,988, time loans of $214,294, and $125,172 in invested funds with seventeen trust accounts and twenty-four agency accounts. When President Nelson died on December 13, 1891, his son, William, filled his father's place on the board of directors and Joseph H. Thompson was elected president.

On October 20, 1899, the bank added a savings department. Its success prompted the bank to offer checking accounts in 1901. Business was so good that the board authorized the purchase of the Sax property on College Street and erected a new building there in 1903.

On March 18, 1917, Joseph H. Thompson died and was succeeded as president by William Nelson, with Percy Warner as first vice president. In 1924, the bank built a new fourteen-story building at 315 Union Street. Nelson died suddenly on October 17, 1926.

The following November, the Fourth & First Bank and Trust Company purchased a controlling interest in the Nashville Bank and Trust Company. Later, the two companies were merged under the name Nashville Trust Company, with James E. Caldwell as president.

In 1930 the company merged again, this time with the American Trust Company under the new name Nashville and American Trust Company. Paul Davis was elected president and Charles Nelson as executive vice president.

Horace G. Hill purchased control of the merged companies on May 17, 1933. He became president, and Nelson remained executive vice president. Hill became chairman of the board in January 1936, and, at the same time, Charles Nelson became the third generation of his family to serve as president. When Hill died in 1942, his son, H. G. Hill Jr., joined the board.

When Nelson died in 1946, William Warner McNeilly became president. A year later, H. G. Hill Jr. was named board chairman.

By 1954 deposits had reached $20,701,172. Two years later, McNeilly became vice chairman of the board and W. S. Hackworth, retired president of the Nashville, Chattanooga & St. Louis Railway and a substantial stockowner, became the company's ninth president. Several months later, the company changed its name to Nashville Bank & Trust Company.

In January 1964 the H. G. Hill Company sold its controlling interest in the company to a group headed by William C. Weaver Jr. of National Life. H. G. Hill Jr. did not know that Weaver intended to merge the trust company into Third National Bank, headed by Weaver's close friend, Sam M. Fleming Jr. The plan called for Nashville Bank & Trust to continue as a branch of Third National. The announcement of the merger was made on March 12, 1964.

The Department of Justice contested the merger as a violation of anti-trust laws. After several years of litigation, a settlement was reached in 1968 under which Third National formed a new Nashville Bank and Trust Company and transferred to it the banking business of three branches, which included the former main office of the Nashville Bank and Trust Company. This amounted to more than $30 million in deposits.

Matt Wiggington, a former director of Nashville Bank and Trust, was elected chairman of the board of the spin-off bank that became known as Nashville City Bank and Trust Company after its merger, in 1969, with Capital City Bank. Joe Howell was elected president of the new bank.

The settlement allowed Third National to keep the trust business acquired in the merger. This was what Sam Fleming Jr. wanted in the first place. Howell was succeeded by James A. Webb Jr., who had been vice chairman and executive vice president of Third National Bank. Webb was Capital City Bank's chairman and chief executive officer through its sale to the Dominion Bank of Middle Tennessee. He retired from Dominion in 1988.

ONE-CENT SAVINGS BANK AND TRUST COMPANY was a black-owned bank that opened its doors to the public for the first time on January 16, 1904. Its first officers were Rev. R. H. Boyd, president; attorney James Carroll Napier, cashier; and Rev. Preston Taylor, treasurer and chairman of the board. The first home of the bank was in Napier's law office at 411 North Cherry Street. In his day, Napier was Nashville's most influential African American politician and its most influential citizen. He would later serve under President William Howard Taft as register of the United States Treasury from 1911 to 1913. Opening day deposits of the One-Cent Savings Bank and Trust Company totaled almost $6,500, a creditable start.

From its name, one would think the minimum deposit was one penny. Actually, it was ten cents. The bank's stated purpose was "to encourage frugality and systematic saving among our people, to secure the safe keeping and proper investment of such savings and set in motion business enterprises."

Growth was restricted by the black community's awareness that, earlier, the black-owned Freedman's Bank had failed in 1874, with customers losing their hard-earned money. At the end of its sixth year, the bank had deposits of only $36,000. Despite having a capitalization of $25,000, only $4,290 had been paid by 1910.

The construction of the Black Powder Plant in Old Hickory in 1917–18 attracted many African American workers and increased the prosperity of the black community in Nashville. The One-Cent Savings Bank and Trust Company's demand deposits and savings accounts doubled between January 1917 and the Armistice in November 1918. After the Great War, the bank reorganized and issued new capital stock. It also changed its name, in 1920, to the Citizens Savings Bank and Trust Company, which still exists today with its main office on Jefferson Street. It is the oldest African-American-owned bank in the United States.

Third National Bank was founded by Frank M. Farris and Walter J. Diehl on July 18, 1927. The bank, one of fourteen in Nashville, opened on the ground floor of the Independent Life building on the corner of Fourth Avenue North and Church Street. Third National was capitalized at $600,000 with $120,000 in surplus. Four tellers recorded deposits of $1,018,140.93 on opening day.

Initially, Watkins Crockett was bank president because Farris felt he was too young to hold the office. Nevertheless, knowledgeable people understood that it was Frank Farris's bank. Convinced that Nashville was starved for an aggressive lending institution, Farris made that a priority. He also initiated a night depository.

Third National was one of four Nashville banks to survive President Franklin Roosevelt's "bank holiday" in 1933. On March 31, 1937, in the bank's tenth year, the bank's deposits had grown to $24,059,736.

Twenty-three-year-old Sam M. Fleming Jr. joined the bank in April 1931 as manager of the credit department. He would go on to become president of the bank from 1950 until 1970, and one of Nashville's greatest bankers and leaders.

In 1987, Fleming recalled that one of the most significant events in the bank's early history was the implementation of branch banking after World War II. The Third National opened their West Nashville branch in 1948 at 4604 Charlotte Pike. The branch offered its customers a drive-through window, the first in Nashville and the second in the country.

After Frank Farris died of heart failure in 1950, forty-two-year-old Fleming succeeded him as president. At the same time, Walter Diehl was named chairman of the board. Energetic and extremely competitive, Fleming instituted a more aggressive approach to commercial banking than Nashville had ever seen.

Third National entered its first merger agreement in 1964 when it acquired Nashville Bank and Trust Company. After a four-year struggle with the US Department of Justice, who opposed the merger, a new Nashville Bank and Trust Company was spun off, but Third National kept the trust department it had acquired during the merger. Third National was then the largest bank in Nashville.

In late 1968 Third National joined the National Life and Accident Insurance Company to set up a one-bank holding company called NLT, which stood for National Life and Third. Two years later, after regulations governing one-bank holding companies were more narrowly defined, Third National was spun off as a separate corporation. John Clay Sr. was named president of the bank when Sam Fleming retired in 1970.

Third National Corporation was chartered in 1972 with Third National as its flagship bank. D. Roscoe Buttrey was named president that same year. In 1975 Charlie Kane came from Louisville, Kentucky, to become bank president, succeeding D. Roscoe Buttrey. In 1976 Kane was elected to the additional offices of chairman and chief executive officer of both Third National Bank and Third National Corporation. Kane was succeeded by Charles W. Cook Jr., as president of Third National Bank in 1979. Cook served as president until 1983. He then served as chairman of the bank from 1983 until 1985, at which time he succeeded Charles Kane as president and chief executive officer of Third National Corporation. He then became

Third National Bank, Main Banking Room, 1930s.
Collection of Ridley Wills II.

chairman and chief executive officer in 1987, a position he held until he moved to Atlanta to become executive vice president of SunTrust.

In 1985, when Tennessee's General Assembly approved regional reciprocal interstate banking, Tennessee bank deposits were almost exactly the same as the banks in North Carolina. Unfortunately, Tennessee's legislature had failed to pass statue-branding legislation in the early 1970s, while North Carolina had a statewide banking system for years. North Carolina had several banks that were at least twice as large as Tennessee's largest bank. This positioned the North Carolina banks as acquirers in the industry's consolidation. Virginia and Georgia also had much larger banks than did Tennessee, putting them in similar positions. Tennessee's banks, particularly those in the attractive Nashville market, were disadvantaged in the competitive consolidation of the banking industry that began in 1985, and which reduced the number of banks from fourteen thousand to some seven thousand today.

In late 1986 Third National Corporation entered into a merger agreement with SunTrust Banks Inc. forming a $24 million holding company. A few years later, Third National's name was changed to SunTrust Bank. John Clay Jr. succeeded Cook in each role at both Third National Bank and Third National Corporation.

On October 7, 1986, Third National Corporation's new twenty-eight-story bank building opened at the northwest corner of Fifth Avenue North and Church Street. The handsome new tower was a joint venture of Third National, the Murphree Company, and the Equitable Life Assurance Society of the United States. At the time, Third National had more than $2.5 billion in assets, 1,243 employees, and thirty-five branches in Davidson and Rutherford County.

BOOKSTORES

BERRY'S BOOKSTORE was established by William Tyler Berry in 1835. He had come from a refined, well-educated family that moved from Maryland to a settlement on Lick Creek near Centerville in Hickman County, Tennessee. Soon the village became known as Little Lot, named for the one-fourth-acre lot that his uncle, Parker Berry, gave for a church.

In 1826 a wealthy and cultured Nashvillian, Wilkins Tannyhill, bought a large amount of land in Hickman County. There, he met Berry, who was about fourteen years old at the time. Since both Berry and Tannyhill enjoyed books, the latter made it a point to know the young man better.

Realizing Berry's potential, Tannyhill brought him to Nashville to enter Tannyhill's printing business. At this time, Tannyhill was a two-term mayor of Nashville, well known for his writing skill.

In 1833 one of Tannyhill's five daughters, Mary Margaret, married William T. Berry. Two years later, backed by his father-in-law, Berry started his bookstore.

Mary's sister, Anne, married William B. Bayless, while another, Eliza Jane, married Albert Gleaves. Both Bayless and Gleaves became partners with Berry and, for a time, the firm was known as Berry, Bayless and Gleaves.

The bookstore prospered and soon became the meeting place where Nashville's most prominent literary and political figures gathered. The store had a reading room, well stocked with the best books of the day. Berry loaned books from the room to his customers free of charge. For the following three decades, the bookstore flourished.

The store's shelves were filled with the works of Bryant, Carlyle, Cooper, Dickens, Emerson, Irving, Longfellow, and Lowell. The works of Charles Dickens outsold all the others. Emerson supposedly wrote Thomas Carlyle that, next to Boston, he sold more of his books in Nashville than anywhere else in America.

Berry bought books from Boston and New York, but his finest ones were imported from London and Edinburgh. He also appreciated fine art and kept works of art in stock for his customers who had similar tastes. Fine leather-bound sets of Shakespeare were on his bookshelves, alongside the works of English and American poets.

John Bell, Aaron Brown, Neil S. Brown, W. T. Cooper, Andrew Ewing, Francis Fogg, Henry S. Foote, Meredith Gentry, Philip Lindsley, John Marshall, and William Strickland were regular customers. Southern planters on visits to Nashville would regularly walk over from the Nashville Inn or the St. Cloud Hotel to Berry's establishment on the public square to buy books they could not find at home.

Writers of the period poured lavish praise on the store. One called it "the best furnished establishment [of its kind] west of the Allegheny Mountains."

Another described it as "one of the finest collections of literary works in the South," while a third called it "the leading bookstore south of the Ohio River."

The Civil War precipitated the beginning of the end of Berry's Bookstore. A staunch Unionist, Berry was distressed that most of his friends were Confederate supporters. He never altered his position and, during the entire war, his political opinions were respected, and he was treated with courtesy. His innate gentleness enabled him to never forget old ties of friendship despite political differences. In a 1978 article for the *Tennessee Historical Quarterly* David Stewart wrote that Berry "condemned the cause but esteemed the individual."

When his favorite son, Ferdinand, joined the Rock City Guards, it must have hurt Berry deeply. That feeling intensified when Ferdinand died in Knoxville in 1863 at age nineteen. In 1865 Berry took his third son, Albert Gleaves Berry, to Washington where he hoped to get him an appointment to the Naval Academy. While in Vice President Andrew Johnson's office, the Berrys learned that Richmond had fallen. A day or two later, in Philadelphia, they learned of the assassination of President Lincoln at Ford's Theater. No one had the time to deal with Berry's request. However, after returning home, President Johnson officially communicated the good news that Albert Gleaves had been accepted at the Naval Academy. This was thought to have been his first official act. Albert Gleaves Berry went on to become a distinguished admiral.

The fate of Berry's Bookstore was sad. During the war, no one in Nashville had time to read books, and the store resorted, in 1862, to selling clothes—including colored alpacas, black silks, melton cloths, gray flannel cloths, shawls, white flannels, Balmoral skirts, linen cambrie, bleached and brown domestics—and umbrellas.

Following the war, the market for the fine books Berry so cherished had virtually disappeared. Although nearly in bankruptcy, Berry paid his debts and was hailed by J. P. Lippincott, the distinguished Philadelphia publisher, as the only bookseller in the South who did so. The doors of Berry's Bookstore finally closed in 1876.

Berry died in 1889 at age seventy-six. One of his many descendants was Catherine (Mrs. Roy) Avery, whom I knew at the Downtown Presbyterian Church. She was a fine amateur historian and the official historian for the church.

DAVIS-KIDD BOOKSTORE was founded on October 28, 1980, by Karen Davis and Thelma Kidd. Located in a thirty-five-hundred-square-foot space at 4012 Hillsboro Road, the bookstore, from the beginning, was a community gathering place for book lovers. In the spring of 1983, Davis-Kidd moved to the Green Hills Mall where they had double their previous space. Their Memphis store opened in 1985, followed by a Knoxville Davis-Kidd in 1986.

In 1988 Davis-Kidd moved to Grace's Plaza on Hillsboro Road. The new store had eighteen thousand square feet of retail space, including a second-floor café, where diners at lunchtime could choose from a variety of homemade soups, salads, and sandwiches. Breakfast offerings included croissants, fruit, granola, yogurt, Danish, or muffins. The bookstore also had additional space for company offices.

With an extensive inventory of books and plenty of chairs and benches, customers never felt rushed and found Davis-Kidd to be an inviting place to relax and visit with friends. The large children's section was a haven for both children and their parents. There were author signings, song writers' nights in the café, storytelling and other events for children, poetry readings, music, dance, and, once, a wedding on the staircase landing.

A few years later, Davis-Kidd moved the offices and warehouse to Grassmere Park, freeing up an additional five thousand square feet of retail space in the Grace's Plaza store. A final expansion came in 1995, when Davis-Kidd opened a store in Jackson, Tennessee. I had a book signing there in 1999 when Martha Sundquist, wife of Governor Don Sundquist, and I toured the state touting my book, *Tennessee Governors at Home*. I remember feeling a sense of pride that Davis-Kidd had a strong presence in Jackson. At its peak, Davis-Kidd had over two hundred employees.

Karen Davis and Thelma Kidd sold their company to Neil Vanuum, owner of Joseph-Beth Booksellers, in 1997. He wisely kept the well-known and respected Davis-Kidd name. A few years later, Davis-Kidd moved back to the Green Hills Mall, but customers found the store less accessible. In December 2010, Joseph-Beth closed the store in Green Hills, having filed for protection in the US Bankruptcy Court for the Eastern District of Kentucky. Nashvillians, who loved Davis-Kidd, were disappointed.

HOOBERRY'S BOOKSTORE opened in 1931 in a small one-story building at 140 Fifth Avenue North. It's founder and proprietor for nearly forty years was Champ Logan Hooberry, a native of Rutherford County, who had already tasted life as an iron molder, a "high class" hobo, and a collector of old Bibles.

Not liking his first name, "Parm," he renamed himself "Champ" for the pro-Confederate guerilla, Champ Ferguson, who was hung in Nashville in October 1865 for the murder of many pro-Union men. Hooberry married in 1904 and graduated from the Nashville YMCA's Night Law School in 1914. He practiced law for a while in Florida, but gave it up to sell law books in North Carolina. All the while, he was studying Greek and Latin, a practice he would continue for seventy years.

Finally, in mid-life, he settled into the comfortable life of selling old books, pictures, coins, glass, ancient weapons, and countless other antiques in his store on Fifth Avenue. The result was that, by 1946, Hooberry had "an uncharted morass" of more than ten thousand items crammed in his small store. By then, he was one of the South's leading authorities on old books and a Civil War expert.

Many of his books were acquired by him driving around Tennessee in a Model-T Ford and stopping at old homes to ask if the families had old books to sell. Bolivar and Winchester were among his favorite stopping places. He had sixty Bibles in his collection, dating as early as 1601, and believed that his Bible collection was the finest in the South. Loving old books, he sold them reluctantly and always refused to sell any of his Bibles. His regular customers included banker Sam M. Fleming, financier Rogers Caldwell, and historian Stanley Horn. If they asked him for a particular book, he could put his hands on it immediately.

If someone visited Hooberry at lunchtime, he would usually find him sitting in an easy chair at the front of the store eating a cold lunch out of a paper bag. It was always the same thing: a cheese sandwich, and peanut butter and crackers, or a butter sandwich, all washed down by water. In the wintertime, he usually didn't turn on the heat until January, and even then he only used a little fan-type heater about nine inches in diameter.

Champ Hooberry in his bookstore. *Collection of Ogden Stokes.*

The store seldom, if ever, was dusted or swept, and if his son, Clayton, ever washed the front window, Hooberry would be out of sorts for weeks.

One of his close friends was Hugh Walker, a much younger man who wrote for the *Nashville Tennessean.* Hugh visited Hooberry two or three times each week and also wrote about him in the newspaper. Hooberry, who was content to live a simple life, always said he intended to run his bookstore until he was a hundred. He didn't make that, but he did run it for nearly forty years and only quit when a broken hip forced him to do so at age eighty-eight.

The entire bookstore stock was sold in September 1971 to Robert Bedford of Indianapolis, who happened to stop in the store after attending the Grand Ole Opry. He bought the stock on a whim and shipped it to Indianapolis.

"Old Man" Hooberry's last public appearance was in October 1972 when he attended the Tennessee Old Book Fair. Despite being feeble and having to get around on a walker, Hooberry stayed much of the day and sold a number of books. Hugh Walker saw to it that the book fair was renamed "The Hooberry Book Fair."

Aware of his own place in history, Hooberry said, not long before he died in February 1973 at age ninety, "Some day people will walk by here and say, 'There's where Old Man Hooberry had his bookstore.'" His funeral was held at First Baptist Church, where he had been a faithful member for decades. Today, there is a surface parking lot where Hooberry "bought low and sold high."

MILLS BOOKSTORE was opened in 1892 across the street from the Southern Turf at 245 Cherry Street. William Rich bought the property for $1,000. Two of his sons and a nephew, Reuben M. Mills, ran this outstanding store. Later, when the Rich brothers went in the printing business, Mills took over its management.

In 1928, when Reuben Mills's daughter, Adelaide "Adele," was twelve, she began working in her father's store. She stayed there for sixty-two years. During World War II, a soldier named Bernie Schweid was stationed near Nashville. While browsing in Mills one day, he began talking to Adele. They married in 1943, and spent their entire working lives making Mills the great bookstore it was. Over the years Mills was located in eight different downtown locations. In 1954 Mills moved from 408 Union Street to 601 Church Street, the former home of Joy's Floral Company. Adele had a radio show on WPLN-FM called *Talking About Books*. Bernie often was a guest on WSM radio. Later, they appeared on local television programs.

During the years when Mills, Zibart, and Stokes & Stockell were the only bookstores downtown, they had a good relationship, sometimes lending each other books when one of them was out of stock. Mills was the first retail store in Nashville to offer a sales position to an African American. Over the years, Mills received many awards and accolades. Adele and Bernie should have gotten one for their assertive roles in the sit-in struggles in the 1960s.

In 1970, Mills closed its downtown store, then at 711 Church Street, and moved to 1817 Twenty-First Avenue South in Hillsboro Village. By then, it had branches in the Belle Meade Plaza Shopping Center, which Adele ran, and in the 100 Oaks Shopping Center. In 1985 Adele and Bernie Schweid received the Haslam Award for excellence in bookselling. Five years later, they retired and a great bookstore closed. After Nashville's new main library opened on Church Street in 2001, a space called "Schweid-Mills Writer's Room" was established in their honor.

Stokes & Stockell Bookshop was a sophisticated bookstore established on September 4, 1928, at 224 Sixth Avenue North by Elsie W. Stokes, president and treasurer, and Alice E. Stockell, vice president and secretary. The invitation to the opening read, "We will open a well-stocked bookstore with fashionable stationery, greeting cards and novelties." Stokes & Stockell also carried a wide assortment of books. The ladies also had a rental library.

In February 1929 Stokes recorded her reflections on her store's first five months. She said, "the opening of Stokes & Stockell Inc. was wonderful. Indeed, it was a miracle of kindness from its inception by the large-hearted John W. Barton, its financing by Charles Nelson & B. Benedict, and its establishment by Alice Stockell and myself. The public have given us hearty support and cooperation, understanding and love. It is an adventure that

Stokes & Stockell Bookshop, showing Elsie W. Stokes, president and treasurer. *Collection of Ogden Stokes.*

has been joyous from the outset and whatever fate is in store for it has already been justified by its fruits in happiness and love." What Stokes didn't say, and what she may not have yet known, was that she and Stockell, both strong-willed ladies, did not get along very well. By 1940 they ended their partnership, and, in the 1950s, Stockell opened her own bookstore at the Maxwell House Hotel.

By 1933 Stokes had gained a national reputation not only as a bookseller but as an expert judge of the value of book manuscripts. She was a confidential advisor on retail trade conditions to the Bobbs Merrill Company of Indianapolis and Harper & Bros. of New York. Many publishers consulted with her before publishing books.

When Stokes & Stockell celebrated its sixth anniversary in 1934, the guest of honor was Irina Skariatina, whose new book, *Little Era in Old Russia*, was for sale in the newly expanded book store on Sixth Avenue North. In its first sixteen years of operation, Stokes & Stockell introduced to the public many famous writers, including Francis Griswold, Robert Self Henry, Marquis James, Christopher Morley, Julia Peterkin, and Irina Skariatina.

In 1936, Stokes invited Margaret Mitchell to come to Nashville and speak at Stokes & Stockell about her new book, *Gone With the Wind*. Mitchell responded in a cordial letter, saying that she had always wanted to visit Nashville but because of having three automobile accidents in the past year, and still wearing a brace, she could not come. In 1937 the bookstore had moved to 212 Sixth Avenue North, and Jane Fleming had assumed Stokes's role as treasurer. The next year, Stokes's bookstore moved to 519 Union Street.

By 1946 Elsie Stokes Cram was assisting her mother in managing the bookstore. In the late 1940s, the bookstore moved next door to 517 Union before relocating, in 1957, to 1802 Twenty-First Avenue South in Hillsboro Village. This was soon after her mother's death in May 1957. Elsie Cram had already assumed management responsibility for Stokes & Stockell following her mother's retirement.

Elsie Cram ran the store until about 1966. Next door to Stokes & Stockell in Hillsboro Village, Patty Warren, a cousin, had a record store. They installed a door between the two stores so customers could have one-stop shopping for books and records.

Zibart Brothers Bookstore began in 1898, when young and ambitious Lee and Sam Zibart, typesetters at the *Nashville American,* decided to buy a small newsstand and tobacco shop directly under the *American*'s second-floor offices at 218 North Cherry Street. At first, they kept their jobs at the *American* and hired an assistant to manage the stand. As business prospered, the Zibarts left the newspaper and worked full-time at the newsstand, which received out-of-town newspapers four or five times daily off the loading dock at Union Station.

As business continued to grow, they opened a second store at the corner of Seventh and Church Streets. This was followed by the opening of as many as a dozen smaller stores, including several in the lobbies of major downtown hotels. Meanwhile, the Church Street location became the main store with a focus on books.

In 1933 the Zibarts moved to a larger store in the Paramount Theater building at 719 Church Street. Their first best-seller in the new store was Margaret Mitchell's *Gone With the Wind.* Copies of Mitchell's book were prominently displayed in a big window facing Church Street. Before autograph parties became popular, Zibart Brothers honored many local and regional writers, including Lon Cheney of Smyrna, Ralph McGill, and Marjorie Kinnan.

Lee's sons, Alan and Carl T., grew up in the main store, occasionally helping in the smaller ones. Alan said, in a *Tennessean* article in 1980, that "With the exception of the war years, practically my entire life has been with the book business."

Carl, who was managing editor of the Vanderbilt *Masquerader* when he was an undergraduate student, worked as a young man in the advertising business in New York and served as an army lieutenant during World War II. He then returned to Nashville to manage Zibart Brothers Bookstore until about 1970 when he left to manage the Vanderbilt Bookstore.

Zibart had a stamp department that Murray Brosius ran for a long time. He was responsible for turning several Nashville kids into lifelong stamp collectors.

When suburban shopping malls began robbing downtown Nashville of its vitality, Alan and Carl went with the trend. They opened a Green Hills store in 1960, and closed their Church Street store nine years later, selling the property to the Martin Theater chain. A second suburban store in Madison was sold to a friend in 1970. By 1980, Carl's son, Henry, worked in the Green Hills store with his partner, Jim Battle, managing most of the day-to-day business. Alan and Carl, then almost sixty-nine and seventy-two, came in almost daily, primarily to visit with friends.

Zibart Brothers Bookstore closed in 1982, when the eighty-four-year-old business was sold to the Bookworld chain.

BREWERIES

WILLIAM GERST BREWING COMPANY began in 1890 when William Gerst and Christian Moerlin, brewmasters with the Moerlin Brewing Company in Cincinnati, came to Nashville and bought a small brewery that they renamed Moerlin-Gerst Brewing Company. The brewery would become the largest in the South. As early as 1891, it had the capacity to produce one hundred thousand barrels of beer annually. In 1892 Gerst bought Moerlin's interest and changed the company's name to William Gerst Brewing Company.

The building was, early in the twentieth century, a landmark in South Nashville. Its brew, hop, malt, and storage houses, cooperage department, ice and bottling works, and stables covered more than five acres between Sixth Avenue South and Ewing Street.

William Gerst, who lived across the street from his brewery, was well known in horse circles. In 1898, when the Hermitage Stud on Franklin Pike had a dispersal sale, he bought New Richmond, a yearling, for $160 and Candidate, a sire. Initially, he kept them and other horses at the Hermitage Stud, which he leased from 1899 until 1904 or 1905. He then moved his trotters and pacers to his own stable near Cumberland Park. In 1910 Gerst's thoroughbred Donau won the Kentucky Derby.

The Gerst Brewing Company's steady growth in the years before Prohibition led to the establishment of Tennessee branches in Chattanooga, Jackson, Knoxville, and Tullahoma. Production grew to two hundred thousand barrels of beer annually with two hundred employees. By then, the company was producing Pilsener, ale, bock, and light beers,

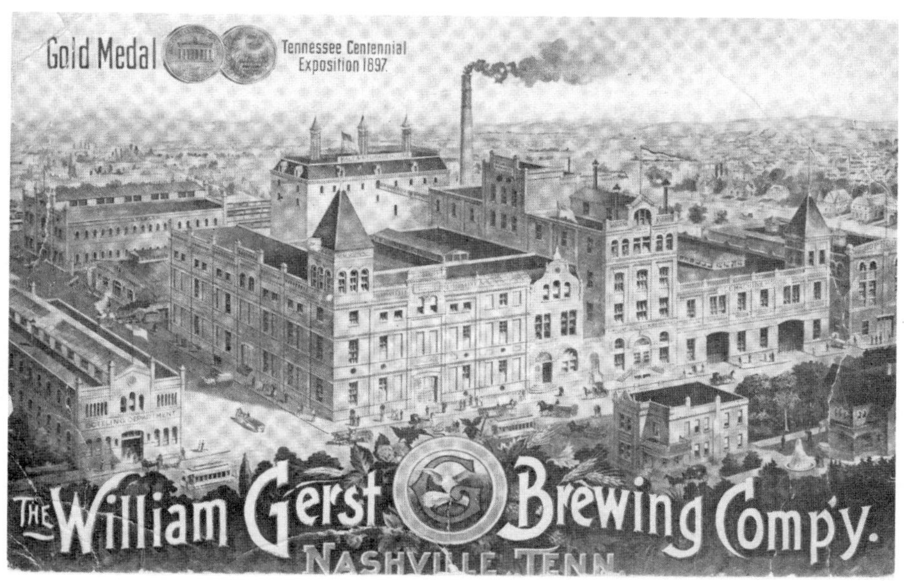

William Gerst Brewing Company, 1897.
Collection of Ridley Wills II.

"Nashville Lager," and "Old Jug Lager from the choicest barley, malt, and Bohemian hops."

Prohibition was a disaster for the company. No longer producing beer, the company instead produced "near beer" and became an agent for ice and soft drinks. Following the repeal of Prohibition in 1933, Gerst never recovered its earlier dominance, as national breweries such as Anheuser-Busch, the brewers of Budweiser beer, garnered an increasingly large share of the national market.

In 1948 the William Gerst Brewing Company, located at 621 Sixth Avenue South, was still a family business with fifty-eight years of service. Its officers were August L. Gerst, president; George J. Gerst and William J. Gerst, vice presidents; and Albert G. Gerst, secretary-treasurer. That year, they advertised their own pale, extra dry Gerst beer.

The Gerst family gave up in 1950, selling their company to a group of stockholders for a reported $400,000. The new owners did not fare any better. They closed the plant in 1954, which remained vacant until it was razed in 1963 by Henry Horrell to build a warehouse that he leased to the Methodist Publishing House.

The Gerst Haus Restaurant at 301 Woodland Street operates as a reminder of the Williiam Gerst Brewing Company's glory years. The restaurant opened in 1955 at 315 Second Avenue North. Its owner was William J. Gerst. The restaurant moved to Woodland Street in 1970, and still serves Gerst beer, brewed by Nashville's Yazoo Brewing Company. The recipe is said to be the same one used by the Gerst Brewing Company a century earlier.

BRICK COMPANIES

W. G. BUSH & COMPANY was founded in 1867 by William G. Bush, a thirty-six-year-old native of the Cane Ridge community of Davidson County. He had been a major in the Confederate army under Gen. Nathan Bedford Forrest. Bush constructed kilns and mined clay for making bricks on twelve lots in North Nashville that cost him $2,000. W. G. Bush & Company delivered the brick in mule-drawn wagons to job sites.

The first clay was dug by hand from pits near where Meharry Medical School now stands. After thousands of tons of clay were excavated for Bush's brick in a nearby location, the depressed area eventually filled with water and became known as Bush's Lake. Nashville's Sewage and Disposal Plant now occupies the site.

W. G. Bush & Company supplied brick to many notable buildings, including the Maxwell House Hotel and Union Gospel Tabernacle (built in 1893 by Capt. Tom Ryman), early buildings on the Vanderbilt campus, and the Tulip Street Methodist Church.

When Bush retired in 1900, Thomas L. Herbert succeeded him as president of W. G. Bush & Company. Herbert, who was married to Bush's daughter, Sarah "Sallie," would serve as president until 1913. One of his innovations was to build sheds around his plant so that he could make brick year-round, unaffected by weather. Consequently, in the early spring, when other brickmakers were just firing up their kilns, Herbert had an ample supply of bricks on hand.

In the early 1900s, Herbert expanded the building materials business by manufacturing clay-based brick at two plants in Nashville and one in Gleason, Tennessee. Their total annual production was eighty million brick. In 1911 Herbert incorporated T. L. Herbert & Sons to dredge sand and gravel from the Cumberland River, while W. G. Bush & Company, incorporated in 1917, continued to supply brick from its three plants. By 1913 T. L. Herbert was so infirm that his last will and testament, written that year, was signed with a very shaky hand. Four years later, following his death, Herbert's son, T. L. Herbert Jr., was elected president. He would remain so until 1949.

When dams and locks were established on the Cumberland River early in the twentieth century, digging sand and gravel by hand was no longer feasible because of the increased depth of the river. Consequently, in 1918, T. L. Herbert & Sons built their first dredge, the "Bertha H.," on W. G. Bush & Company property at the foot of Van Buren Street in North Nashville. In 1925 the company sold the "Bertha H." and built a new diesel electric dredge, "Herbert," and a new diesel-powered tugboat named "Harvey." Both boats were designed by Harvey Herbert and built by the Nashville Bridge Company.

Sometime in the 1920s, T. L. Herbert & Sons began operating another dredge on the Tennessee River and built the "Sally H." at the Jeffersonville Boat Works in 1928. When the "Herbert" caught fire and burned to the deck in 1928, the dredge was rebuilt with steel and served well until April 14, 1941, when a barge loaded with gravel turned over on it, causing the "Herbert" to sink in thirty feet of water at Double Island near Gallatin. Completely rebuilt a second time, the "Herbert" operated for many years as a sand and gravel dredge on the Tennessee River near Dennison's Landing.

During the Depression, Herbert's fleet was idle as demand for sand and gravel almost vanished. At that time, several boats were leased to other companies for towing. To add to the company's woes, the W. G. Bush & Company's brick plant, located on First Avenue North, was completely destroyed by fire on March 14, 1933. The loss was estimated at $50,000.

Since the Depression, the company, renamed Herbert Materials, became a leader in the waterways industry with giant sand and gravel operations and raw material plants. In time, the company acquired a concrete block manufacturing company in Shelbyville, Tennessee, that later included a ready-mix concrete plant. In 1949 John S. Herbert succeeded his uncle, T. L. Herbert Jr., as president.

In the 1950s, W. G. Bush & Company owned McWhorter Weaver. Larry Mulhall, the president of McWhorter Weaver Company, became active in the management of Herbert Materials as well as at McWhorter Weaver. Later, he bought McWhorter Weaver back from the Herberts. In these years W. G. Bush & Company and T. L. Herbert & Sons were located at 174 Third Avenue North.

John S. Herbert would serve as president of Herbert Materials for twenty-one years. During the last years of his life, he would often tell his friends that brick making went back over six thousand years, and that his family had been involved in the brick business in Nashville for over one hundred years. There are "Herbert bricks" all over, he would say.

James A. "Buddy" Skinner Jr., a grandson of R. D. Herbert, succeeded John S. Herbert in 1970. Skinner represented the fifth generation of his family to command this position. In 1979 W. G. Bush & Company was producing more than three hundred thousand bricks a day from three plants.

Herbert Materials Inc. and its predecessor company, W. L. Herbert & Sons, had maintained a banking relationship with First American for more than forty years when it ran into financial difficulty in 1981. The company reputedly owed the bank $3.5 million. The housing market, which absorbed 90 percent of the company's brick production, was soft. First American agreed to lend Herbert Materials another $2.5 million but insisted on control over Herbert Materials' operations and management as a condition of the additional financing.

Although Herbert Materials complied with the "business plan" by selling some assets and cutting costs, First American told the company that "it could no longer provide working capital funding for any brick manufacturing." First American declared all of the company's loans in default on September 5, 1982, and "captured all incoming funds to pay off those debts." Herbert agreed to sell its Gleason, Tennessee, brick plant, much of its other real estate, and "all non-essential equipment" in order to stay in business. Herbert Materials did so at prices significantly below market value. Cumberland & Ohio Company, of Justiceburg, Texas, purchased what was left of Herbert Materials.

One exception was SanGravl Company Inc., which John B. "Jack" Herbert began operating in June 1983 with some used equipment and $400,000 in debt. Thirty years later, in 2013, SanGravl Company Inc. is still in operation, owned by Ingram Materials.

R. D. Herbert & Sons, which separated from T. L. Herbert in 1947, was run for a number of years by R. D. "Bobby" Herbert III and Frank Wilk. In 1988 their company, the largest sheet metal and roofing firm in Nashville, built a new $1.3 million building on Third Avenue North where it operates today. Later, Wilk sold his interest to his wife's cousin, Bobby Herbert. When Herbert died, his widow, Betty Herbert, ran the business before turning it over to their son, Houston Herbert, who is chief executive officer today.

CIGAR STORES

Best & Russell Cigar Company was located at 2 Arcade in Nashville in 1912. Charles J. Ransom was the manager. By 1914 H. S. Edwards had succeeded Ransom. That year, the company established two branch locations, one in the lobby of the Maxwell House Hotel and another in the lobby of the Hermitage Hotel. By 1916 William L. Smith had become manager. The stand sold newspapers, pipes, cigars, smoking tobacco, out-of-town and local newspapers, postcards, and popular magazines such as *Harper's Weekly* and *Collier's Weekly*. Best & Russell was still operating its Hermitage Hotel cigar stand in 1918, but there is no mention of the company in ensuing city directories. A competing cigar stand, the Volunteer Cigar Company, was located at the Hermitage Hotel in 1914 and 1917. In later years, the Hermitage Hotel cigar stand had the concession from about 1924 until 1937.

CLOTHIERS

CHARLES DAVITT & COMPANY, on the southeast corner of Sixth Avenue North and Union Street, was one of the city's most popular men's clothing stores in the 1950s. It featured Hickey-Freeman clothes, Cavanagh hats, Hathaway shirts, and French Shriner shoes. Davitt's remained on Sixth Avenue North until the exodus of retail stores from downtown that followed the development of suburban shopping malls in the 1960s. In 1964 Charles Davitt Jr. was president.

I often wondered how James "Slick" Welsh was so effective in selling men's clothing to conservatively dressed Nashville businessmen, given the fact that he had a penchant for wearing outrageously colored clothes, including purple, lime green, and pastel three-piece suits.

One of local sportswriter Fred Russell's greatest practical jokes involved Davitt's and its owner, Slick Welsh. One day, Max Benson, public relations director for General Shoe Corporation, went to Davitt's and bought a top-of-the-line size 7 1/8 Cavanagh hat. Realizing how proud Benson was of his new hat, Welsh called his good friend, Russell, about an opportunity to have some fun at Benson's expense.

So, Russell went to the store and bought the identical hat, except it was size 7¼, a bit larger than Benson's hat. He then had Benson's initials put in his hat to exactly match Benson's newly purchased hat. Russell then drove to Benson's office and, without Max Benson knowing he was there, swapped Benson's hat hanging on the hat rack with the one he bought.

Russell then invited Benson to lunch. When Benson went to the hat rack and put on his hat to go to lunch with Russell, the hat was a little too big, slipping down on his head. After checking for his initials to be sure it was his, he went in the restroom and put some tissue paper in the sweatband so it would fit properly.

At lunch, after they were seated, Russell excused himself and slipped in the coatroom where he switched hats, putting the tissue paper in the smaller hat. When Benson left the restaurant and put on his hat, it didn't feel right, being too tight. He couldn't figure out what was going on. He looked again at his initials to be sure he had the right hat and, after swearing under his breath, took the tissue paper out, threw it away, and went back to his office.

Realizing that the prank had been wonderfully successful, Russell continued swapping the two hats at Vanderbilt basketball games and elsewhere for two weeks. Finally, Benson went to see his doctor, complaining that something was wrong with his head!

Charles Davitt & Company went out of business in about 1978.

Joseph Frank & Son began late in the nineteenth century, when Joseph Frank moved his family from Murfreesboro to Nashville and opened a clothing store on Cedar Street. In 1897 Frank's eighteen-year-old son, Ernest, became a porter in his next clothing venture, Frank & Morse Company.

Ten years later, the company reorganized as Joseph Frank & Son. By this time, Ernest Frank was managing the store that was located in the Jackson Building at the corner of Church Street and Fifth Avenue North.

Across Fifth Avenue North, the First Presbyterian Church faced Church Street. In the 1920s and 1930s, the church had a sign out front that read "Jesus Saves." If someone was walking up the sidewalk on the south side of Church Street approaching the church, the "Jesus Saves" sign seemed to be imposed above the "Joseph Frank Clothes" sign across Fifth Avenue North. So, if you were not paying attention, you might think there was a single sign that read "Jesus Saves Joseph Frank Clothes"!

In the 1920s, Joseph Frank & Son sold Knox hats and Florsheim shoes in addition to suits, slacks, coats, and accessories. The company's advertisement in the 1925 *Commodore* claimed, "The Majority of the Better Dressed Vanderbilt Men Have Bought Their Clothes from Joseph Frank & Son."

In 1937, Joseph Frank & Son moved to 209 Sixth Avenue North. There, Ernest Frank put his desk in the middle of the store. When asked why, he explained, "I want to be in a position to see everything that is going on."

In 1949, Joseph Frank & Son advertised itself as having "Nashville's Largest Selection of Well-Known Brands in Men's Sportswear and

Clothing." Ernest Frank managed Joseph Frank & Son until 1959, when he was eighty years old. At that point, he turned the management over to his son, Joseph Frank Jr.

In the 1960s, I bought most of my clothes from Joseph Frank Jr. I remember him as a soft-spoken gentleman. He ran Joseph Frank & Son until he closed the store upon his retirement in 1976.

EVERETT HOLZAPFEL'S SHOP FOR MEN was an upscale men's clothing store opened in 1961 in partnership with several "good customers" and by borrowing against Everett Holzapfel's life insurance policy. In 1964, if you shopped at Everett Holzapfel's Shop for Men in Belle Meade Plaza, you would have been waited on by Holzapfel, Maurice Ball, James "Slick" Welsh (who had come from Charles Davitt & Company), or Bill Hathaway. Holzapfel also had a store in the Mall at Green Hills from 1982 until 1990.

In 1977 John "Hosey" Holzapfel and Morgan Holzapfel were both salesmen at their father's store, as were Rick Campbell, Mike McGrady, and Russell Carpenter. Campbell was there from 1962 until 1996, when Holzapfel closed.

The store was still a viable business, but Hosey Holzapfel cited several challenges, including increasing "rent prices, competition from mail-order companies and larger retailers, and changing attitudes toward attire." He said, "Young people seemed to be more concerned with price and labels than service."

TOWN AND COUNTRY SHOP OF NASHVILLE was an elegant ladies' specialty shop opened in 1931 by Binnie (Mrs. Robert) Lusk and Julia (Mrs. Richard) Dake, two Nashville social leaders who had no previous business experience. They started the company during the Depression as a means of providing supplemental incomes for their respective families. Each invested $250 in what was initially a small French dress shop in two rooms of A. Herbert Rodgers' interior decorator shop at 2410 West End Avenue.

The first shop of its kind in a suburban Nashville location, Town and Country initially sold dresses bought from an exclusive store in New York

City. A year or two later, Lusk, who had impeccable taste, conceived the idea of having clothes sent to Town and Country on consignment from shops in other cities. From selling these clothes, Town and Country was able to build up its working capital.

At the end of the first year, Town and Country had outgrown its limited space, so they leased the first floor of a house at the corner of Twenty-Third and West End Avenues. When West End United Methodist Church purchased the house in 1937 to build a new sanctuary, Town and Country moved to a house at 2412 West End Avenue that Binnie Lusk had purchased.

When Julia Dake retired in 1950 for health reasons, Binnie Lusk bought her interest and became sole owner of the store that she incorporated. Her initial employees were May Buntin (later Mrs. Horace G. Hill Jr.), Helen Cheek (later Mrs. Eugene Forker), and Blanche Keffer, who succeeded May Buntin as bookkeeper. Elizabeth Christmas managed the store's alteration department for many years.

Carolyn Barr, Lusk's daughter, became president of Town and Country when her mother died in 1968. Her husband, Richard A. Barr Jr., became vice president at the same time. She had grown up in the business as a buyer who made trips to New York a few times a year for twenty-five years, and also served as a bridal consultant. In 1972 Carolyn Barr said if she decided to write her memoirs, she would name the book *Of Girls and Girdles* "because I never had a customer try on a dress who failed to say, 'I don't have on my good girdle.'"

When the store closed on January 1, 1973, upon Barr's retirement, many Nashville ladies had wonderful memories of purchasing beautiful trousseau and wedding dresses there, as well as remembering fashion shows staged by Town and Country. Carolyn Barr recalled that, in the early years, "girls going away to college would come in with their mothers who'd advise them about correct clothes. These consisted, usually, of matching sweaters and skirts, dresses for sorority teas or tea dances, a formal or two, and always a good suit for traveling."

COAL COMPANIES

ST. BERNARD COAL COMPANY, founded by James R. Love, provided soft coal to Nashville homes and businesses for many decades. Known as St. Bernard Mining Company in 1916, its symbol was a knight in armor riding a horse and holding a St. Bernard banner. Its motto in 1916 was "Leads Them All." Love was succeeded by his son, Hooper Love, who was president of West Kentucky Coal Company, of which St. Bernard Coal was then a division. Hooper's son, James R. "Jimmy" Love III, was vice-president of West Kentucky Coal until he left the company in 1952. In the 1950s and 1960s, St. Bernard's office was at 2400 Charlotte Avenue. The last Nashville City Directory entry for the company was in 1970 when Gilbert P. Hurt was manager.

COFFEE COMPANIES

AMERICAN TEA & COFFEE COMPANY had its beginning when David S. Bubis, who started as a peddler, began roasting green coffee beans in 1919. That year he created Bluebird Coffee. Unable to register his brand under that name, he changed it to American Ace Coffee to honor the airmen he called "the exciting American aviator heroes of World War I." David's two brothers, Kolman and Israel, were initially his business partners, but he later bought them out.

David's son, Marvin Bubis, began working at the company as a teenager. Following college and three years of military service in World War II, Marvin joined the company full time. When David died, Marvin assumed control of American Tea & Coffee Company.

Under the leadership of David and Marvin Bubis, the company's advertising staff coined two phrases that brought American Ace name recognition across the South and Midwest. Those phrases were, "If you don't get your American Ace Coffee, go back to bed," and "Elmer! Don't forget the American Ace Coffee!" I remember hearing these jingles over the WSM radio station when Roy Acuff and Minnie Pearl were Grand Ole Opry spokesmen for American Ace Coffee. During the 1940s and until about 1951, American Ace was one of the biggest sponsors of the Grand Ole Opry, Saturday nights, 7:30–8:00 p.m.

In 1951, American Tea & Coffee Company, located at 2422 Charlotte Avenue, began using the new medium of television to advertise. At that time, the company expanded its institutional and restaurant coffee service and also produced Big Chief Peanut Butter.

Marvin Bubis, who was with the company for fifty years, sold American Tea & Coffee Company, then located at 2500 Heiman Street, in 1996.

Cheek-Neal Coffee Company was founded by Kentucky natives Joel O. Cheek and John Neal. Cheek was born in Burkesville in 1852. After attending Transylvania College for one year and teaching school for two years, he moved to Nashville in 1873, where he got a job as a traveling salesman for Webb, Hughes & Company, a wholesale grocery firm. His territory was in mountainous East Kentucky, where there were few roads. Consequently, he rode on horseback with his samples on one side of his saddle bag and his clothes on the other. His customers were general store owners, with whom he earned a reputation for fairness.

Cheek married Minnie Ritchey, also of Burkesville, Kentucky, in 1874. The couple would eventually have eight sons and three daughters, eight of whom lived to adulthood.

In 1884 Cheek moved back to Nashville, where he joined a firm later called Cheek, Webb & Company. While employed there, Cheek and an English coffee broker named Roger Nolley Smith began experimenting with Brazilian, Columbian, and Mexican coffees to find the perfect blend. By 1892 Cheek believed he had found what he was looking for.

He approached the food buyer for the Maxwell House Hotel and persuaded him to take twenty pounds of his coffee on a trial basis. The trial convinced the hotel's chef that Cheek's coffee was simply a better blend than what the hotel dining room had been using. Accordingly, Cheek gained a longer trial. At the end of six months, the chef was completely satisfied with Cheek's coffee and Mr. William K. Black, the hotel's manager, reluctantly acceded to Cheek's request that the coffee be named the Maxwell House Blend.

Encouraged by this success, Cheek resigned from the wholesale house and went in partnership with John Norton to form a wholesale house specializing in coffee. In 1900 they were joined by John Neal, a fellow-Kentuckian, who had once sold for Cheek. The next year, Norton left the partnership, and Cheek and Neal formed the Nashville Coffee and Manufacturing Company, specializing in Maxwell House Coffee.

In 1903 the partners changed the company's name to Cheek-Neal Coffee Company. The company incorporated in 1903 with a capital stock of $300,000. Finding success in the Nashville market, Cheek-Neal opened roasting plants in Houston, Texas (1905), Jacksonville, Florida (1910), and Richmond, Virginia (1916).

One by one, six of Cheek's sons joined their father's firm. In the 1920s, one of them, Robert S., was vice president and manager of the Nashville plant.

Joel Cheek's greatest strengths were his advertising and promotional skills. By 1907, his advertisements were appearing in Nashville newspapers. On October 22 of that year, President Theodore Roosevelt visited Nashville on a five-hour stop. He was met at Union Station by a huge crowd, including Governor Malcolm Patterson and the mayor Thomas O. Morris. The grand marshall led a parade of fifteen carriages and twenty-four automobiles to the Ryman Auditorium, where the president spoke to an estimated six thousand people for thirty-two minutes.

He then went by car to the Hermitage. There, he visited Andrew Jackson's tomb and then went upstairs in the house to the front gallery for a photo shoot.

After coming downstairs, the *Nashville Banner* reporter wrote, "Mr. Roosevelt was ushered into the dining room, where he called for a cup of coffee. 'I like this coffee,' he said, as he sipped the amber fluid, which had been poured by Mrs. John M. Gray Jr. and handed to him by Mrs. Rachel Jackson Lawrence. 'This is the kind of stuff I like, by George, when I hunt bears.'"

Joel O. Cheek and his eight sons, six of whom were active in the Cheek-Neal Coffee Company. Seated, left to right: Joel O. Cheek Jr.; Leon Cheek, vice president, Jacksonville manager; Joel O. Cheek Sr., president; Robert Cheek, vice president, Nashville manager; and William Cheek, vice president, Richmond manager. Standing, left to right: John Cheek; Newman Cheek, secretary; Frank Cheek, vice president, New York manager; James Cheek, vice president, Los Angeles manager. *Collection of Picksley Cheek.*

President Roosevelt then was served lunch in the dining room by members of the Ladies Hermitage Association. They naturally used General Jackson's silver service and china. After he received a number of gifts, including a bottle of Tennessee whiskey, the president left the Hermitage to return to Union Station to board his special train.

He did not stop at the Maxwell House Hotel while in Nashville and, while at the Hermitage, probably never mentioned by name Maxwell

House Coffee or Fit For A King Coffee, which was sold by the H. G. Hill Grocer & Baking Company. Nevertheless, both Joel Cheek and Horace G. Hill were quick to put ads in Nashville newspapers touting their respective coffees. The first H. G. Hill Grocer & Baking Company ad ran in the *Nashville American* on October 20. It read, "While in Nashville the president will drink only one kind of coffee. That will be the grade that always gives satisfaction. Fit For A King Coffee." On the twenty-fifth, three days after the visit, the H. G. Hill Grocer & Baking Company's ad in the *Nashville Banner* read, "The president at the Hermitage told the ladies he had often taken lunch at other places than the White House, but he had never tasted such good coffee. Of course, the ladies were pleased. So that's what everybody says when they have a cup of Fit For A King Coffee."

President Theodore Roosevelt at Andrew Jackson's tomb, the Hermitage, October 22, 1907.
Collection of Ridley Wills II.

The next day, Cheek-Neal Coffee Company's ad in the *Nashville Banner* countered the H. G. Hill's ads. The Cheek-Neal ad correctly quoted what the president said about the coffee served him at the Hermitage, and went on to say, "The above is an extract from the *Nashville Banner* of October 22, and relates to the coffee served President Roosevelt by the Ladies of the Hermitage Association during his visit on that day to the home of Andrew Jackson. This was Maxwell House Blend Coffee." We will never know whose coffee Roosevelt drank that day. It undoubtedly was either Maxwell House Coffee or Fit For A King Coffee, the two most popular brands in Nashville.

Roosevelt probably never uttered the words, "Good to the last drop." The first Maxwell House Coffee ad to use this slogan would not appear until about 1921. In 1908 the Coca-Cola Company called its beverage, Coca-Cola, "Good to the Last Drop." As the Coca-Cola Company had been incorporated by Asa Chandler in 1892 and, by 1908, had a national reputation, it seems highly likely that Joel Cheek heard the slogan and decided to use it, attributing it to Teddy Roosevelt. Regardless of what President Roosevelt said or didn't say, he has ever since been given credit for saying that Maxwell House coffee is "good to the last drop."

Joel Cheek was a promotional genius. He hired Edna Moseley, "a soft-spoken Southern Belle," to push the virtues of Maxwell House Coffee at state fairs across the South.

By 1914 the sixty-one-year-old Cheek had become wealthy. He built a house at 209 Louise Avenue, next door to the house my grandfather, Ridley Wills, one of the founders of the National Life and Accident Insurance Company, built in 1914 at 217 Louise Avenue. Soon people were calling that block of Louise Avenue "Millionaire's Row."

Cheek was elected vice president of the National Coffee Roasters Association and later, in 1921, president of that association. In speeches, Cheek often expressed sympathy for traveling salesmen, explaining he had been on the road himself for twenty-eight years.

By the early 1920s, Cheek-Neal, whose Nashville headquarters was in Cummins Station, had established additional branches in Los Angeles, Chicago, and Brooklyn. The establishment of the Brooklyn plant in 1921 put the Cheek-Neal Coffee Company into the national advertising field. The company launched an aggressive advertising campaign in the East with daily big-city newspaper advertising, a big Maxwell House coffee cup sign on Broadway, and full page magazine advertisements in color. From 1921 until 1928, when the company was sold, Cheek-Neal spent $1 million annually on advertising. When radio became popular later in the decade, Cheek-Neal launched a "high-class and expensive advertising program on the air."

In fiscal year 1926–27, Cheek-Neal's gross sales were approximately $28 million and net profits were about $3 million. This caught the attention of the Postum Company that, in 1928, acquired Cheek-Neal Coffee Company for $45 million. Postum changed Cheek-Neal's name to the Maxwell House Products Company, with headquarters in New York City. A year later, the Postum Company changed its own name to General Foods Corporation.

When Joel O. Cheek died on December 14, 1935, in Jacksonville, Florida, at the age of eighty-three, his obituary was in newspapers across the country. In January 1936 the *Tea & Coffee Trade Journal* in New York wrote that Cheek had been in retirement for the last eight years, and that he "was a generous contributor to educational, civic, and charitable enterprises." A Chicago trade journal, in December 1935, called him "one of the most outstanding figures in the industry" and said that "he was well known to the trade throughout the country." In Nashville, Cheek had been honored in 1918 by the Nashville Conservatory of Music, which had named its new recital hall the "Joel O. Cheek Auditorium."

CONSTRUCTION COMPANIES

FOSTER & CREIGHTON COMPANY began in January 1885 when Major Wilbur Fisk Foster and Robert Thomas Creighton, his former rod man on engineering projects, formed a partnership to conduct a general contracting business. The company's initial working capital was only $1,500 with each partner investing $500. On some of their jobs, Creighton would take his family to live in a tent on the construction site.

In 1895 the country was in the grip of a deep recession. Foster & Creighton had no work. Salvation came when the company was given a contract to build the foundation for the Parthenon at the 1897 Tennessee Centennial Celebration, where Creighton was chief engineer.

In 1906 Foster & Creighton brought on Chauncey C. Foster, Wilbur Foster's son-in-law, and Wilbur Foster Creighton, oldest son of R. T. Creighton, as associates. Wilbur F. Creighton had worked for the firm on summer construction jobs since he was twelve years old.

After Wilbur Foster retired at age seventy-two, the company was incorporated under the name of Foster & Creighton with a capital stock of one thousand shares of $100 par value stock. R. T. Creighton became president and Chauncey C. Foster took the role of secretary-treasurer.

With road contracts to provide thousands of tons of ballast and fluxing stone, Foster & Creighton purchased a stone quarry near Columbia, Tennessee, in 1906, and later ones on Carter's Creek and at Darlington in northern Alabama. The company gained profitable contracts to grade and macadamize streets in Murphy's Addition on Church Street and J. C. Bradford's Belmont Land Company subdivision on Sixteenth Avenue South. The company also had contracts to build the substructure and superstructure for the Jefferson Street and Sparkman Street Bridges in Nashville.

In 1920, when R. T. Creighton relinquished control of the company, its capital and surplus was $373,000. Wilbur F. Creighton succeeded his father as president, and A. D. Creighton was elected secretary-treasurer. Wilbur F. Creighton, who was born in 1883, lived until 1968. He called himself a stonecutter by trade, civil engineer by profession, and builder through heredity.

During the Roaring Twenties, Foster & Creighton built bank buildings for the Chattanooga Savings Bank, the Nashville Trust Company, Caldwell & Company, the Birmingham Trust and Savings Company, and the Merchants National Bank of Jackson, Mississippi. The company also built bridges and highways and an immense quantity of other construction work during the 1920s and 1930s. One of the highways Foster & Creighton built in the 1920s was the concrete pike between Columbia and Mt. Pleasant. The twelve-inch slab is still there, visible when repairs are made on the highway. During World War II, "Foster & Creighton alone, and with associates, did forty-one million dollars worth of work for the War Department."

Wilbur Creighton was succeed by his son, Wilbur Foster Creighton Jr. (1906–2004), as president on March 1, 1958. During the 1950s and 1960s, bridge work constituted an important part of Foster & Creighton's work.

In 1972 Wilbur F. Creighton III was elected president of the company, becoming the fourth generation in his family to hold the top management position. A year later, the company was contracted to build the First American National Bank Tower, the largest building complex in Nashville. This seemed fitting since Creighton's grandfather, Wilbur Creighton Sr., built the Fourth & First National Bank building on the same site fifty-seven years earlier.

Both Wilbur Jr. and Wilbur III made their marks in buildings and structures across the country. Wilbur III was in charge when his company built the New River Gorge Bridge in West Virginia that, at the time, was the longest steel arch bridge ever constructed.

Foster & Creighton was liquidated in 1984. Wilbur Creighton III said that large construction companies were taking over the construction industry so fast that it would be very hard for companies such as his to compete.

OMAN CONSTRUCTION COMPANY had its roots in 1876, when John Oman, attracted by the limestone in the Middle Tennessee basin, moved his family to Nashville and entered the cut stone and stone masonry business. In 1881 his company received a contract to build a bridge for the Nashville, Chattanooga & St. Louis Railway. Other contracts came to build bridges, embankments, tunnels, and railroad facilities. After the mass production of automobiles began in the first quarter of the twentieth century, Oman Stone Company added highway construction to its capabilities.

John Oman Jr. became the first second-generation member of the Oman family to enter the family general contracting business. In 1929,

John Oman Jr. founded the Crab Orchard Stone Company. His experience in that job helped him when he, his brother, Stirton Oman Sr., and John's son, John Oman III, started Oman Construction Company in the 1940s. The company was on McMurray Avenue, later renamed Oman Street, near Centennial Park.

In 1942–43 Oman Construction strung telephone lines along fifteen hundred miles of the Alcan Highway. This critical war-time work went on all year long. During the winter, Oman trucks had to be kept running twenty-four hours a day to prevent the gas and oil from freezing solid. During the summer, Oman Construction workers had to contend with mosquitoes, bears, and moose.

When John Oman Jr. died in 1949, his brother, Stirton Oman Sr., succeeded him as chief executive officer. In 1950 Oman Construction Company was incorporated. One of the company's most visible local projects in the 1950s was building the handrails and lighting system and laying the concrete slabs and the bituminous surface for Victory Memorial Bridge that first opened to traffic on May 1, 1955. A year earlier, Oman began its first international project in Portugal's Azores Islands for the US Army Corps of Engineers. Oman would return to the Azores in the 1960s and 1980s on projects for the US Navy.

Stirton Oman Jr. joined the family business in 1958, after serving four years in the US Air Force. At this time, his father was chairman of the board and John Oman III was president. Stirton Oman Jr.'s brother, Jack A. Oman, joined the company in 1959.

In March 1960 Mr. and Mrs. John Oman III and Mr. and Mrs. Sam Fleming attended a cocktail supper hosted by Mr. and Mrs. Allen Dobson in honor of the Argentinan ambassador Dr. Emilio Donato del Carril and his wife and two other Argentinan couples. As a courtesy, John Oman III, a veteran pilot, agreed to fly the visitors to Muscle Shoals, Alabama, using both of his company planes. The Oman Company pilot flew one, and Oman flew the other. On the return trip to Nashville, as Oman began his approach to Berry Field, the plane encountered an ice storm near Brentwood and crashed, instantly killing him and Sammie Menzies, an employee.

NLT Tower excavation, completed by Oman Construction Company, 1968. Left to right: John H. Tipton Jr., Walter Bearden, Stirton Oman Jr., Andy Sutton, unidentified, William C. Weaver Jr., Stirton Oman Sr., Jack A. Oman, unidentified, and C. E. Howard.
Collection of Ridley Wills II.

In 1960 Stirton Oman Jr. was placed in charge of the company's overseas operations, most of which were located in the Middle East. Oman Construction organized a joint venture partnership with other large American contractors to build the Trans-Asian Highway from Kabul to Kandahar, Afghanistan, a distance of three hundred miles; the Dhahran Air Terminal in Saudi Arabia; and the Trans-Alaskan Pipeline, the largest privately funded construction project in history. Oman and its joint venture partners constructed a 152-mile section of the pipeline from the north bank of the Yukon River to a point forty miles southeast of Fairbanks, across the

Salcha River. Despite a temperature range from a winter low of -70 degrees Fahrenheit to a summer high of 80 degrees Fahrenheit, Oman got the job done.

Oman Construction and seven other contracting companies formed a consortium in April 1962 to successfully bid on the construction of a 735-foot-high dam to span the Feather River Canyon in Oroville, California. When completed in 1968, the Oroville Dam was the highest earth-fill dam in the world, and Oman had been the lead contractor.

Locally, Oman Construction Company excavated the site of the NLT Tower in the late 1960s. Jack Oman estimated in 2012 that in the 1980s and 1990s, Oman Construction did 80 percent of all commercial excavation work in Nashville.

Stirton Oman Sr. relinquished the presidency of Oman Construction Company to Stirton Oman Jr. in 1972. The senior Oman remained as chairman of the board until his death in 1977. Not many people know that in the 1960s and early 1970s, Oman Construction Company, through a subsidiary, Vine Street Realty Company, owned the Belle Meade Shopping Center.

Stirton Oman Jr. became Oman Construction Company's board chairman in 1977. When he retired in 1984, his brother, Jack, succeeded him as chief executive officer and board chairman. During Jack Oman's tenure as chief executive officer, two of the company's biggest projects were a section of Interstate 65 south of Birmingham, Alabama, and the Farley Nuclear Plant in Dothan, Alabama.

In 1989 Jack A. Oman announced that Oman Construction Company was moving from its Crab Orchard stone headquarters on Oman Street, that his great-grandfather had built in 1939, to a new ten-thousand-square-foot building constructed by DcDevitt & Street Company, of Nashville, at 200 Forty-Second Avenue North.

After Oman Construction Company sold six thousand acres of land in Florida and liquidated all its assets in 1997, the Oman headquarters building was purchased by Sherman-Dixie Concrete Industries. Four generations of the Oman family had run the Oman Construction Company and its predecessor company for 122 years.

WILSON-WEESNER-WILKINSON COMPANY was preceded by Wilson Ingram & Company, which was formed in 1907. Wilson Ingram was started by partners George M. Ingram II and John A. Wilson to enter the construction products distribution business. Immediately after being formed, the company furnished steel for the Sparkman Street and Jefferson Street Bridges in Nashville.

Even before starting the new company, Ingram employed a young paving superintendent, A. M. "Mike" Weesner. Weesner worked for Ingram at two other companies he owned until Ingram's death in 1916. At that point, Wilson became the sole proprietor of Wilson Ingram & Company. During the next year or so, he and Weesner attended construction job lettings around the South.

Early in 1918 John Wilson invited Weesner to join Wilson Ingram & Company. Weesner accepted that February. Four years later, Weesner obtained a 10 percent partnership interest in the company that changed its name to Wilson-Weesner & Company. The company sold earth movers, mule-drawn scrapers and graders, small rock crushers, steam rollers, and small concrete mixers. For the next few years, Wilkinson designed and sold reinforcing steel, as well as machinery. To handle business from the State Highway Department, the company hired Wilbur C. Sensing, a 1924 graduate of Vanderbilt engineering school, as a sales engineer.

Later in 1925 Wilson-Weesner & Company moved to 108 Fatherland Street. That same year, E. B. Wilkinson, a young civil engineering graduate of the University of Colorado, and an excellent salesman, joined the firm as a partner with a 10 percent ownership interest. He would head the firm's Knoxville office. To reflect Wilkinson's ownership position, the company changed its name to Wilson-Weesner-Wilkinson (WWW).

On Christmas Day 1926 the Cumberland River was rising at an alarming rate. The management team and office staff at WWW, fearful of a devastating flood, began to scramble to safeguard records and get equipment out of harm's way. On January 1, 1927, the Cumberland crested at 56.1 feet at the foot of Broadway. The river washed out the dedicated rail line that WWW used to bring heavy equipment to the plant. The rail line had to be rebuilt, but the plant was saved.

John Wilson died of a heart attack in 1928 at age forty-eight. In his will, written the night before his death, he had stated that Weesner and Wilkinson should be allowed to buy the business, that had assets of $145,000, and they should allow Wilbur Sensing to have an interest in the company if he so desired. Sensing was interested, and the three men successfully raised the money to buy out Wilson's heirs.

The year 1929 was a good one for Wilson-Weesner-Wilkinson. The company had $1,394,611 in sales with $47,178.94 in profits, a 32.5 percent return on assets. Company officers elected at the annual meeting on May 11, 1929, were Mike Weesner, president and treasurer; E. B. Wilkinson, vice president and general manager; and Wilbur C. Sensing, vice president and secretary.

In 1931 Wilson-Weesner-Wilkinson acquired the W. C. Caye Company, of Atlanta, that was in a similar business but was in financial difficulty. W. C. Caye was elected a director of Wilson-Weesner-Wilkinson, who operated W. C. Caye Company as its Atlanta branch. The company also had an office in Knoxville, and was doing quite a bit of business in Memphis.

The Depression hit the construction business in Tennessee hard. In 1931 WWW suffered a net loss of $10,229.10. In 1932, salaries were trimmed and expenses were cut. Still, the loss that year was $40,236.19. In 1933 salaries were cut in half, the company's Knoxville warehouse was sold, and inventories were reduced. These measures helped, as losses in 1933 were not as bad, totaling $13,074.97.

In 1932 WWW supplied steel for WSM's 878-foot radio tower which was dedicated on November 12, 1932. Wilson-Weesner-Wilkinson also received a contract to design the reinforcing steel for the roof of the US Post Office on Broad Street. The company rebounded in 1935–36, making small profits both years. During the 1930s, WWW had a subcontract to provide concrete for a handsome concrete bridge built by Oman Construction Company on Hillwood Boulevard over Richland Creek. By 1938 profits edged up to $10,033.17, and the worst of the Depression seemed to be over. At an October 25, 1940, board meeting, a $1,600 bonus was declared for each officer, and salaries were restored to earlier levels.

In 1939 the five-member Nashville Electric Power Board created the Nashville Electric Service (NES). After World War II, plans were under way for a new NES building at 1214 Church Street. WWW received a contract to supply steel for this project, and George Weesner, of WWW, designed the dome, which was completed in 1950.

In 1951 Mike Weesner was still president and secretary-treasurer of WWW, E. B. Wilkinson was vice president and general manager as he had been more than two decades, and Wilbur C. Sensing was vice president. At this time and for nearly forty years in the future, the company headquarters and main warehouse were at 310 South Second Street.

Probably the most exciting WWW contract in the 1950s was that of supplying reinforcing steel for the thirty-story Life and Casualty Tower at Fourth Avenue North and Church Street. Completed in 1956, Life and Casualty Tower was, at that time, the tallest office building in the Southeast United States.

By 1960 E. B. Wilkinson was board chairman, Wilbur C. Sensing was president, and Mike Weesner was honorary board chairman. Other officers were Richard W. "Dick" Weesner and George W. Weesner, Mike's sons, who were executive vice president and treasurer, respectively. Thomas R. Raines and Walter D. Kerrick were vice presidents, while Edwin B. May was secretary. Two years later, E. B. Wilkinson retired.

W. C. Sensing resigned in 1965 to become president of ENCO Materials. He took with him the reinforced steel portion of the business in an amicable arrangement worked out with E. B. Wilkinson earlier. Dick Weesner succeeded Sensing as president. He would serve in this capacity until his death in 1989. He was succeeded as president by his brother, George W. Weesner, who would serve as president or board chairman until 1993, when he retired.

Throughout the 1970s and 1980s, WWW employed about ninety people in four offices, although most of the staff worked at the headquarters at 310 South Second Street. Frances Seavey was company secretary or secretary-treasurer during much of this period. When George Weesner became board chairman in about 1977, Charles R. "Charlie" Sheley succeeded him as president and held that position through 1987.

Weesner and Sheley remained as WWW's board chairman and president until Weesner's retirement. In 1988 Frances Seavey, who had worked for the company since 1958, was secretary-treasurer. During the 1980s and early 1990s, Wilson-Weesner-Wilkinson was still in the business of selling contractor's equipment and road machinery. After Ingersoll-Rand took over operations in 1993, Wilson-Weesner-Wilkinson remained a shell corporation for several more years but was no longer an active business.

COTTON MILLS

Tennessee Manufacturing Company began on November 19, 1871, when Samuel D. Morgan, for many years one of Nashville's leading wholesale merchants, opened a large, brick, four-story cotton factory in North Nashville. Morgan, the president of the company, had superintended the construction of the building as he had previously done during the construction of the State Capitol. Serving with him on the Tennessee Manufacturing Company executive committee were A. G. Adams, James Whitworth, and Robert H. Gardner, all prominent Nashville businessmen.

Initially, the factory would accommodate 13,820 spindles and four hundred looms. Power was furnished by two two-hundred-horse-power steam engines. The cotton mill, sitting on fourteen acres of land, was viewed by experts as a model of efficiency, and the company quickly gained the reputation of producing sheets, shirts, and other cotton goods equal in quality to any in the country.

In October 1872 Morgan, then seventy-three years old, resigned as president and was replaced by Whitworth, who, after purchasing additional equipment, began the manufacture of heavy brown cotton sheetings, drills, and shirtings. For the fiscal year ending September 1, 1873, the factory consumed 2,328 bales of cotton and employed a workforce of 268 people, including 202 females. The 1873 net profits were $11,300.

In 1875 James C. Warner became president of the Tennessee Manufacturing Company. A grandson of Robert Cartwright, who had come to the Big Salt Lick in 1780 as a member of John Donelson's party, Warner had been in the hardware business in Chattanooga before the

Civil War. He moved to Nashville in 1863 due to the illness of a daughter who could not get adequate treatment in Chattanooga. Since 1868, he had been an officer in the Tennessee Coal and Railroad Company, serving part of that time as general manager. In 1874 he resigned from this position because of poor health. After a year's rest, Warner recovered and accepted the presidency of the Tennessee Manufacturing Company, an entirely new business for him. After one year's service as president, he retired with the satisfaction of knowing that the company was in a prosperous condition.

By 1880 the factory workforce had increased to four hundred people, and thirteen bales of cotton were required daily to keep up with production. To accommodate the growth, a three-story addition was built in 1881–82.

In 1882 Joseph B. "Jo" Morgan and James O. Hamilton started a small wholesale paper and twine business on Market Street as a partnership named Morgan & Hamilton Company. Four years later, Hamilton developed tuberculosis and was forced to move to El Paso, Texas, where he died in 1890. At his death, Morgan & Hamilton was incorporated and a relative of Hamilton's and his childhood friend, Joseph H. Thompson, was elected president, with Mr. Morgan treasurer and manager. Hamilton was also president of the Nashville Trust Company. In 1906 Morgan & Hamilton Company moved for the fourth time to the factory in North Nashville built by the expiring Tennessee Manufacturing Company.

When Thompson died in 1917, Jo B. Morgan succeeded him as president. Morgan was a director of the Nashville, Chattanooga & St. Louis Railroad and one of the founders of West End Methodist Church. When he died in 1927 at age seventy-one, his son, Jo B. Morgan Jr., became president of Morgan & Hamilton Company.

The *Nashville Tennessean* announced on February 1, 1928, that, effective January 31, Morgan & Hamilton Company, one of the leading manufacturers of cotton bags in the country, had been acquired by Werthan Bag Company in one of the largest business transactions in the history of Nashville. The merger brought with it a complex of 1860–80 era textile mill buildings on Eighth Avenue North.

Meier Werthan, the founder of Werthan Bag and Burlap, began business in Nashville in 1868 as a rag dealer. A year later, he and his brother-in-law, Sigmund Godhelp, operated a produce store at 143 Market Street called Godhelp & Werthan. After the death of Godhelp in 1895, Werthan renamed his business as M. Werthan and Company, and brought his sons, Morris and Joe, in the business. Meier Werthan changed the name of the company to Werthan Bag Company in 1911, and opened a small plant on Second Avenue North near the public square. The business grew rapidly and, in 1914–18, made sandbags for the war effort.

In 1928 Werthan Bag purchased the Tennessee Manufacturing Company and the Wariota Cotton Mills, described as the second largest cotton bag plant in the United States. Morris Werthan was the merged company's president, Joe Werthan was vice president and treasurer, and Bernard Werthan was treasurer. The new company, initially named the Werthan-Morgan-Hamilton Company, was perhaps the largest manufacturer of all kinds of bags in the world. Werthan Bag Company went on, under the leadership of four generations of Werthan family members, to be an important and respected Nashville industrial concern throughout the twentieth century.

During World War II, Joe Werthan purchased two large homes on Elliston Place and opened the Joe Werthan Servicemen's Center on the corner of Elliston Place and Twenty-Third Avenue North. The center provided lodging, food, and entertainment free of charge. Between December 5, 1942, and 1946, it had hosted more than one million servicemen.

Werthan built a multi-wall paper bag facility in 1952 and established a textile mill division during the decade. In the 1960s, the company diversified by building a plant to manufacture plastic bags and expanded into check printing and auto part sales. As a result of this diversification into printing on paper and plastics, the company changed its name to Werthan Industries Inc.

During the 1970s, Werthan closed its textile mill division. Later in the decade, Werthan had as many as fifteen hundred employees. The company sold its packaging division to Bernard Werthan Jr. in 1989, and sold the buildings that housed the textile mill and textile bag plant to Charles Jones in 1998. Jones sold the buildings to Core Development Services some years later. Core Development converted part of the old factory building into handsome condominiums, and continues to do so today.

Werthan Bag Company, 1954.
Metropolitan Nashville Archives.

In 2009, under chief executive officer Don Belmont and Chairman Tony Werthan, the company continued to be one of the major producers of multi-wall paper bags for the pet food industry. This was still the case in 2013, when Werthan had operations both in Nashville and White House, Tennessee.

DEPARTMENT STORES

BURK & COMPANY was started in Baltimore in 1843 by Charles Burk. A Nashville branch was opened in 1879 by a nephew of Burk named Joe Fensterwald. The store sold men's and women's wear, sporting goods, and uniforms. In 1921 Burk & Company was located at 416–22 Church Street, on the site of the old Masonic Hall and Theater. Burk & Company was then the exclusive furnisher of uniforms for Nashville police, firemen, and the Boy Scouts of America.

In 1930 the company's marketing area covered all of Middle Tennessee. That summer, Burk & Company was the official outfitter for Camp Alpine, a mountain camp for girls eighty-eight miles southeast of Nashville in Monteagle, Tennessee. By 1948 Burk & Company provided men's and boys' clothing and furnishings, uniforms, sporting goods, trunks and bags, shoes, camera and photographic supplies, hobby craft, and ladies' "ready-to-wear" clothing.

I remember shopping at Burk & Company with my mother in the 1940s. The store owners, brothers Bernard and Ralph Fensterwald, sons of Joe, had rigged up a series of wires, pulleys, baskets, and vacuum tubes that sent merchandise, cash, and paperwork from the apparel sections of the store to the cash register. It was fascinating to a young boy. In 1949 a Burk & Company advertisement read: "Everything For Correct Sports, Campus, Street and Formal Wear."

When Bernard Fensterwald died in May 1951, Ralph purchased the half interest from his brother's estate, intending to keep the business in the family. The next year, however, Harveys bought Burk & Company and renovated the air-conditioning system and the elevators. By 1956, Robert Belser was manager, and Greenfield Pitts was secretary-treasurer. When Harveys closed Burk & Company in 1961 and leased the space to Gus Meyer, Greenfield Pitts became treasurer of Harveys.

Cain-Sloan Company was founded in 1903 and became the city's first complete department store. That year, Paul L. Sloan, John E. Cain, and Patrick H. Cain bought Kalmbach's Beehive, a dry goods store at 233 North Summer Street. They renamed the store Cain Sloan & Company.

On November 16, 1903, the new store's ad in the *Nashville Banner* read: "We will offer great values in Gloves, Hosiery, Underwear, Corsets, Leather and Fancy Goods, to make room for new lines of Dry Goods arriving daily."

In 1907 the company moved to a six-story "double warehouse" at 207–211 Fifth Avenue and incorporated the store as Cain-Sloan Company.

Cain-Sloan Company and the Tennessee Theater, circa 1972.
Collection of Kermit C. Stengel Jr. Estate.

By the 1920s the owners' advertisements heralded the store as "Nashville's most popular department store." In 1915 and again in 1936, the store acquired more frontage on Church Street.

Upon the death of Paul Sloan in 1933, his son, John E. Sloan, who had joined the company as a salesman in the men's department, became vice president. In 1937 he was elected president, a position he would hold until his retirement in 1969. In the same year Sloan became president, Cain-Sloan installed a fur storage department. Previously their customers had to ship their fur coats to large cold-storage plants in the East.

In 1944 Cain-Sloan secured a ninety-nine-year lease on property directly across Church Street that my grandmother Elizabeth Jackson Buckner's family owned. In 1949 John Sloan announced that Cain-Sloan would erect a $1 million store on the site. The Jackson Building was razed and a parking garage was built as phase one of the new project. A shortage of steel during the Korean War halted construction.

Finally, a merger with Allied Stores, announced on July 28, 1955, enabled Cain-Sloan to build an exciting new building. On October 25, 1957, Cain-Sloan moved, with great fanfare, to its new $8 million building at the southwest corner of Fifth Avenue and Church Street, which was a much larger building than had been anticipated in 1949.

Chief Executive Officer John Sloan, who was a handsome man of high intelligence, and with a quick wit, promoted the store as "the greatest store of the Central South." Cain-Sloan became known for its unique window displays, its three-thousand-cars-a-day parking garage, and its fashion shows in the Iris Room Restaurant. To counter Harveys innovations, Cain-Sloan had an animated "Bunnyland" display in the toy department at Easter and a "Breakfast with Santa" in December.

In 1965 Cain-Sloan opened its first suburban department store in the new Green Hills Shopping Center. John Sloan was named Nashville's "Merchandiser of the Year" in 1968. Sloan retired in 1969.

John Dubuisson succeeded him as president. A few weeks later, Dubuisson suffered a fatal heart attack and was succeeded by Frank Harvey in 1970. A year later, Cain-Sloan opened an anchor store in Rivergate Mall. A store in Hickory Hollow came in 1978.

In 1987 Cain-Sloan was sold by its owner, Allied Stores, to Dillard Department Stores, Inc., of Little Rock, Arkansas. Jack Curtis, who had succeeded Frank Harvey as president, remained as president of Dillard's Nashville stores until 1990, two years after the downtown Cain-Sloan store closed.

Realtor Tony Giarratana purchased the property then sold it to Allright Parking but retained exclusive rights to buy it back. The building was imploded on April 24, 1994, and remains a two-hundred-space parking lot today.

CASTNER-KNOTT was opened in 1898 by Charles Castner and William Knott at the northwest corner of Church and Summer Streets. The same year, Knott established a buying office in New York, an unusual move for a Southern dry goods store. In 1906 Castner-Knott moved to its handsome new five-story store at 618 Church Street, on the corner of Church and Capitol Boulevard. The new store had a complete men's shop and a department devoted to furniture, rugs, draperies, and upholstery.

In 1910 a postcard advertised Castner-Knott's rest room on the second floor as "the finest in the South." A 1915 ad in the Vanderbilt *Commodore* scaled back the earlier claim, only proclaiming the dry goods store as "Nashville's Shopping Center." In 1928 the men's department on the main floor offered a suit with two pair of trousers for $22.50.

Mercantile Stores Inc. of New York bought Castner-Knott in 1933. In 1955, in the face of stiff competition downtown, Castner-Knott underwent a $3 million expansion.

Castner-Knott opened its first branch store in 1961 in Donelson Plaza. Their second suburban store opened in Harding Mall in 1966. Next came stores in Rivergate in 1971 and Hickory Hollow in 1979. Castner-Knott remained aggressive, establishing stores in Bellevue in 1990 and in Cool Springs in 1991. The company did so even though many analysts theorized at the time that the department store concept was outmoded.

When Sears closed its store on Lafayette Street in 1991, Castner-Knott became downtown's only department store. Ralph Glassford served as president of Castner-Knott from 1975 until his retirement in 1992. In

Castner-Knott Dry Goods Company, 1907. *Collection of Kermit C. Stengel Jr. Estate.*

September 1994 Mercantile Stores, Castner-Knott's parent company, was purchased by Dillard Department Stores Inc. of Little Rock, Arkansas. Because Dillard's also owned Cain-Sloan, anti-trust laws forced the chain to divest itself of one of their two Nashville stores. Castner-Knott closed its doors on September 30, 1998, exactly one hundred years from the date its first store opened its doors in Nashville.

That same year, Nashvillian Michael Shmerling bought the downtown Castner-Knott building for a reported $1.5 million and restored it to its original grandeur. Michael's Adventure 3 Properties rents the building today for office and retail use.

HARVEY'S began when Fred Harvey moved to Nashville in 1942 to open the department store.

One day, a gentleman approached James R. Kellam Jr. at his desk at Commerce Union and asked to see Potter, the bank president. Kellam, who

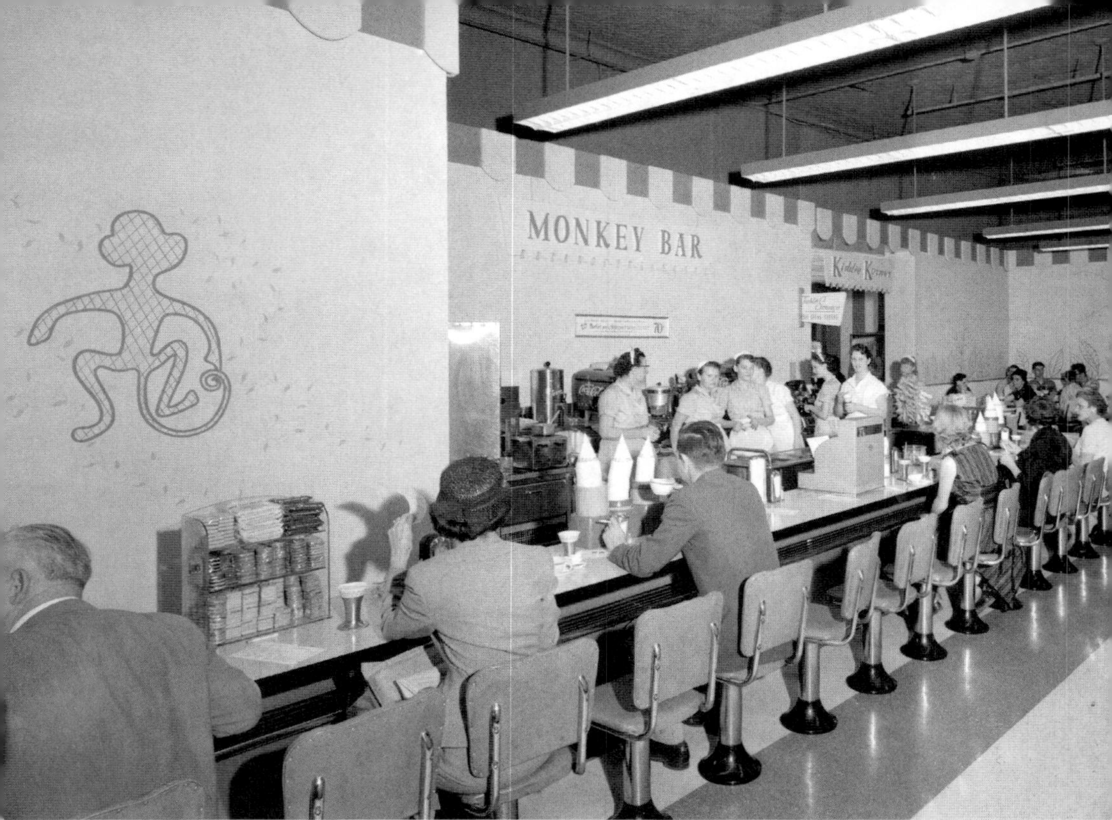

Harvey's Monkey Bar.
Collection of Grannis Photography.

was cashier of the bank, explained that Potter didn't come to the bank on Saturdays. The man identified himself as a department store broker and said that it was important for him to see Potter. Impressed with his story, Kellam drove him to Potter's house, where he was cutting wood in the barn. When the man asked, "Where is Mr. Potter?" Potter answered, "He's in the house." Potter then followed the man to the house, where the stranger explained that he had a client, Fred Harvey, who might want to take over the Lebeck property located at 514–24 Church Street.

Potter asked him to bring Fred Harvey, manager of the basement store at Marshall Field & Company, to Nashville for an interview. When Harvey came, Potter asked him how much he was prepared to pay in as capital if he obtained the lease. Harvey replied, "Everything I have in the world, about $65,000."

Potter was pleased, as he took a dim view of any borrower who sought bank funds without first committing his own money to the fullest extent. Harvey got the loan, leased the property, and moved to Nashville in 1942 to open the department store known as Harvey's.

Fred Harvey's modern merchandising and entertainment skills made his store a serious competitor to the city's established department stores but not without some cost to his son. When Fred "Rick" Harvey Jr. graduated from Parmer School in 1946, his father made him attend West End High School rather than the elitist Montgomery Bell Academy, where most of Rick's friends went. Nevertheless, Fred Harvey bought the P. D. Houston mansion on Belle Meade Boulevard and put his name on an oversized mailbox.

In 1946 Harvey's installed the first escalator in Tennessee. I was thrilled to go downtown to ride it. By then, Harvey's had the full attention of Nashville shoppers because of the escalators and his other promotional tactics that ranged from unusual to bizarre. They included putting a cage of monkeys beside the store's snack bar, and installing carnival mirrors and children's rides, including a merry-go-round. The *St. Louis Post Dispatch* once wrote that shopping at Harvey's was "more fun than a case full of monkeys."

In 1953 Harvey's placed dozens of larger-than-life-sized nativity scene figures on the east side of the Parthenon, facing West End. For fourteen years, Nashvillians came in droves to slowly pass by the white nativity scene each Christmas to see the display, which was bathed in spot lights. The display was removed in 1967 because of the deterioration of the figures.

In 1957, after Cain-Sloan moved to its new building on the southwest corner of Fifth and Church, Harvey's bought Cain-Sloan's old building across Church Street. Harveys then occupied the entire north side of Church Street between Fifth Avenue North and Sixth Avenue North. During the 1950s and 1960s, Nashville kids loved the fun-house mirrors, the elephant slide, live monkeys, and the merry-go-round horses. Harvey's was then the city's largest store, having grown to twenty times its size in 1942.

Fred Harvey died in 1960 at age fifty-seven. Two years later, the store opened its first branch in the Madison Square Shopping Center. In 1967 Harvey's built a suburban store to anchor 100 Oaks Shopping Center. In the latter half of the decade, Harvey's also built stores in several Middle

Tennessee towns where competition was not as fierce as in Nashville. In 1984 Harvey's, then run by Fred Harvey's son, Rick Harvey, closed its Church Street store. Four years later, W. S. Peebles, a thirty-nine-store Virginia-based chain, bought the nine Harvey's stores and renamed them. An exciting era had ended.

KUHN'S BIG K was a wholesale conglomerate started as Kuhn Brothers Company in 1917. It was founded by three brothers, Lee, Gus, and Ike Kuhn, who earlier had three different stores at three different locations: Lee in Columbia, Tennessee; Gus in Harriman, Tennessee; and Ike in Decatur, Alabama. When these companies were merged in 1917, they decided to consolidate in one central location and chose Nashville, where they established an office/warehouse/store at 309 Broad Street.

By 1929 Kuhn Brothers Variety Stores had thirty-three employees at its downtown location. By then, Gus's brother-in-law, Simon S. Weil, was a partner. During his long career at Kuhn's, he would serve as store manager, buyer, superintendent, director, and finally president of Big K stores.

Jack and Gus Kuhn Jr., second-generation members of the Kuhn family, and Weil greatly expanded the company, launching their Big K Stores. In 1962, it had forty-two stores in four states. They, however, kept some of their old stores, including Kuhn's Variety Store at 4816 Charlotte Avenue in Nashville. It operated there from 1942 until the building burned in 1977.

The Kuhns, with their sons and sons-in-law, Gilbert Fox and Carl Goldstein, decided in the 1960s to give discounting a try in the Southeast. So they began opening new stores in the region under the name Big K Discount. By 1976 they had over one hundred stores, seventy-nine of which were called Big K. Following Walmart's strategy, they placed their Big K stores in small- to medium-sized towns in Alabama, Georgia, Kentucky, and Tennessee. In 1978 they opened an enormous warehouse/office complex in MetroCenter. Soon they had 145 stores.

A downturn in the economy and an increase in the interest rate were two of the factors that caused Kuhn's Big K Stores Inc. to sell out to Walmart in 1981.

Lebeck's handsome new store, 1907.
Collection of Ridley Wills II.

LEBECK BROTHERS INC. was founded in 1874. Its owners, Michael S. "Mike" Louis and Samuel Lebeck, operated their store in a four-story building at 38 South Union Street, then the center of retail activity in Nashville.

Their store prospered. Deeply committed to their community, the owners were known for their philanthropy.

In 1880 Lebeck Brothers was selling dry goods and notions at a new location, at the corner of Market Street and the Public Square.

In January 1897 a devastating fire broke out in the four-story Lebeck building, destroying it and eight other buildings and damaging the south end of the Market House.

Lebeck Brothers regrouped and, in time, relocated to a new store at 514–24 Church Street. Outgrowing their space there, they built a new four-story building on the same site in 1922.

Late in the 1920s, ads urged Vandy co-eds to visit Lebeck's Style Shop and Vanderbilt men to visit the men's section.

In the 1930s, Lebeck Brothers was hammered by the Depression, accumulating a sizeable debt to Commerce Union Bank. Unable to pay, the company filed a petition in bankruptcy. As a result of the court action,

Commerce Union was awarded all the stock of Lebeck Brothers. The bank also was awarded the company's only remaining asset, its building on Church Street, which had been vacated in 1940.

LOVEMAN, BERGER & TEITLEBAUM was a fashionable store founded by David Loveman, as D. Loveman & Company, in 1862, to make hoop skirts. The store, originally located at 16 Public Square, later moved to 412–14 Union Street. In 1906 Loveman had two partners, Henry Teitlebaum and Samuel W. Berger. A year later, the establishment, having broadened its merchandise to include children's and women's apparel of all kinds, moved to a larger building at 241–45 Fifth Avenue North.

In about 1913 the three owners changed the name of the company to Loveman, Berger & Teitlebaum to reflect their respective ownership positions.

Loveman's smart clothes and fashion accessories attracted a large and discriminating clientele. After World War II, ladies from surrounding towns would give their children a quarter and tell them to investigate the five-and-dime companies on Fifth Avenue North while they shopped at Loveman, Berger & Teitlebaum.

In 1959 when Robert Teitlebaum Sr. was president, Loveman's opened a Belle Meade store on Harding Road. Two years later, the company's downtown store closed.

In 1976 after being in business for 114 years, Loveman's closed.

MCCLURES started as an offshoot of Neely, Harwell & Company, a wholesale dry goods business run by Sam K. Harwell Sr. and his sons, Robert and Sam Jr., and their cousin, William B. Harwell. Neely, Harwell & Company relied on its drummers (early in the twentieth century traveling salesmen were called "drummers") and primarily served small town dry goods stores in the mid-South area. During the Depression, many of these stores closed, leading the Harwells to start the McClure's chain of stores in Middle Tennessee as outlets for Neely, Harwell's goods.

In 1949 McClure's, located at 1801 Twenty-First Avenue South, advertised itself as "Nashville's Largest Suburban Department Store," offering Kirsch Venetian blinds, Armstrong linoleum and asphalt tile, drapery and hardware, men's furnishings, ladies' "ready-to-wear" clothing, and gifts of all kinds.

McClure's was headed in the 1950s by the Andrews family, including Sam Harwell Jr.'s daughter, Evalina Andrews; her husband, David Andrews; and his brother, Nelson Andrews. Evalina was a pioneer as one of the few women to operate a business the size of McClure's. Eventually, there were four McClure's stores in Hillsboro Village, Madison Square, Franklin, and Madison Furniture Store. McClure's appealed to a clientele looking for moderately priced clothes, fabrics, toys, and Boy and Girl Scout uniforms and accessories.

In 1973 McClure's opened a thirty-thousand-square-foot store in Belle Meade, which was larger than all the other McClure's stores put together. This store offered a more sophisticated selection than any of the others and generated large fashion ads in the Sunday *Tennessean* to gradually change the company's image.

David Andrews IV, who became manager of the new store, was determined that excellent customer service would become a company hallmark. Within a few years, McClure's was recognized as one of the leading independent department stores in the United States. In the 1980s, McClure's opened a store in Brentwood and, at its peak, grossed sales of over $20 million.

The company closed in July 2002, as its customer base had dramatically changed shopping patterns. Former customers still miss the Easter bunnies, the mystery sale, special Christmas boxes, party dresses, the piano player in December, and the outstanding, friendly staff.

Rich, Schwartz & Joseph was Nashville's finest upscale women's clothing store. It was founded March 17, 1902, by Leo Schwartz, who had grown up in Chattanooga, and Julius Rich, who had for many years worked for Nashville's D. Loveman and Company. Rich-Schwartz, located at 227 North Summer Street, was the first exclusive specialty store south of Louisville, Kentucky, and the first store in Nashville to carry ladies' "ready-to-wear," a term Leo Schwartz coined. Earlier, Nashville ladies were dependent on dressmakers for their fine clothes.

Three years later, when Arthur Joseph bought into the business, the company name was changed to Rich, Schwartz & Joseph. The store quickly gained a reputation for "class and couture." One Christmas, when a little boy was asked who the three wise men were, he answered, "Rich, Schwartz & Joseph." Arthur Joseph, who was responsible for the financial side of the business, retired in 1926.

By 1936 the 200 block of Fifth Avenue North had become dominated by dime stores. This caused Rich, Schwartz & Joseph to move to 204 Sixth Avenue North. There, the company built a sleek, new steel and concrete building designed by a Chicago architect. It featured handsome bronze doors and mellow wood paneling inside. The company cleverly advertised itself as being on "Smart Sixth Avenue." Two innovations were that Rich, Schwartz & Joseph had the first built-in air-conditioning system and the first Muzak, state-of-the-art background music system in the city.

That same year, Emmette Vance Plumlee was promoted to an executive position in the firm. He did most of the buying of fine coats, suits, and furs until his death in 1948.

After Julius Rich died in 1937, Leo Schwartz bought his interest in the company. Having earlier acquired Joseph's interest, he then had full control. The corporation's name, however, remained Rich, Schwartz & Joseph, although most people called the store Rich-Schwartz.

In 1949 Schwartz hired a talented young designer named Betty Jo Patten from Grace's. Her charge was to open Nashville's first bridal department. She did so and quickly gained the confidence of Leo Schwartz and his son, Morris Frank Schwartz. In 1950 Betty Jo married Morris's son, Frank, who also worked at the store.

When the brilliant merchant Leo Schwartz died in 1952, Morris Schwartz succeeded him as president. He had been with Rich, Schwartz & Joseph since 1922.

Three of Rich, Schwartz & Joseph's frequent customers in the mid-twentieth century were Jean Faircloth McArthur, wife of Gen. Douglas McArthur; Sara Mac Jarman, the stylish wife of Maxey Jarman, chairman of the board of Genesco; and Sarah Cannon, known to so many Americans as "Minnie Pearl."

One of Morris Schwartz's longtime assistants was Mamie Mallory, who did all the elegant window decorations that featured life-sized mannequins posed on hardwood floors and small area rugs. Mallory, who was always well-dressed, contributed to the elegance of the store.

For many years, Rich, Schwartz & Joseph employed a full-time artist to draw sketches of elegant dresses and gowns that appeared as full page ads in the *Nashville Tennessean* and *Nashville Banner*.

Before integration, the store opened a dressing room specifically to accommodate their affluent African American clientele, many of whose husbands were physicians, professors, and attorneys. Rich, Schwartz & Joseph was the first predominantly white store in Nashville to do this.

In 1955 Rich, Schwartz & Joseph, realizing that they would be unable to renew their lease at 204 Sixth Avenue North, made the decision to move to a new "uptown" location at 2400 West End Avenue, closer to where a majority of the store's clientele lived. The new location had been the home of E. Gray Smith's Packard dealership. The interior was designed by Sydney H. Morris and Associates of Chicago, the same company that had designed the Sixth Avenue store. To make certain that the interior design was "right," Morris Schwartz sent his daughter-in-law, Betty Jo, to Chicago thirteen times in thirteen weeks to work out details with the architect's interior designer. When the store opened on March 5, 1956, it looked exquisite and showcased a fine line of quality dresses, furs, lingerie, accessories, and shoes. There were comfortable chairs scattered about and large couches in the coat, suit, and fur departments.

At the time of the opening, Morris Schwartz promoted Ellen Woodson, a capable African American maid, to cashier. Another valued African American employee, Zach Primm, walked to and from work every morning from his home near Ward-Belmont because he refused to ride on segregated city buses. He became the first African American bonded in the South and was given responsibility for hiring, training, and firing all the company's African American help.

When Morris Schwartz died in 1957, his son, Morris Frank Schwartz Jr., became the third generation of his family to become president of Rich,

Schwartz & Joseph. Frank was a Vanderbilt graduate, who had served in the US Navy in World War II.

In 1960 Oman Construction Company approached Rich, Schwartz & Joseph about building a second store as the anchor tenant in their proposed Belle Meade Shopping Center. Schwartz turned down Oman two or three times because he didn't feel he could afford to build and furnish the store. Oman persisted and negotiated a loan/purchase deal that finally convinced Rich, Schwartz & Joseph to make the move. Schwartz entrusted his wife, Betty Jo, with decorating and furnishing the store that opened in 1961 under her management. The Belle Meade store maintained the same high standards of hand selection of quality merchandise as did the 2400 West End store. It, however, put greater emphasis on younger customers' tastes and budgets, and included children's and maternity wear, a photographic studio, and a beauty salon.

Betty Jo Schwartz had to find someone to handle the bridal department since she had assumed the management of the Belle Meade store. She hired Jeanne (Mrs. Bob Dudley) Smith to do so in about 1966. Jeanne Smith recalled, in 2012, that she traveled in the company's white station wagon to weddings all over the Midsouth. The station wagon had the name "Rich, Schwartz & Joseph" painted on its sides and the words "All Our Brides Are Beautiful" painted on the back. Smith had worked for Rich, Schwartz & Joseph, as a teenager, at its Sixth Avenue North store after school and on Saturdays. To her, Rich, Schwartz & Joseph was a world of elegance and beauty. From 1966 until 1969, when Betty Jo and Frank Schwartz Jr. divorced and Betty Jo left the company, Betty Jo had been Jeanne Smith's mentor and, in her words, "Rich, Schwartz & Joseph's driving force."

Rich, Schwartz & Joseph did not do well after Betty Jo Schwartz left. In 1976, Frank Schwartz Jr. sold it to a man and his son from Lexington, Kentucky, who continued operating Rich, Schwartz & Joseph until 1986, when the business closed, ending a nine-decade-long run of upscale fashion merchandising.

SERVICE MERCHANDISE COMPANY was a catalogue/showroom business that grew out of a Ben Franklin five-and-dime store founded by Harry Zimmerman in Pulaski, Tennessee. With two cousins, he formed a partnership, Shainberg & Zimmerman Company, that expanded to ten stores. Zimmerman's wife, Mary, ran the stores while he served in the South Pacific during World War II.

After the war, Harry Zimmerman dissolved his partnership with his cousins and moved to Nashville, where he went into the wholesale business, selling jewelry and other goods directly to dime stores. Harry Zimmerman, by then joined by his son, Raymond, left the wholesale business and opened, in 1960, the Service Merchandise Company showroom on Lower Broadway in Nashville.

Harry and Raymond Zimmerman took the store public in 1971 and grew it into a national concern that had, at its height, 140 catalogue showrooms in twenty-eight states. In the early 1980s, the company moved its headquarters to Brentwood. In December 1995, Raymond Zimmerman, chairman of the company's board, made the tough emotional decision to close the original Service Merchandise store at 305 Broadway that his father had opened in 1960. By 1995 Service Merchandise had grown into the country's largest catalogue showroom retailer, with more than $4 billion in sales in 1994.

Nevertheless, Service Merchandise was hammered by the strength of such giant discount stores as Walmart, K-Mart, and Target. Zimmerman countered by restructuring his company's retail format. Still, Service Merchandise went into bankruptcy and, finally, into liquidation in 2002.

P. J. Tinsley Millinery Company was a department store that started in 1888 as Tinsley Brothers & Gilbert. Located at 200–202 Broadway, the store sold dry goods, boots, and shoes. The partners were Ellis F. Tinsley; his brother, Phillip J. Tinsley; and William J. Gilbert, a neighbor on Woodland Street. By 1894, Tinsley & Gilbert had moved to 207–209 Broadway, and advertised itself as a wholesale millinery and notions store.

About this time, Phillip Tinsley had assumed full ownership of the company and changed its name to P. J. Tinsley Millinery Company. When he sold his company a few years later, the business moved to 322 Union

Tinsley Millinery Company, interior view, 1915.
Collection of Ridley Wills II.

Street but retained the name, P. J. Tinsley Millinery Company. Its president in the 1920s was O. D. Kirk, who was recognized as a great salesman.

By 1925 Tinsley Millinery moved to its final location at 701 Church Street. Thirty years later, two managers at Harveys acquired bank financing and purchased Tinsley's for an estimated $200,000. The store then had annual gross sales of an estimated $1 million.

Before 1960, when Hart Stores Inc. of Mobile, Alabama, purchased Tinsley's, Melville Morris (who owned a string of jewelry stores across the South, including Jacob Jewelry Company in Nashville), owned a majority of Tinsley's stock. The purchase did not work well for Hart Stores Inc., so the company closed the store.

The 13,500-square-foot building was vacant for many months before it became home, in 1964, to Gold & Silver Company, founded in about 1954 by Paul S. Gold and Dave Silver.

DRUGSTORES

Demoville's Drug Store was, in the 1890s, Nashville's most prominent drugstore. Located at the corner of Church and Cherry Streets, it was founded in 1859 by S. L. Demoville, who ran the business until 1896, when he retired. His son, James L. Demoville, succeeded him and later brought into the firm, as junior members, brothers John and Paul Stumb, who operated the cigar stand.

The store occupied one half of the basement and the first floor of a four-story building thirty-five by one hundred feet at 200 North Cherry Street in the heart of the city. The first floor featured walnut wall cases, plate glass showcases, and handsome counters. Complete in every respect, Demoville's carried drugs and druggist's articles, perfumes, medical supplies, and surgical instruments.

The onyx soda fountain, built at a great expense, was to the right of the front door. Cigars, both domestic and imported, and smoking tobacco were displayed in a glass counter to the left of the front door. In the rear was the pharmacy, where prescriptions were filled and where patent medicines were sold. Demoville's was also a wholesale dealer in mineral water. The most popular brands were Bethesda, Boro Lithia, Ozonate Lithia, and Willow Brook. In the 1890s, Demoville's had eight employees. It was succeeded by Stumb Soda and Cigars that opened next door.

Ford-Musgrove Drug Store was owned by brothers-in-law Dr. Jesse Hill Ford Sr. and Dr. Robert L. Musgrove Jr. This drugstore was located at 5211 Harding Road for many years. Their slogan was "Rely on Us—Your Doctor Does."

When I was a boy in the 1940s, my best friend, Jim Meadows Jr., and I would ride our bicycles over to Ford-Musgrove on Saturday afternoons and listen to college football games while sipping Cokes. We loved listening to University of Alabama games as the Crimson Tide's star left halfback, Harry Gilmer, was an All-American who had perfected the "jump pass." In 1946, Gilmer led Alabama to a 34–14 Rose Bowl victory over the University

Demoville & Company.
Nashville Public Library, Special Collections.

of Southern California. Robert Musgrove was not as enamored over Alabama's gridiron success as we were; he was an Auburn man.

Some of the regulars who drank coffee every morning in the 1960s and 1970s at Ford-Musgrove were Charlie Broome, John Eddie Cain, Charlie and Nick Daugherty, Bill Elliston, Rufus Fort, Carl Haury, Pete Holt, John Phipps, Tom Plaster, and Reese Smith. They loved to play jokes on each other and gamble on football games.

Ford-Musgrove Drug Store. Left to right: Charlie Daugherty, Dr. Robert Musgrove, Nick Daugherty, Pete Holt, and John Ramsey. *Collection of Charlie Daugherty.*

In 1974 the Federal Bureau of Investigation (FBI) raided Ford-Musgrove, mistakenly thinking that gambling done there was on a greater scale than was the case. Inside the drugstore at that time was a louvered door on which the regulars who sat nearby put a sign that read "Bored of Directors." One of the FBI agents asked, "What's behind that door?" The regulars said, "Nothing." When he opened the door, he was staring into some electrical equipment. One of the regulars, perplexed as to why the FBI would bother to raid Ford-Musgrove, quipped, "Now I know why you can't find Patty Hearst."

Ford's son, Jesse Hill Ford Jr., became a noted writer of Southern literature. In 1961 he spent a year at the University of Oslo as a Fulbright Scholar and published his first book, *Mountains of Gilead*. In 1964 he wrote the script of *The Conversion of Buster Drumwright*. A year later, he wrote *The Liberation of Lord Byron Jones*. Ford-Musgrove hosted a book signing when the book was published. It was Ford-Musgrove's finest hour.

After Jesse Ford Sr.'s death in the 1960s, Musgrove continued to run Ford-Musgrove until his retirement in about 1975. At that time, some of the regulars who had coffee there every day, including John Eddie Cain, gave a retirement party for Musgrove at Hillwood Country Club. Musgrove's brother came from Alabama to help negotiate a sale of the drugstore to Henry Birdsong, who owned West End Drugs at 2914 West End Avenue.

MOON DRUG COMPANY INC. was Located in the Belle Meade Theater building. This drugstore was opened in 1940 by its owner, Dr. Clyde K. Moon.

In the 1940s, there were many fraternity parties and dances at the Belle Meade Country Club. Sometimes, at intermission, boys, with their dates beside them, would race their cars down both sides of Belle Meade Boulevard (which was usually almost empty), to get ice cream sundaes or milk shakes at Moon Drug Company. On Saturday afternoons, before and after "The Happiness Club" matinee at the Belle Meade Theater next door, dozens of children could be seen sprawling on the floor at Moon's reading comic books. Youngsters also mobbed Moon's after Friday night movies.

In 1947 Moon Drug was the city's largest and most modern drugstore with seven major departments that sold prescriptions, cosmetics, household needs, and sundries. The drugstore also featured a US Post Office.

In 1962 Moon moved his store to the west end of the building. There, Betty Lou Layne continued serving lunches until 1981. Moon sold his interest in 1970 but continued to work in the pharmacy every morning, serving customers whose parents and grandparents had been his customers in earlier years.

In the 1970s, Moon Drug Company was still going strong in the Belle Meade Shopping Center, the Medical Arts Building at 1211 Twenty-First Avenue South, at 2010 Church Street in the Mid-State Medical Center, at 3900 Hillsboro Road in Green Hills, and in the 100 Oaks Shopping Center.

In 1991 Cliff Edward, Moon Drug Company's owner, moved the store back to 4309 Harding Road, closer to its original location. He sold the drugstore in 1997 to Clearwater, Florida–based Eckerd Drugs. Moon, then eighty-eight years old, said, "I was really saddened to see them close. I suppose that's just what's happening—everything is big business."

STUMB SODA AND CIGARS was created when a young man, John P. Stumb, formed a partnership with his younger brother, Paul A. Stumb, to operate a cigar stand in the Demoville's Drug Store on Cherry Street, which in December 1904 had its name changed to Fourth Avenue. Being quite successful, they secured, by 1910, a long-term lease in the same building, next door to Demoville's at 202 Fourth Avenue North. There, they built up a fine trade under the firm name of Stumb Soda and Cigars, with John being the senior partner. The restaurant sold fountain drinks; food; ice cream; Whitman's candy; W.D.C., Sasieni, and Dunhill pipes; and fine cigars. It was a popular meeting place for men, particularly at lunch hour.

In about 1919, their younger brother, Andrew J. Stumb, joined the firm. He ran the company's ice cream business, making ice cream in hand-operated freezers. Stumb ice cream was the first "home-made" ice cream for retail sale in Nashville. One of their customers was the Centennial Club. At their luncheons, the women's club served Stumb ice cream molded in the shape of flowers.

John Stumb died in 1922 at age fifty-one. Paul, who was also a principal in Stumb-Cawthon Motor Company, retired in 1926, leaving Andrew to run the family business. By 1928, the business had closed, and Andrew was running the Andrew Stumb Company out of his home at 3116 Gallatin Road. That year or the next, the building at 202 Fourth Avenue North was torn down to build the Noel Hotel.

Warner Drug Company was founded in the 1880s by J. W. Warner Sr., who prepared for his life's work by clerking in a drugstore one year without pay. When he felt prepared, he formed a partnership with J. G. Greener under the firm name J. G. Greener & Company.

Later, Warner bought out his partner and renamed the company Warner Drug Company. His first store was in the Warner Building, built in 1887 at 401 Public Square on the northwest corner of College and Cedar Streets. Warner Drug Company was incorporated in 1902. Its business included the handling of crude drugs, seeds, paints, and glass. Warner's second store was on Church Street in the center of a fashionable retail shopping area. The third Warner Drug Company was on Fifth Avenue at the entrance of the Arcade.

By 1925 Warner's management responsibilities were shared by his brother, L. A. Warner, who was vice president; another brother, C. Bowling Warner; and J. W.'s son, J. W. Warner Jr., who was treasurer. The Warners opened, in July of that year, a fourth store at the corner of Third Avenue North and the Public Square. A big crowd visited on opening day, many coming to congratulate Warner Sr. on his store's forty years of progress. Warner always realized that the foundation of the company's success was his prescription department and his Squibb line of products—pharmaceuticals, chemicals and biologicals that were prominently displayed in his show windows.

In 1928 the Warners sold all of their stores to the Walgreen Drug Company. All but the one at the Arcade were repurchased in 1932, presumably at lower prices due to the Depression. In 1949, the company still had four stores: 2800 West End Avenue, 1813 Hillsboro Road, 219 Public Square, and 401 Public Square. All offered drugs, lunches, fountain service, and gifts for all occasions. When these stores were sold in August 1953 to Wilson Quick Pharmacy, the company name and other assets were retained by J. W. Warner Jr., who continued to operate his own Warner's Pharmacy in Donelson.

On November 1, 1956, W. J. "Billy" Warner III and his father opened a modern six-thousand-square-foot drugstore on the east side of Franklin Pike near Battlefield Drive and next to a new H. G. Hill supermarket. J. W. Warner Jr. was president, and Billy Warner was store manager and secretary.

In 1967 Billy's nephew, Tom Hudson Jr., then a student at Montgomery Bell Academy, worked at the store that had a thriving breakfast and lunch business. Hudson remembers cooking breakfast daily for 120 customers that summer. When Interstate 65 was built in the late 1950s and early 1960s, the Tennessee Department of Transportation (TDOT) took part of the building. The store continued to operate, however, until December 1994, when competition from nearby chain stores caused Billy Warner to sell the one-time chain's last store on Franklin Road to Revco Drug.

DRY GOODS STORES

LARDNER CLARK'S DRY GOODS STORE was the first dry goods store in Nashville. It was established by Lardner Clark in 1786. He brought his merchandise—piece goods, needles, and pins—over the Appalachian Mountains from Philadelphia on ten horses. His building served as a store, tavern, and dwelling. It was located at what is today 214 Second Avenue North.

Lardner Clark was in business for about six years. In June 1790, Clark and J. C. Mountflorence leased the salt works they owned on low ground near the Cumberland River to a Captain Hart who produced salt there. In 1786 Clark was one of the original trustees of Davidson Academy.

ELECTRICAL COMPANIES

Braid Electric Company was founded by Scottish-born James W. Braid in 1879. Braid and another bright young Nashvillian, Edward Barnard, were working for Poole's Photographic Gallery on the corner of Cherry and Union Streets. Poole was frustrated because Barnard was crazy about astronomy, while Braid was equally crazy about electricity. Barnard went on to become an internationally acclaimed astronomer, famous for discovering the fifth satellite of Jupiter.

Braid and a friend in Louisville, Kentucky, conducted a telephone conversation with each other in 1878, although nearly two hundred miles separated them. Inspired by his friendship with Alexander Graham Bell, Braid made history as his phone call was the first between the cities of Nashville and Louisville.

In 1879 Braid left Poole's Photographic Gallery to start his own business that initially manufactured watchman's clock tape, commutator compounds, and signal equipment. Initially located at 133 Union Street, Braid Electric Company soon moved to Market Street.

In 1882 the company introduced the incandescent light to Tennessee only three years after Thomas Edison received a patent for the incandescent bulb. Baird installed the first electric lightbulb in a prominent window in the State Capitol. He followed up, in 1885, with the much more ambitious project of successfully installing long-distance telephone lines between Nashville and Louisville. In 1890 Braid Electric installed a generator in the Maxwell House Hotel, generating enough power to light the dining room, lobby, and halls. The company also became the first phonograph dealer in Nashville in 1895.

Encouraged by their success, J. W. Baird, W. W. Gambill (who joined the company in 1890), Thomas Jones, E. C. Andrews, and W. W. Woolwine incorporated Braid Electric in 1898. Two years later, Braid, more entrepreneur than businessman, sold his business to Gambill.

Between 1900 and 1923, Braid Electric focused on wiring large buildings, including the Polk and Watauga Apartments, for electricity; installing power plants in neighboring towns; and doing contracting work. In 1918 Braid began selling electric washing machines. By 1923 the company was selling radios. The first radio news program had been broadcast only three years earlier on station BMK in Detroit. (Note: Station BMK, which was believed to be the first station to broadcast news reports regularly, later became station WWJ 950 AM.) The company was definitely on the cutting edge.

In 1923 Gambill decided to drop the contracting work and go into the electrical supply business as well as the rapidly expanding radio and appliance businesses. By this time, his son, Ben, was working full time at the company in the city sales department, handling contractor, industrial, and appliance accounts. When his father died in 1933, Ben S. Gambill Sr. became president of Braid Electric.

His executive secretary, Alma Lewis, who had worked for his father, said that Ben Gambill "is the man who pulled the business out of the Depression." When he became president, the company had a single store and seven employees. Later in the decade, conditions improved somewhat, buoyed by Braid Electric selling the first large order of fluorescent lighting in Nashville.

By the late 1940s, the business had grown to the point that a new and larger building was essential. In 1950, Braid Electric moved into a modern building at 1100 Demonbreun Street.

When Braid Electric celebrated its seventy-fifth anniversary in 1954, it was solidly in the air-conditioning business, having started distributing air conditioners in 1951. In its first expansion outside Nashville, Braid bought controlling interest in Triangle Electric Company of Bowling Green, Kentucky, in 1960, and changed its name to Power-Lite Electric Supplies Inc. A twenty-six-thousand-square-foot expansion of the headquarters on Demonbreun Street was completed in 1969.

Ben S. Gambill Jr., a graduate of Washington and Lee University, succeeded his father as president in 1972 when Gambill Sr. became board chairman. During the next four years, Braid expanded its presence in Central Kentucky and Middle Tennessee by establishing a branch of Power-Lite in Danville, Kentucky, and opening electric supply and lighting branches in Cookeville and Shelbyville, Tennessee.

When Ben S. Gambill Sr. retired in 1977, he had been with the company for forty-four years. He had seen it grow from seven employees to more than one hundred, and seen the company provide a full line of electrical and electronic supplies, lighting, and major appliances to customers in two states. His son Ben had become chief executive officer, while another son, Tom, became vice president in charge of operations.

Braid Electric celebrated its one hundredth anniversary in 1979, marking the occasion by the acquisition of Clarksville Electric and Plumbing Supply Inc.

With steady growth fueling the move, Braid Electric moved in 1989 to a seventy-five-thousand-square-foot warehouse, lighting showroom, and corporate headquarters at 299 Cowan Street near the Cumberland River. That year and the next, Braid Electric opened its fifth and sixth locations in Columbia and Murfreesboro.

In 1990 Ben S. Gambill Jr. was elected president of the National Association of Electrical Distributors for 1991–1992.

In 2004, the company, which had about 130 employees, was acquired by Rexel, a worldwide leader in supplying electrical solutions and supplies to industrial, residential, and commercial markets.

ENGRAVING COMPANIES

Gulbenk Engraving Company was founded by Roupen Gulbenk, who had come to America in 1896 at age thirteen. He made the voyage in the hold of a ship, not knowing that hours after he left his home thirty miles from Istanbul, Turkey, his father, an Armenian Christian, was decapitated by Muslims because he refused to renounce his faith in Jesus Christ.

The young boy landed in Boston, Massachusetts, where he lived in the attic above an Armenian restaurant. As an apprentice to a photo engraving union, he studiously learned his trade. With those skills he next got a job with the United Brethren Publishing House in Dayton, Ohio, where he started adding color to his engravings.

Someone at the Methodist Publishing House in Nashville admired the young man's work. That resulted in Gulbenk (who had recently married Mildred Metcalf, of Dayton, Ohio) being offered a job at Nashville's Capitol Engraving Company, a firm that did work for the publishing house. He accepted the job and moved to Nashville with his wife in 1911.

When the Gulbenks had a son in 1920, they named him Roupen. To avoid confusion, the senior Gulbenk changed his first name to Reuben. When the baby was one year old, Mildred Gulbenk died. Reuben Gulbenk never remarried and reared his son with the help of a nurse and his mother-in-law, who moved to Nashville to help. Many times, Gulbenk brought his baby in a crib to the plant.

By working hard at Capitol Engraving and living frugally, Gulbenk saved enough money to buy a small engraving plant from Foster & Parks Printing Company. The sellers made one stipulation: Gulbenk had to promise that an African American employee named Willie Horatio Hollins would always have a job at Gulbenk Engraving Company. Gulbenk, who ran a union shop, agreed, and insisted that the International Photo Engravers Union accept Hollins as a member. Reluctantly, the Union did, and Hollins became its only black member.

Gulbenk was joined in the firm by his brother, Baldrig Gulbenk, who took care of the business side while Reuben, who was very creative, handled production and sales.

One of Gulbenk Engraving Company's early customers was the Sunday School Board of the Southern Baptist Convention. Gulbenk Engraving made the plates for the board's Sunday school material, including the Kind Word series. The relationship, begun in 1919, would last for seventy years. Other customers were the Southern Baptist Sunday School Publishing House and the National Baptist Publishing Board.

Gulbenk Engraving Company initially was housed in the garret of the Kirkman Building on Union Street, where the Gulbenks lived, and where the Tennessee Performing Arts Center is today. During the work week, Reuben spent much of his time soliciting work from printers and publishers. He worked late each night and delivered plates the next day for the cash he needed to buy material and food for himself and his son. Gulbenk Engraving Company's fast, efficient service brought more business and the company prospered. At some point, Gulbenk opened branch plants in Atlanta and Dallas that were later sold to key employees in those locations.

Reuben was sufficiently successful that he was able to put his son, Roupen, through Peabody Demonstration School and Vanderbilt. After a stint in the military, Roupen joined Gulbenk Engraving Company as a salesman in 1946.

A few years later the company opened a branch in New York City. By then, Gulbenk Engraving Company was located on the second floor of the Chamber of Commerce building in Nashville. Expansions led to the company taking over the third and fourth floors as well. Later, the company moved to a building they purchased at 418 Commerce Street. Gulbenk Engraving would remain there until 1980, when the company was sold.

During the 1960s, approximately half of Gulbenk Engraving Company's sales were in New York City. During this decade, the company employed one hundred skilled plate-making craftsmen, recruited from all over the country. Reuben Gulbenk still came to work every day in his work clothes, but as an octogenarian in declining health, he left management decisions to his son.

When Reuben Gulbenk died in 1970, his son took control of the company. He realized that, while he was an excellent salesman, he had shortcomings as a businessman, having relied heavily on his uncle Baldrig to oversee that aspect of the business. But, Baldrig had died, too, leaving his share of the business to Roupen.

Roupen Gulbenk changed the name of his company to Gulbenk Graphics since engraving work had almost disappeared. The company's focus by then was on making lithographic plates, computer typesetting, and letter-pressing. Gulbenk Graphics performed work for 150 monthly publications. Gulbenk discovered, however, that increasing his volume of business did not automatically result in higher profits. In 1979 the company earned $70,000 on several million in sales.

Feeling his company had become too big, he sold Gulbenk Graphics in 1980 to two former executives of the Nashville Bridge Company. The new owners gave Roupen a three-year management contract to help ease the transition to new management. This ended earlier with Gulbenk being bought out.

Interested in antiques since he was a boy, Gulbenk would later open Cinnamon Hill Antiques on Highway 100 in the Westgate Shopping Center. Gulbenk Graphics went on to merge with Dixie Electrotype Company, which was later owned by James R. Meadows Jr.

ENTERTAINMENT

The **HIPPODROME** was announced on October 31, 1905, when Nashvillians read in the *Nashville Banner* that the coliseum for indoor athletic events would be built on West End Avenue opposite Centennial Park. The building opened for business on February 5, 1906, with Jack Price as manager. Located at 2613 West End Avenue, the building was sold to movie-house baron Tony Sudekum, owner of the Crescent Amusement Company.

On May 5, 1914, the *Nashville Tennessean* and the *Nashville American* announced the construction of a brick building to replace the original wooden structure. It would feature an auditorium, 100 feet wide by 350 feet long, that would seat twenty thousand, giving it the second largest seating capacity in the South. The building was designed for conventions, indoor athletic events, and exhibitions, including automobile shows. Because of its gigantic size, the structure, that covered 4.5 acres, had forty exits. Between events, the building was used as a skating rink and dance hall, with the skating rink in the front and the dance hall in the back. Construction of the new building was completed in the winter of 1915–16.

Vanderbilt began using the original auditorium, which players remembered as "cold and drafty and ill-equipped for large crowds," for their varsity basketball team during the winter of 1907–08. Vanderbilt continued to play in both the old and the new Hippodrome until about 1948. Pinky Lipscomb, an All-SEC forward in 1938–39, and again in 1940–41, recalled what it was like to play in the Hippodrome. He said it "was completely inadequate for the game. After all, it was a skating rink. Crepe paper hung from the rafters during some games, and the ball would strike the paper if shot with any arc. The floor had an oil slick coating for the skaters and that was hell for rubber-soled basketball shoes."

In the late 1930s, Benny Goodman and other big-name bands came to the Hippodrome for one-night events. From 1934 until the late 1960s, Golden Gloves boxing championships, professional wrestling, high school dances, and Clinic Bowl events were held at the Hippodrome. Once, there was even an indoor baseball game. The Hippodrome's primary use, with basketball gone, was for skating.

I went to many skating parties there in the late 1940s and thought the Hippodrome was pretty neat with its mirrored wall and forty-foot ornamental plaster ceiling with thousands of little lights. I also remember how dirty the place was.

During World War II, the Hippodrome was a mecca for servicemen. Sometimes, as many as three thousand skaters were on the floor at once. On such occasions, it was "so crowded you could hardly fall down."

Fats Domino performed there in the 1950s, as did Chubby Checker.

In June 1962 the Southern Regional Roller Skating championships were held at the Hippodrome. In February 1968, not long before the building was torn down, a sign to the left of the entrance read "Skating, every night 7:45 to 10:00."

In January 1968 Red O'Donnell wrote in his column in the *Nashville Banner* that the Hippodrome Skating Rink "is about to slide into oblivion." The building was demolished in the summer of 1968 to make way for a Holiday Inn Select hotel.

Vaulxhall Gardens was established by Messrs. Decker and Dyer in 1827 as a place of public entertainment. Located south of Demonbreun Street near present-day Ninth Avenue South (formerly Vaulxhall Street), the gardens covered several acres and included a ballroom, a dining hall that could seat fifteen hundred, and, in later years, a miniature railroad.

On March 4, 1929, the day Andrew Jackson was inaugurated president of the United States, there was a dinner and program at Vaulxhall Gardens to celebrate the event. Public receptions were held for President Jackson here in 1832 and 1834.

Henry Clay made a famous "Vaulxhall Gardens" speech on May 23, 1835. On the same occasion John Bell, of Nashville, spoke. These speeches were thought to have been a factor in Hugh Lawson White, of Knoxville, carrying the state over Van Buren in the 1836 election. The gardens lasted for more than a decade.

FAST-FOOD COMPANIES

MINNIE PEARL'S FRIED CHICKEN was launched by John Jay Hooker in 1967 with front-page publicity in the *Nashville Tennessean*.

The colorful Nashville attorney and 1966 Democratic candidate for governor conceived the idea of this company based on his thought that, if Pepsi-Cola Bottling Company could make billions of dollars by copying Coca-Cola, he could do the same thing in the fast-food business by copying Kentucky Fried Chicken. In the back of his mind, Hooker also thought about the financial empire Nashvillian Rogers Caldwell had built in the 1920s. He had attended weekend lunches at Caldwell's home on Bridge Street in Franklin some years before and admired the financier.

Hooker convinced Sarah Cannon to lend the company her stage name, "Minnie Pearl." He boldly predicted that the company would have five hundred stores by 1970. In the fall of 1967 the *Nashville Tennessean* reported on franchise sales from Florida to California. In those heady days, a single franchise cost $20,000, with 10 percent down. By the following February, Minnie Pearl's Chicken Systems had sold nearly three hundred franchises, only five of which were in operation. John Jay Hooker and his brother, Henry, each owned 650,000 shares, while Sarah Cannon had 96,000.

On May 2, 1968, the company went public and, on the first day, the stock shot up from $20.00 to $40.50 per share. By then, twelve states had approved the public sale of 300,000 shares. Tennessee had not, having misgivings about the offering price of $20 per share. The Hookers' friends in Nashville, who had stock, watched the market intently that summer, trying to decide whether to cash in or hang on for the ride.

The brothers, thinking they had Minnie Pearl's Chicken Systems under control, began to branch out before having even one Minnie Pearl's Fried Chicken restaurant open in their hometown. First, they announced a new chain of Mahalia Jackson Fried Chicken franchises aimed at the African American market. Next came Minnie Pearl's Roast Beef, patterned after Arby's.

Although press coverage in Nashville remained positive, *Fortune* magazine sounded a caution note in its October 1968 issue when it cautioned, "Profits from actual food sales are still very slim, but profits from franchise sales have been very strong. . . . If the food does not agree with the people who are supposed to patronize all these outlets, then Minnie Pearl's will find itself with a balance sheet full of deserted buildings."

Because the brothers were focused on selling franchises, at which they were very good, John Jay Hooker talked his best friend, Ed Nelson, executive vice president of Commerce Union Bank, into joining the company to look after internal operations. Ed did so, but it was not long before he began to worry whether or not Minnie Pearl's had the capacity to manage the less glamorous side of the business of selling chicken, perfecting recipes, developing an advertising strategy, and supporting the franchisees.

When 1969 came around, less than forty restaurants were open and none were yet profitable. That January, Minnie Pearl's Chicken Systems changed its name to Performance Systems Inc. (PSI), to let the public know that this was not just a fast-food company.

As more Minnie Pearl's Fried Chicken restaurants opened, including six in Nashville, customers began to realize that there seemed to be no consistency of recipes from store to store, and that the chicken didn't always taste good. Many franchisees, who had gone into business with borrowed money, were having trouble making a profit. By August 1969, banks and stock analysts began to have serious doubts about the company and the stock fell almost as fast as it had originally risen. It became available for $10 a share.

On August 21, 1969, John Jay Hooker resigned from his position at PSI to make another run for the governor seat. Other companies the brothers owned were falling apart. Whale filed for bankruptcy and Temco laid off most of its employees. Nashville Bridge Company, once a proud company with a long history, had been taken over by a bank and sold to the American Ship Building Company in Ohio.

PSI failed to file a report to the Securities and Exchange Commission (SEC), due in April 1970. When the report was filed in September, it revealed that PSI had lost more than $30 million in 1969. In November 1970 Winfield Dunn defeated John Jay Hooker in the general election for governor, becoming the first Republican to hold the office since Henry Horton was elected in 1927. Dunn won, in part, because he was able to depict Hooker as a failed businessman.

By 1975 PSI had sold most of its assets to satisfy creditors and became inactive. In 1977 Richard Chambers bought what was left and converted it into a small computer company named DSI Corporation.

FIVE-AND-DIME STORES

WOOLWORTHS, which opened its first store in 1878, had two stores in the Nashville area by 1931. One was at 311 Third Avenue North, while the other was at 221–23 Fifth Avenue North.

The store's segregated lunch counter was a focal point in the city's sit-ins. On February 13, 1960, Nashville African American students convened at the Arcade on Fifth Avenue North and entered Kress's, Woolworths, and McClelland's. After making small purchases, they occupied lunch counter seats. By 2:30 p.m., all three stores closed their lunch counters, without having served the students, who departed peacefully. The sit-ins continued on Fifth Avenue, and the students suffered verbal and physical abuse, arrests, fines, and incarceration. The Nashville sit-ins, the second in the South, were successful, but African Americans continued to associate Woolworths with segregation. To counter that, the downtown Woolworth moved to Church Street.

In 1993 the New York–based retailer announced that the company would close or redesign 970 stores across the country, including all 11 in Tennessee. The 3 Nashville stores on Church Street, Lebanon Road, and in the Madison Square Shopping Center all closed by January 31, 1994.

FLORISTS

TOM HARRISON FLOWERS, a well-known florist, was located for many years at 210 Sixth Avenue North. It was founded in 1940 by Tom C. Harrison Sr., who had earlier worked for Harrison Brothers Florists and Joy Floral Company. Harrison's wife and two of their children, Tom C. Harrison Jr. and Anne Harrison Cooper, worked there from the company's founding. In its early years, funeral arrangements made up a large part of the company's business. By the early 1980s that percentage had dropped to about 18 percent.

Harrison Brothers Florists, 1920s.
Collection of Ridley Wills II.

Tom Harrison Flowers moved to 2020 West End Avenue in about 1950. That year, its officers were Phillip M. Harrison, president; Clifford J. Harrison, vice president; and Sarah B. Harrison, secretary-treasurer. A member of the Florists Telegraph Delivery Service (FTD), Tom Harrison Flowers advertised in 1950 that they could send "Flowers by Wire Anywhere." They could do so because FTD used telegraph lines to transmit orders.

Tom Harrison Jr. and his sister, Anne, began running the company in 1963. They would do so until the store closed on November 30, 1984. During those twenty-one years, Cooper handled customer contacts, sales, and arranged flowers, while her brother was the store manager and active in local, state, and national florist organizations, including a term as president of FTD. In the early to mid-1960s, they deliberately kept the business small enough that one of them could personally handle every order.

A major change came when twenty Nashville florists formed a pool for deliveries, sending a single vehicle to every area of the city rather than have every florist maintain their own fleet of vans. This enabled Tom Harrison Flowers to reduce its work week from seven days to six. The floral company also subcontracted a lot of work and, beginning in 1967, began using a computerized bookkeeping service operated through Florists Transworld Delivery. These changes enabled Tom Harrison Flowers to reduce its number of employees to three people. With the advent of air freight, flowers became available from South America, the Middle East, and Africa to all the Nashville wholesale florists.

The decision that Tom Harrison Jr. and Anne Harrison Cooper made to close their store on November 30, 1984, was prompted by the December 31, 1984, expiration of the lease on their building at 2020 West End Avenue, and the realization that they would likely be confronted with major repair expenditures for equipment if they renewed the lease. As Harrison said on October 21, 1984, "We determined to quit while people would say they are sorry to see you go."

FOOD INDUSTRY

Lay's Potato Chip Company had a plant at 1700 Portland Avenue (today's Athlete's House) in the 1930s. Retired Nashville bank chief executive officer Sam M. Fleming recalled, in 1983, his first memory of Herman Lay. It was, Sam said, "when he lived around the corner from me on Granny White Pike. He had a small pickup truck and used it to deliver potato chips to a few customers that he developed. He was always extremely pleasant—one of those people whose company you always seek."

Lay was tremendously enthusiastic and persuasive, so much so that he convinced Ed Johnson, who had an Esso service station at 2001 Belmont Boulevard, to take stock in his new company, rather than cash for the gasoline that Lay needed but had no money with which to pay. The stock that Johnson took in lieu of cash would, in time, make him a millionaire.

Fleming continued, "We financed Lay in the early days when he grew in Nashville and then when he went to Atlanta, and on to Dallas. The bank [Third National] never had a more loyal customer."

H. W. Lay Distributing Company was last located in Nashville in 1935 at 1023 Fifth Avenue North. Lay merged with the Frito Company in September 1961, creating the largest-selling snack food company in the United States, the Frito-Lay Corporation. Herman Lay, who was chairman and chief executive officer of the company, later became a loyal member of the board of Third National Bank.

Martha White Flour pioneered the development of self-rising flour, self-rising corn meal, and later the packaged mixed southern hot bread. In 1941 Cohen E. Williams and his sons, Cohen T. and Joe, purchased Royal Flour Mill and its premier flour brand, Martha White, from Richard Lindsey. (He had named the flour for his daughter, Martha White Lindsey). Williams renamed his company Martha White Flour and kept the picture of Martha White Lindsey on every bag.

In 1947 the company began sponsoring the "Martha White Biscuit and Cornbread Time" on WSM at 5:45 a.m. Martha White sponsored its first show on WSM's famous Grand Ole Opry in 1948. In 1953 Martha White Flour hired Lester Flatt, Earl Scruggs, and their band the Foggy Mountain Boys to tour the South promoting their products. This group, which became closely identified with Martha White, went on to become the country's number-one bluegrass music group.

Cohen E. Williams was chairman of the board until 1947, when his son, Cohen T. Williams, who had been president, succeeded him. Cohen T. Williams's son-in-law, James R. King, became president at the same time. Upon King's death in 1972, he was succeeded as president by Williams's son-in-law, Robert V. Dale.

After the Foggy Mountain Boys disbanded, Tennessee Ernie Ford became spokesman for Martha White and a good friend of Cohen T. Williams. When in town, Ford would stay at Williams's home, and, on weekends, they would often go to the Belle Meade Motel for supper. Ford continued as the company's spokesman through the 1980s.

In 1975 Martha White Flour merged with Beatrice Companies Inc. becoming a wholly-owned subsidiary of Beatrice. Between then and 1984, company ownership changed hands several times, with Robert V. Dale remaining president until the company was sold by Windmill Holding Company to the Pillsbury Company in 1994.

MEADOW GOLD ICE CREAM had a factory located at 1710 Church Street since 1940 that closed in February 1995. Founded in the late 1920s as an independent dairy, Meadow Gold was acquired by Beatrice Foods. In 1958, Wallace N. Rasmussen was Beatrice's Nashville district manager. In 1983 Beatrice sold its Nashville factory to Borden Inc., an Ohio-based giant in the food industry.

By the early 1990s, Borden was laying off workers and closing plants. Borden lost a combined $1 billion in 1992 and 1993. Severance packages were negotiated with the Nashville factory's forty-one hourly workers and sixteen salaried employees, and it closed.

Meadow Gold Ice Cream Company district manager Wallace Rasmussen and Nashville Mayor Ben West, 1958.
Metropolitan Nashville Archives.

Odom's Tennessee Pride Sausage, a Nashville institution since 1943, had a plant in Dickson, Tennessee, with about 400 employees, and a plant in Little Rock, Arkansas, with about 280 employees. Larry Odom, the company president, was the grandson of the company founder, Douglas Odom Sr. One of Larry's aunts drew the original farm boy figure in the 1950s.

From 2008 to 2012, Odom's Tennessee Pride became the second largest producer of frozen breakfast sandwiches in the United States. The company had annual sales in excess of $190 million. Larry Odom, who started working for the company in 1974, said he had been thinking about retiring. Because he did not have anyone in his immediate family interested in taking over management when he did retire, he was susceptible when ConAgra came to him with a proposal to acquire the company.

When it was announced on April 19, 2012, that ConAgra, the giant Omaha, Nebraska, food chain, was buying Odom's Tennessee Pride Sausage, a company spokesman assured the sausage company's customers that ConAgra would keep the farm boy figure that had been featured on Odom's sausage packaging and in their advertising for decades. Nevertheless, the Odom Company would disappear as one more local company that had been swallowed up by a national one.

RUDY SAUSAGE COMPANY was incorporated in 1945 by brothers Dan and Frank Rudy at 2607 McGavock Road. Frank took charge of the actual hog kills, while Dan was responsible for sausage production. They sold hot and mild sausage and specialized in country sausage and bacon.

A few years later, the Rudy brothers built a twenty-seven-hundred-square-foot sausage plant. By 1950 they were producing about five thousand pounds of sausage a month. In 1962 a more modern plant was built to handle the volume of business. At its peak, Rudy Sausage Company employed about 175 people making thousands of pounds of sausage.

Rudy Sausage was sold to Kahn's Meats, of Cincinnati, then a subsidiary of Consolidated Foods. In 1990 the new owner, Sara Lee Corporation, moved the production of sausage from the Nashville plant to Newbern, Tennessee.

FOUNDRIES

BRENNAN FOUNDRY AND MACHINE SHOP, owned by Samuel P. Ament, was at 37 South College Street. It was acquired by Thomas M. Brennan, probably in the early 1850s. In 1855 Brennan Foundry and

Machine Shop, at the same address, had the following ad in the *Nashville Business Directory*: "Having lately added a machine shop, I am prepared to execute orders for steam engines and boilers, mill and gin gearing, and shafting, water-wheels, corn-shellers, straw cutters, corn and crib crushers, and agricultural machines generally."

Francis Strickland, who carried on his father's work after William Strickland died on April 7, 1854, had the iron work on the tower of the State Capitol cast by Brennan Foundry and Machine Shop. The tower was completed on July 21, 1855.

The 1857 business directory lists Thomas M. Brennan as proprietor of the "Nashville Foundry" at 37 College Street. Then, in the 1860–61 *Nashville City Directory*, Brennan's company is listed as "Claiborne Machine Works," without giving an address. Sometime after 1857, Brennan Foundry relocated to the northeast corner of Broad and Front Streets.

During the early months of the Civil War, before Nashville was occupied by Union forces, the Brennan Foundry cast cannon tubes for the

Brennan Foundry, on the southeast corner of Broad and Front Streets. Francis Strickland had the iron work on the tower of the State Capitol cast here. During the brief months of the Civil War before Nashville's occupation, Brennan cast cannon tubes for the Confederacy. Two of these are on exhibit at the Tennessee State Museum. *National Archives.*

Confederacy. The Tennessee State Museum has two in their collection, the tube for a six-pounder (undated) and the tube for a twelve-pounder cast in 1861.

On February 21, 1862, with the Confederate evacuation of Nashville nearly complete, Gen. Nathan Bedford Forrest took responsibility for saving as many supplies as he could before the Federal Army arrived. His soldiers went to Brennan Foundry and loaded on wagons "about fourteen Brennan cannons, some of them unfinished," and a new rifling machine built at the machine shop. It had been constructed according to plans and specifications stolen from the Fort Pitt Foundry near Pittsburgh by a Confederate spy. These items and others from the Nashville Armory were taken on the cars (Nashville & Chattanooga and Western & Atlantic Railroads) to Atlanta for use by the Confederate Army.

When the Federal Army arrived in Nashville by steamboats on the morning of February 25, 1862, the captain of the Eighth Indiana Battery was ordered to go to the Brennan Foundry on Front Street and salvage what he could. One of his soldiers reported on the expedition: "They had finished ten 130-pounders, but left them spiked. There were others partially finished and a large amount of shot and shell in the foundry." The Union Army made no effort, however, to use the foundry to produce ordinance but used the building for other purposes.

On March 30, 1862, brothers Thomas M. and Joseph Brennan, both Confederate sympathizers, were arrested, paroled, and summoned to a hearing. The results of the hearing are unknown. On July 1, 1864, Federal authorities offered for sale at auction some machinery from Brennan Foundry. A year earlier, "a lot of cannon axles and other valuable pieces of iron," probably from Brennan's, had been sold in Nashville. Resting in a barrel of iron, undetected, was a steel die for the first Great Seal of the State of Tennessee. The Indianapolis man who bought the iron discovered the die and apparently returned it to Military Governor Andrew Johnson.

Both Thomas M. and Joseph Brennan survived the Civil War. By 1870, the two brothers had reestablished Brennan Iron Works on South Front Street near Broad. The foundry was listed in both the 1870 and 1871 city directories, but disappeared from sight after that.

FUNERAL HOMES

Finley Dorris & Charlton Company had its beginnings in 1902. Finley M. Dorris was born in Clarksville. He began his career as an undertaker at age seventeen when he entered the employment of his uncle, William R. Cornelius, of Nashville, whose funeral home, W. R. Cornelius & Company, was at 214 North Summer Street at the turn of the century. Finley worked for his uncle for twenty-two years before starting his own business in 1902.

In the spring of 1906 Finley Dorris received the largest commission in his professional life. He was asked to move from the mausoleum at Belle Meade Farm the bodies of thirteen Harding and Jackson family members and rebury them in Mt. Olivet Cemetery. Included were the remains of the plantation's founder, John Harding, and his wife, Susannah Shute Harding; Gen. William Giles Harding and his wife, Elizabeth Irwin McGavock Harding; and my great-grandfather, Justice Howell E. Jackson. Having accomplished this in a flawless manner, Finley Dorris became the most prominent white funeral director in Nashville.

The next year, in 1907, he established a partnership with George A. Karsch. At that time, the funeral home was at 616 Church Street. In 1927, the funeral home, named Dorris Karsch & Company, was in a handsome two-story house at Ninth Avenue North and Commerce Street that had been built in 1901.

Later, Dorris changed the name of his company to Finley M. Dorris and Company. Dorris died in 1939.

In 1951 the company, renamed Finley Dorris & Charlton, was located at 2423 West End Avenue. Associated with the funeral home then were E. Carter Dorris, E. Dorris Charlton Sr., E. D. Charlton Jr., H. C. Moseley, L. L. Ball, and W. W. McMahon.

By 1975 the company's name had changed again, having merged with Roesch-Patton & Cosmopolitan Funeral Home to become Roesch Patton Dorris & Charlton Funeral Service at 1715 Broadway. Its president was Milton Austin. Today, the site is occupied by a Hilton Garden Inn.

TAYLOR AND COMPANY UNDERTAKERS was located at 316 North Cherry Street.

After the Civil War, an African American named Thomas Winston operated an undertaking shop to insure that Nashville African Americans were treated with dignity and respect when they died. His funeral business closed after he died in about 1888.

To fill that void, Preston Taylor, a black minister who had moved to Nashville in 1885, opened Taylor and Company Undertakers. A year later, he purchased land on Elm Hill Pike about one mile east of Mt. Ararat Cemetery, where he founded Greenwood Cemetery for which he served as superintendent.

By 1892 Taylor and Company Undertakers was the largest and most respected African American funeral home in town. When three black firemen lost their lives in a downtown fire that year, Taylor, by then a member of Nashville's black elite, constructed a special carriage to carry their bodies in a public funeral procession to the cemetery.

In 1904 Preston Taylor was one of the founders and the board chairman and treasurer of the One-Cent Savings Bank and Trust Company.

The next year, after the State Legislature passed a Jim Crow law authorizing cities to racially segregate passengers on streetcars, Taylor and other black leaders organized a street boycott of streetcars and formed the Union Transportation Company, for which Taylor served as president. The company purchased their own electric streetcars to serve three African American neighborhoods.

In response, the city council passed a privilege tax of $42 per car. That, and the failure of the boycott in 1907, forced the Union Transportation Company into bankruptcy.

The indefatigable Taylor also founded Greenwood Park in 1905. It became the largest black-owned recreational park in the state. His Lea Avenue (Disciples of Christ) Church in South Nashville was popular, attracting members of both the working class and the elite class. In 1917 Taylor and several other prominent African Americans bought the Duncan Hotel and refurbished it to house the Colored YMCA.

FURNITURE STORES

HARLEY HOLT FURNITURE COMPANY had its beginning in 1897 when W. H. and H. J. Harley opened a small, secondhand furniture store at 311 Broadway. New management, headed by Robert E. Moore, officially incorporated the Harley Furniture Company in 1904.

Edwin Lee Holt was vice president of the new firm. He was also a member of the Davidson County Court and one of the founders of Big Brothers. In 1911 he organized Harley Holt Furniture Company at 317 Broadway. Within two years, Harley Holt had expanded to include the 319 Broadway building. The company's slogan was "a dollar or two a week will do," emphasizing Harley Holt's easy payment plan. The company also erected, as a signal of the easy payment plan, a sign of "Two Fingers" on the front of the building to attract customers. Deliveries were made in a one-horse wagon until 1914, when a large Kissell truck was added.

From then until 2003, when Harley Holt closed, the store was one of Broadway's oldest, largest, and best-known businesses.

The Victorian building later featured a façade of black Italian marble and an iconic neon sign that boldly declared "Good Furniture." Inside was a large freight elevator that doubled as a passenger lift.

When Edwin Holt died in 1938 at age sixty-four, his son, Thomas Malone Holt, took over the business. Tom had earned a bachelor degree in civil engineering at Vanderbilt and a master's degree from MIT. He and his wife, Mary Louise Nooe Holt, operated the business for fifty years. The company prospered, as those years included the heyday of furniture retailing on lower Broadway when three dozen home furnishing stores were located there. In 1959 Holt and four other furniture merchants on lower Broadway purchased a ground parking lot at 315 Broadway for the convenience of their customers.

Their son, Edwin Lee Holt II, joined the firm in 1960 after attaining a bachelor of science degree in civil engineering from Vanderbilt. In 1987, a year before his father died, Ed and his wife, Lois, purchased the buildings. Three years later, they undertook a complete exterior restoration under historical guidelines. This restoration was one of the first major renovations made in the successful effort to revitalize what had become a blighted area.

In 1994 Ed and Lois Holt's daughter, Marion Holt Wilmoth, became the fourth generation of the Holt family to enter the furniture business. She graduated from Auburn University with a degree in interior design. She immediately added an exciting element and fresh approach to furniture retailing in Nashville. One example was the introduction of a Christopher Lowell Home Gallery at Harley Holt in 2002, offering a more contemporary, urban custom design and functional lifestyle.

Unfortunately, the innovations came too late. By the mid-1990s, the Holts realized that the era when Nashville homeowners came downtown to purchase sofas, tables, and bedroom suites was over. Competition from suburban shopping centers and malls lured buyers away from lower Broadway. Facing this reality, the Holts sold their building and parking lot early in 2004, and closed the business that October after ninety-two years in business.

Harley Holt Furniture Company's legacy is that customers from years gone by still tell the Holts how much they enjoyed shopping at Harley Holt, and how pleased they were with the quality of the furniture they purchased from the Holt family.

GROCERY STORES

GREEN HILLS MARKET opened at 3909 Hillsboro Pike in 1939. It was owned and managed by partners A. Roy Greene and Roy T. Primm Sr. Green Hills Market, Green Hills Pharmacy, and the Green Hills Theater gave the area the name "Green Hills." The market advertised itself as "The House that Quality Built."

Roy Primm Jr. started bagging groceries there when he was fifteen years old. Back then, he heard adults tell his father that he was out of his mind to build a store so far out of downtown Nashville. The gamble worked, however. Roy Primm Jr. said, in 1989, it did so because "for the first few years, we had a delivery service. We had five trucks and a wide range of delivery until 1952."

Green Hills Market.
Collection of Grannis Photography.

Roy Primm Jr. began working full-time at his father's store in 1950. When his father retired, he ran the market until it closed in 1989.

In 1971 Green Hills Market built a new store at the site of the old store, in effect, doubling its space. In 1975 Emma Fry Primm was chairman and treasurer, Roy T. Primm Jr. was president, Dorothy M. Primm was vice president, and James C. Dale Jr. was secretary.

The company closed on June 1, 1989. When asked why he decided to close the well-patronized store, Roy T. Primm Jr. said, "I decided to close the door because I turned sixty-six years old last year, and all my management team were either older than me or close to my age, and I couldn't find younger people who were interested in taking over." When he retired, Primm leased the building to Raymond Zimmerman's Service Merchandise Company.

Some of Green Hills Market's long-standing customers were distraught. Joan (Mrs. Randall) Yearwood was one of them. She said, "I've been shopping here all my life, and I'm just teary over this. It's a special place; the people make it like a home."

H. G. **HILL & COMPANY** began in November 1895, when twenty-two-year-old Horace G. Hill went into the grocery business. He first bought on credit the stock of a grocer who was going out of business and opened a grocery at the corner of State and McTyeire Streets. With only ten dollars in capital, he ran the store on a credit as well as a cash business. By 1899, Hill had decided to build a chain of grocery stores and to operate them strictly on a cash basis.

He owned fourteen stores by 1907. Each was on a corner lot on the right-hand side of streets in alignment with street car traffic. They were strategically placed on the corners where the streetcars stopped.

Hill incorporated the H. G. Hill Grocery and Baking Company in 1907 with a capital of $100,000. At about the same time, he leased the five-story Berry & DeMoville Building on the public square at First Avenue North for seven years. The building, one of the largest in town, and with a commodious basement, became the company's distribution center, housing a large wholesale grocery, an up-to-date coffee roasting plant, a bakery, and a retail grocery operation.

During the first decade of the twentieth century, Nashville businesses operated under a set of "blue laws" that would remain in effect most of the century. Hill followed these laws faithfully, closing his stores on Sundays and refusing to sell beer at all. For many years, H. G. Hill sold its own brand of coffee, Fit For A King Coffee, roasted and blended daily.

By 1913 Hill operated twenty-eight H. G. Hill Grocery Stores in Davidson County, one in Columbia, Tennessee, and six in Birmingham, Alabama. Four years later, during World War I, he set a trend by eliminating grocery delivery service.

The next ten years brought unprecedented growth. In about 1920, Hill bought a wholesale grocery business, Phillip Trawick Company. By 1923, Hill was chief executive officer of the largest grocery corporation in the South with 308 stores, mostly in Middle Tennessee but also in Chattanooga (Red Food Stores) and Knoxville, Tennessee, and in Birmingham, Huntsville, Montgomery, and Tuscaloosa, Alabama. He even had a store in New Orleans, Louisiana. Hill had sent his brothers, J. B. and Nelson, to Birmingham to run the stores there and convinced his son-in-law, W. E. Penick, a New Orleans native, to run the New Orleans operation. In 1923

H. G. Hill & Company, wholesale and retail grocers, 628 Fatherland Street, Nashville, circa 1908.
Collection of Wentworth Caldwell Jr.

Hill's father, who years earlier had been in the grocery business on a small scale, went to work for his son as the head of H. G. Hill's produce and fresh vegetable department.

The H. G. Hill Company and a relatively new H. G. Hill Realty Company weathered the Depression well. When H. G. Hill died in 1942, he was known for his business acumen, his philanthropy, and for being one of Nashville's wealthiest men.

Horace's son, H. G. Hill Jr., was in the army when his father died. He was given a discharge because of the H. G. Hill Company's importance as a food producer and the fact that he was needed at home to run the company. He returned as chief executive officer.

By 1955 he had consolidated the company's small stores into a smaller number of supermarkets, including thirty-one in Nashville, and many more in the midstate. In 1960 he had twenty-seven Nashville stores, thirteen outside of Nashville, and $30 million in annual sales. In each store, H. G. Hill still sold the company's Fit For A King Coffee during the 1960s and 1970s, something they had done for over fifty years.

In 1971 H. G. Hill Jr. built a $3 million distribution center on Sidco Drive. Hill also successfully fought off efforts to unionize his company. The last store he opened before his death in 1993 was an H. G. Hill Food Store that opened in Brentwood in 1983. More conservative than his father, and much less innovative, Horace Hill Jr. was a man who would be remembered for his dedication to worthy causes. He was chairman of the board of George Peabody College for Teachers and the greatest benefactor of the YMCA of Middle Tennessee.

Following his uncle's death, Wentworth Caldwell Jr. ran the grocery business and John B. Hardcastle ran the realty company. Freed from his uncle's conservative business restraints, Caldwell opened H. G. Hill supermarkets on Sundays and began selling beer. In 1999 the H. G. Hill Company announced the sale of its food stores to Fleming Companies Inc. In its 103-year history of being in the food business, H. G. Hill Company had an enviable reputation as a favorite shopping place for Nashvillians.

Although the H. G. Hill grocery business is gone, H. G. Hill Realty Company, located at 3011 Armory Drive, remains as a major player in the Nashville real estate business. Under the leadership of John Hardcastle and Wentworth Caldwell and, more recently, James Wentworth "Jimmy" Granbery, chief executive officer of H. G. Hill Realty, the company developed an upscale residential complex called "Hill Place" in West Meade. It also has numerous commercial properties, the two most visible being the Hill Centers located in the Green Hills and Belle Meade Shopping Centers.

HARDWARE STORES

PHILLIPS & QUARLES opened on Fourth Avenue in 1919 with wooden display cases and a manual cash register. In 1963 the store moved to 106 Broadway, where it remained for thirty years.

The rejuvenation of Lower Broad put pressure on Phillips & Quarles to move to a less expensive site. Robert Harwell, president of Phillips & Quarles, decided to relocate the store.

When Hard Rock Café acquired their building in 1993, Max Vick, manager of the downtown Phillips & Quarles, put a banner on the store's front door that read "From Hardware to Hard Rock" and began a moving sale, with all merchandise offered at a 25 percent discount. Phillips & Quarles was left with two Phillips & Quarles Home Centers, one on Hillsboro Pike and one on Franklin Road.

HARNESS COMPANIES

Early-Cain Harness Company was a wholesale and retail business organized in 1902. It had as its specialties horse boots, track harnesses, and imported saddles and bridles.

Located at 315 Second Avenue North, the building was three stories tall and had a freight elevator in the back. On the second floor, men sat on benches in front of tables full of large leather hides and made harnesses. All kinds of curious tools and leather scraps were usually scattered on the floor.

John Early, the company president, gave his daughter, Margaret, a new imported English saddle and bridle every Christmas from the time she was a teenager until she married Hubert Wyatt and quit showing horses.

Early rode his horse, The Emperor, to work every day from his home, Ponotoc, on Greenwood Avenue in East Nashville. He was said to be the last businessman in Nashville to ride a horse to his office. When Main Street was paved, Early experimented with all kinds of horseshoes in an effort to keep The Emperor from falling. Nothing worked, and before Early finally gave in to driving a car to work, The Emperor had fallen so many times his knees had no hair on them.

After graduating from Vanderbilt, Early began his career at the Methodist Publishing House. In addition to running Early-Cain Harness Company, he was also a partner in Early and Berry, a fire liability, bonds, and livestock insurance firm. In 1906 Early was one of the founders of the Tennessee State Fair and, for many years, was starting judge for the harness races there. From 1923 until 1930, he was chairman of the board of Montgomery Bell Academy. In 1930 he resigned because he was preoccupied with disposing of his harness business on Second Avenue.

In September 1933 Early had the pleasure of watching his daughter, Margaret Wyatt, set a world's record for lady drivers, riding J. E. Vonian in a mile-long, three-heat harness race at the Tennessee State Fairgrounds. John Early died in December 1934, soon after his store closed.

HOTEL COMPANIES

PRITCHETT-THOMAS COMPANY was organized in 1917 by John A. Pritchett, Col. Joseph W. Pritchett, and George G. Thomas, all natives of Jonesboro, Tennessee. Initially, they rented an office in Nashville for $12.50 a week. Partially under Thomas's guidance, the company grew rapidly.

In 1925 the Pritchett-Thomas Company built the Memorial Apartment Hotel on the corner of Seventh Avenue North and Charlotte Avenue. It consisted of two hundred units of one to five rooms, bachelor and efficiency apartments, furnished or unfurnished, that rented by the day, week, or month.

During the 1930s and 1940s, the hotel was managed by William A. "Bill" Pritchett. In later years, the building was owned by the State of Tennessee, and still later by the National Life and Accident Insurance Company. NLT ultimately demolished the building to build the NLT Center in 1969. I had an office in the building when I worked for National Life.

In 1927 the Pritchett-Thomas Company built the Sam Davis Hotel on the corner of seventh Avenue North and Commerce Street. It had 250 outside guest rooms.

The company then built, in 1929, their third hotel in four years, the James Robertson at 117 Seventh Avenue North. This was a commercial hotel with 225 outside rooms, each with a private bath, and twenty-five kitchenette suites. The James Robertson featured a coffee shop, two private dining rooms, and its own basement garage with elevator connections to

Seventh Avenue Garage, operated by the Pritchett-Thomas Company. "South's largest garage. . . . Convenient to churches, theatres, and business district. . . . More than a garage. Spacious lobby, ladies' lounge, and rest rooms. Free check room for parcels. Twenty-four-hour service." *Collection of Ridley Wills II.*

the lobby and rooms. Thomas managed the James Robertson while Joseph Pritchett managed both the Memorial and Sam Davis hotels.

The combined cost of the three new hotels on Seventh Avenue North was more than $2 million. As a result of the Pritchett-Thomas Company's efforts, Seventh Avenue North was widened and a new lighting system was installed on the street by the city.

In 1948 the Pritchett-Thomas Company had 110 employees, with a majority of the key persons having between ten and fifteen years' experience with the company. It had built more than one hundred residences, and also had construction interests in Arkansas and Virginia. Thomas, who was president of the Tennessee Hotel Association in 1946 and 1947, had this motto: "A hotel is no better than its personnel."

In 1950 the Sam Davis Hotel was managed by J. C. "Jim" Pritchett, while the Memorial Apartment Hotel was managed by W. A. "Bill" Pritchett.

J. W. Pritchett was managing director of both hotels. By then, however, the Pritchett-Thomas Company had apparently ceased to exist. It was last listed in the *Nashville City Directory* in 1947.

HOTELS

ANDREW JACKSON HOTEL opened in 1925 at the southeast corner of Sixth Avenue North and Deaderick Street. This four-hundred-room hotel immediately became a major competitor of the Hermitage Hotel, which had opened fifteen years earlier.

Throughout the next few decades, the two wings of the Democratic Party housed their headquarters in one of the two hotels. In the November 1926 gubernatorial campaign, Hill McAllister's name adorned the side of the Hermitage Hotel, while Austin Peay's name was inscribed on a banner across the front of the Andrew Jackson. Senator Albert Gore also used the Andrew Jackson as his campaign headquarters.

I remember watching from the NLT Tower as the Andrew Jackson Hotel was imploded on June 13, 1971. The James K. Polk State Office Building occupies the site today.

DUNCAN HOTEL was a four-story, seventy-five-room hotel built in 1890 by William M. Duncan, a wealthy Nashville broker, to compete with the Maxwell House and the Nicholson House for supremacy as the city's finest hotel. Located on the southwest corner of North Cherry and Cedar Streets, the brick and stone-trimmed hotel was known for its pink and marble staircase that led to a seventy-five-foot by one-hundred-foot ballroom on the second floor. The ballroom, site of many cotillions, was adorned with massive fireplaces and "lake-like" mirrors.

In 1896 L. C. Garrabrant was manager. Convenient to business, the hotel bragged about being the only one on a streetcar line running to Centennial Park. Its rates were three dollars to five dollars per day.

At some point after the 1893 national financial crisis, the ownership of the hotel changed, and by 1910, the hotel's glory days had ended. Originally located in the jobbing district, not far from the retail district of downtown

Nashville, the neighborhood changed early in the twentieth century to become the heart of the Negro business district. The One-Cent Savings and Trust Company, organized in 1904 by several members of Nashville's Negro Business League, first operated out of James C. Napier's law office at 411 North Cherry Street. The Duncan closed its doors in 1916 and was refurbished as the home of the Colored YMCA and the One-Cent Savings and Trust Company.

The building was damaged by a 1933 tornado, losing its distinctive turret dome. In the early 1970s, the building was torn down as part of the downtown urban renewal. A state office building on Citizen's Plaza occupies the site today.

Maxwell House Hotel, located at the northwest corner of Church and Cherry Streets, was the brain child of Col. John Overton Jr., of the historic Travellers Rest plantation. Begun before the Civil War, the hotel was taken over by the Confederate army and renamed Zollicoffer Barracks. After Nashville fell in February 1862, the barracks were used to house Federal troops. In 1863, Federal authorities used the building to house captured Confederate soldiers.

After the war, Overton resumed construction and his hotel opened for business in 1869. With its two hundred rooms elegantly furnished and well ventilated, the hotel became one of the South's greatest hotels.

Nathan Bedford Forrest, a lieutenant general in the Confederate army, was supposedly named the "Grand Wizard" of the Ku Klux Klan at an 1867 meeting of the Nashville Den in room 10 of the hotel. For the next several decades, the Maxwell House was known as a place for important political meetings and as the stopping place for governors, eight presidents, and other celebrities.

Its management was always of the very best. After John Thompson married Overton's daughter, Mary McConnell, in 1878, he supplied the Maxwell House dining room with vegetables from his Glen Leven farm.

In 1896 the Maxwell House's advertisement in the July issue of the *Confederate Veteran* described itself as the city's largest and most centrally located hotel and bragged that its cuisine was unsurpassed and that it was newly furnished and re-frescoed throughout. Interestingly, its base rate of

Andrew Jackson Hotel lobby, 1930.
Collection of Kermit C. Stengel Jr. Estate.

$2.50 was 50 cents less than the base rate at the Duncan, whose advertisement in the same *Confederate Veteran* issue claimed it was "acknowledged to be the best hotel in the South."

O. Henry's "A Municipal Report," published in 1909, gives an eloquent description of the Maxwell House. The short story is considered O. Henry's best. Beginning in 1921 Joel Cheek began using the slogan "good to the last drop" to advertise his Maxwell House Coffee, named for the hotel. For years, the hotel's Oak Room Men's Bar served Jack Daniel's whiskey, another famous Tennessee product. The hotel, more than a half century past its prime, burned on Christmas night, December 25, 1961. Seven years later, Third National Bank erected a twenty-story building on the site as its new headquarters.

Duncan Hotel Lobby, circa 1910.
Collection of Ridley Wills II.

MUD TAVERN stood very early in the nineteenth century on the road from Nashville to Lebanon near the intersection of today's Elm Hill and McGavock Pikes. It is not known who built the tavern, but he is thought to have used mud and cedar logs to build it, hence the name. Court records show that Richard Smith bought the property in 1810. Court records in 1816 and 1832 suggest that he operated a tavern there.

Andrew Jackson is supposed to have stopped at the tavern frequently while traveling the road between his home at the Hermitage and Nashville. Jackson is also supposed to have spent two nights at the tavern in 1806 while preparing for his duel with Charles Dickinson.

A small community grew up around the tavern, and it, too, became known as Mud Tavern. Wilbur F. Foster's 1871 map of Davidson County shows Mud Tavern on the line of the Tennessee and Pacific Railroad and on a branch of Mill Creek.

NASHVILLE INN was Nashville's earliest grand hotel. It was established by Maj. William T. Lewis in 1796, the year Tennessee achieved statehood. Then it was a tavern and inn operated for a time by L. A. Parker. In 1806, the tavern became Winn's Inn. A few years later, the name was changed to the Nashville Inn. In 1822 the *Nashville Clarion* announced that Alpha Kingsley had taken possession of the inn.

Three years earlier, President James Monroe, the first president to visit Nashville, was the guest of honor at a dinner given at the inn. Andrew Jackson often brought his prize roosters to the inn for cockfights. After being shot on the public square by Jesse Benton in 1813, Jackson recuperated in the inn. In May 1825, a banquet for the Marquis de Lafayette was held here. President James K. Polk and future president Andrew Johnson also stayed there. Sam Houston roomed in the Nashville Inn with his bride, Liza, when he was running for reelection as governor in 1828. When William Strickland came to Nashville in April 1845 to build the Tennessee State Capitol, he stayed in the famous old hotel, then the Democratic party headquarters.

The three-story hotel, with balconies on each level, was destroyed by fire on April 13, 1856.

Scene of many historic events. On June 6, 1819, James Monroe, president of the United States, was the guest of honor at a dinner given at the Nashville Inn. *Nashville Public Library, Special Collections.*

NICHOLSON HOUSE, designed by the architectural firm of Thompson & Gibel, cost $80,000. Six stories high with 160 rooms, the hotel replaced a "high class" boarding house that had been there since the 1860s. Contracts for the new hotel at the northeast corner of Spruce and Church Streets were let in April 1892.

The Nicholson House was owned and managed by Isaac C. Nicholson, a former dry goods merchant. It hosted Tennessee Centennial Celebration visitors, vaudeville stars, State Supreme Court judges, Southern league baseball teams, and football teams coming to Nashville to play Vanderbilt.

In about 1918, the Nicholson House, under new management, was completely renovated and renamed the Tulane Hotel. Upon completion, it had two hundred rooms and an exterior of brick, terra cotta, and cut stone. In the 1920s, the Tulane was advertised as Nashville's best popular-priced hotel with rates from $1.50 to $2.00.

In 1956, about the time the hotel closed, Houston Bond, who once had been an elevator operator at the Tulane, spoke of its clientele. Bond said, "The Tulane changed hands several times, and there were politicians, traveling salesmen, show girls from the old Princess Vaudeville, dignitaries, a few criminals hiding from the law, a suicide or two; the Tulane got them all." The hotel site is now a surface parking lot.

NOEL HOTEL was built by brothers Oscar F. and John H. Noel in 1930 at 200 Fourth Avenue North, on the northeast corner of Fifth Avenue North and Church Street. The hotel was thirteen stories tall, had 220 rooms, and was connected with a five-story parking garage that had already been completed behind the hotel. Years earlier, Adelicia Acklen's town house occupied this site. Opening day for the Noel was on November 1, 1930. Each room was equipped with a tub and shower, ceiling fan, circulating ice water, and radio loud speaker. The Noels advertised their hotel as "Nashville's Newest and Finest." After forty-two years as a hotel, the building was remodeled in 1973 to house the Hamilton Bank. Later, Prudential Securities occupied the building. In 2012 FirstBank was headquartered there.

Nicholson House.
Collection of Ridley Wills II.

ST. CLOUD HOTEL was in its palmy days in the latter 1850s. The hotel was built in about 1851 by making additions to the home of Dr. "Red-Head" Martin on the northwest corner of Church and Summer Streets.

Jane Thomas lived at the St. Cloud from 1851 until 1855. She spoke of the ladies entertaining the gentlemen boarders with piano renderings of "Coming Through the Rye," and recollected her charming dinner partners. She also reported with pride on the prominent and intelligent legislators who were part of the group.

In December 1864 Union Gen. George Thomas stayed at the hotel. On the night of December 14, he assembled his staff in his hotel room and plotted strategy for the battle that began the next day. On the fifteenth Thomas paid his bill at the hotel early in the morning and rode off on his horse to command the Union army that overwhelmed Gen. John Bell Hood's Army of Tennessee on December 15 and 16.

In 1869 Daniel F. Carter and C. A. R. Thompson, the hotel's new owners, tore down the corner building of the two-part St. Cloud and built a handsome three-story building they called the St. Cloud block. In 1871 the original hotel, next to the three-story wing, was remodeled.

Competition, particularly from the Maxwell House, was fierce. In 1889, the owners sold the property to the Hall-McLester Company that tore down the original part of hotel and replaced it with a six-story

Pictured from left to right are the Maxwell House Hotel, the Noel Hotel, the Third National Bank, and in the foreground the excavation for the L & C Tower is shown circa 1954.
Collection of Grannis Photography.

merchandising mart that was hailed by Nashville newspapers, in 1890, as the "biggest and most imaginative retailing and wholesaling adventure south of Cincinnati." This building was used in succession by three leading department stores, Castner-Knott, Cain-Sloan, and Harveys. Today it is named St. Cloud Corner and is rented for commercial use.

UTOPIA HOTEL, an Italianate, six-story-tall hotel located at 206 Cherry Street, was built in 1890–91. It had a beautiful stone façade designed by Nashville architect Hugh Thompson. Only 25 feet wide, the hotel had a depth of 175 feet and had sixty rooms.

Originally managed by Ike Johnson, the Utopia was located in the "Men's Quarter" of the city, where men gathered, primarily at the Southern Turf, the Climax, and the Utopia, to eat, drink, and gamble. Johnson later managed the Southern Turf Saloon down the street.

Utopia Hotel and Stumb's Soda and Cigars, 1929,
Fourth Avenue North at Church Street.
Collection of Ridley Wills II.

In 1911, after the new manager of the Utopia, William R. Polston, died, the hotel changed its name to the Bismark Hotel and Café. It became the Utopia again in 1920. Two years later, in the *Nashville City Directory*, the hotel's listing read, "European Hotel and Restaurant, Saloon, Cigars and Tobacco." The Utopia, though vacant, still stands at 206 Fourth Avenue North, a mute testimony to a different time.

HOSPITALS

MILLIE HALE HOSPITAL opened on July 1, 1916, on the second floor of the home of Millie Hale and her husband, Dr. John Henry Hale, professor of clinical medicine and surgery at Meharry Medical College. They lived at 523 Seventh Avenue North.

Millie Hale established the twelve-bed hospital to serve African Americans who had been turned away by white hospitals. A Fisk graduate who received a nursing degree from the Graduate School for Nurses in New York City, Millie Hale was the hospital's head nurse and administrator.

By 1923 the hospital had grown to twenty-three beds and was a training center for African American nurses. The hospital issued a periodical called the *Hale Hospital Review and Social Service Quarterly*. In 1930, after Millie Hale's death, her husband managed the hospital. It later closed in 1938 when he was appointed chief of surgery at Meharry.

PROTESTANT HOSPITAL was founded by L. A. Bowers, Leslie Cheek, E. B. Craig, R. M. Dudley, and John A. Pitts, who applied for a charter on December 12, 1918. For $210,000, they purchased ten and one-half acres of the Murphy Addition that included the large Samuel M. Murphy home that faced Church Street between Twentieth and Twenty-First Avenues North. The tract was described as being "in the heart of the very best residential section of Nashville."

The Murphy home was initially used as the nurses' home, and three-story additions were built on either side. The new hospital was managed by a board as "a public welfare institution for the training of nurses and caring for the sick and afflicted." A new, modern hospital building was completed in 1927.

Evander M. Sanders, physician and surgeon, was a driving force at Protestant Hospital, which had financial difficulties in the 1930s and 1940s. The hospital was eventually forced into receivership. Its assets were acquired by the Tennessee Baptist Convention in 1948, and it was renamed Baptist Hospital.

US ARMY HOSPITAL NO. 8 was Nashville's largest military hospital during the Civil War. On January 4, 1863, one day after the Confederate retreat from Murfreesboro following the Battle of Stones River, the US Army commandeered Nashville's First Presbyterian Church for use as a US Army hospital. The Army returned the building to the church officers on August 19, 1863, but confiscated it again on October 14, 1863, and used it, along with the Masonic Hall across Spring Street, and the Cumberland Presbyterian Church on Summer Street at Cumberland Alley as the city's largest military hospital until April 27, 1865. The pews in the church's sanctuary were removed so that cots could be placed there for convalescing Union soldiers. Other soldiers were housed on cots downstairs. On the east side of the church, a two-story wooden latrine was built for the ill and wounded soldiers.

On April 12, 1864, Elvira J. Powers, a volunteer nurse from Massachusetts, visited U.S. Hospital No. 8. She toured the part of the hospital in the Masonic Hall first. After passing the guard, she ascended a broad flight of stairs to a second floor ward where she met a matron from Ann Arbor, Michigan, who was responsible for building maintenance. The matron's staff consisted of seven Negro women and two Negro men. Powers saw only a few patients, including a fifteen-year-old boy, who asked the matron to bring him some dried peaches. She agreed to do so but would not accept his offer to pay for the peaches with money he had hidden under his pillow. Miss Powers then crossed the street to visit patients in First Presbyterian Church, which she was told "is notable for the promulgation of seccession sentiments from its pulpit in other days." She and a fellow nurse responded by singing the "Star Spangled Banner" accompanied by the church organ. This, Elvira said, gave "much pleasure to the sick and wounded soldiers." The following September, when Miss Powers was back in Nashville, the matron at US Hospital No. 8 was Miss Annie Bell, described as "possessing a really noble and independent nature."

I grew up in First Presbyterian Church and remember seeing elderly couples from the Midwest who, in the summers during the 1940s, visited the church to see where their grandfathers, who were Union soldiers, recuperated from battle wounds and illnesses.

On July 1, 1865, Captain T. Wing, of the Quartermaster's Department in Nashville, gave Robert Lusk, treasurer of First Presbyterian Church, a check for $7,500 to settle the church's claim for damages done to the church during its use as a Federal hospital. The minutes of deacons meetings indicate the money was accepted and used for repairs, including the purchasing of new cushions, repair of the church organ by its builder from Boston, interior painting, and replacement and revarnishing of the pews that had been stored elsewhere. It took the congregation until Sunday, November 12, 1865, to restore the church building to a condition suitable for worship. That morning, for the first time in three years, the doors were thrown open for the worship of God.

In 1914, Congress voted to give the church an additional twelve hundred dollars for wartime damages.

INVESTMENT BANKING

J. C. Bradford & Company was founded by James Cowden Bradford and Walter Robinson. During his second year of law studies at Vanderbilt in 1912, J. C. Bradford dropped out of school to become a salesman at Paul M. Davis & Company. When the United States entered World War I, he volunteered for service. After completing officer training school (OTS), he received a commission and was posted to Fort Sill, Oklahoma, where he served as an artillery instructor for the rest of the war.

He then returned to Nashville to become a partner with Paul Davis in Davis, Bradford and Company, an insurance agency in the American Trust building.

In August 1923, at age thirty, Bradford was unexpectedly chosen by Davis to succeed Clarence Saunders as president of Piggly Wiggly Stores Inc., a Memphis-based grocery company that was losing money at the rate of $1 million a year. After engineering a turnaround in a remarkably short time, Bradford returned to Nashville in March 1925.

In 1926, Bradford accepted Paul Davis's offer to join Nashville's American National Bank as a vice president. Finding the pace there "a little slow," Bradford bought, in partnership with Walter Robinson (an experienced stock broker), a securities firm owned by the estate of Joe Palmer, who had unexpectedly died in April 1927. The cost was $10,000. On May 25, 1927, they founded J. C. Bradford & Company. He was the managing partner, while Robinson was the general manager. Bradford's intent was to cash in on the booming stock market.

J. C. Bradford & Company had five other employees, two salesmen, two clerks, and a bookkeeper, Margaret Craig, who was Bradford's half sister. They worked in two rooms on the twenfth floor of the Nashville Trust building on Union Street, then called the "Wall Street of the South."

The new company specialized in Southern municipal bonds and regional stock sales. In September 1929 Leslie Cheek told Bradford that a major correction in the market was about to occur. The next week Bradford sold off all his risky issues. On "Black Tuesday," October 29, 1929, the stock market plummeted as Cheek had warned.

Unsure of the future of the business, Bradford and Robinson dissolved their partnership on December 1, 1929. At that point, Bradford became the company's sole owner, although Robinson continued working there, managing the bond business.

In 1932 Melville M. "Mel" Barnes, a twenty-one-year-old Nashvillian, joined J. C. Bradford & Company, after dropping out of Vanderbilt University. Mel became a partner in the 1960s and remained as such until his death in 1992.

Early in 1930 Bradford went to New York to visit bankers, brokerage firm executives, and New York Stock Exchange officials. Encouraged by what he heard, he decided to purchase a seat on the New York Stock Exchange. J. C. Bradford & Company purchased the seat for $400,000 on

J. C. Bradford Jr., senior partner; Luke Simons, managing partner; and Norris Nielsen, partner, at J. C. Bradford & Company, early 1980s. *Collection of "Tootie" (Mrs. James C. Jr.) Bradford.*

March 20, 1930. His was the first Nashville company to do so. Bradford's fledgling company survived the Depression by cutting expenses to the bone and by using his personal capital of $500,000. Bradford said, "I was pumping practically everything I had" into the business. Although J. C. Bradford & Company lost money from 1931–33, the firm made money in 1934 and continued to be profitable every year until 1974.

When Life and Casualty Insurance Company of Tennessee was close to failure in 1934, the state insurance commissioner named J. C. Bradford as the chairman of a voting trust that took over the management of the company. Bradford served as board chairman of Life and Casualty from 1934 until 1951. In that position, he gained an understanding of insurance accounting that would serve him well when J. C. Bradford & Company began investing in insurance companies in the 1950s.

When the stock market crashed in 1937, J. C. Bradford took the unheard-of step of putting all his salesmen on salary, realizing that there was little business to be sold until the market turned around. When the market improved, he put them back on commission.

In 1941 a Knoxville broker named Bob Maher approached J. C. Bradford about opening a branch in Knoxville that Maher would manage. Bradford told Maher, "If the Russians hold the Germans at Moscow, I'll do it." That November, the German army got within nineteen miles of the Kremlin before being thrown back. Bradford kept his promise and opened J. C. Bradford's first branch in Knoxville with Maher its manager in 1943. The second branch was opened in Memphis in 1946. Twenty-four years later, there were, in addition to those two branches, offices in Chattanooga, Clarksville, Jackson, and Kingsport, Tennessee, along with ones in Atlanta, Georgia; Birmingham, Alabama; Greeneville and Spartanburg, South Carolina; Greensboro, North Carolina; Columbus, Gulfport, Jackson, and Meridian, Mississippi; and New York City.

In 1956 Bradford, then recognized as one of the nation's leading experts on insurance investments, took advantage of his knowledge by setting up Life Insurance Investment Inc., a mutual fund to invest exclusively in life insurance stocks. The initial offering was $21 million. By 1967 the Life Insurance Investment Inc. fund had assets of more than $125 million and more than forty-five thousand stockholders. That asset number would peak at $135 million. Bradford also organized Nationwide Corporation, a holding company for five life insurance companies that had about $4 billion in insurance in force.

While life insurance stocks were a company mainstay and J. C. Bradford & Company was one of the leading insurance company specialists in the industry, the company also handled virtually all other types of financial transactions, including over-the-counter securities, tax-free municipal bonds, new issues, mutual funds, and new money for corporations through public offerings or private placements.

In 1959, J. C. Bradford & Company pioneered the industrial revenue bond field by managing one of the largest issues for a $9.5 million General Tire plant. Big New York and Boston investment banking houses didn't like industrial revenue bonds because they felt that Southern investment bankers wanted to use them to steal industries from the North and East. Municipal bonds maintained a large proportion of J. C. Bradford's business.

Bradford found tremendous satisfaction in helping people create valuable estates. By January of 1967 J. C. Bradford & Company was serving people through approximately six thousand open accounts. Approximately 20 percent of the company business was in odd lot transactions involving less than one hundred shares. To service its customers, the company had 220 personnel, half of them in Nashville. There were, in 1967, twenty executives and eight market analysts who made stock and bond recommendations.

In 1968 J. C. Bradford & Company moved into the former Third National Bank building on the southeast corner of Fourth Avenue North and Church Street, renaming it the J. C. Bradford Building. Bradford's office was on the twelfth floor. Although his office was uncluttered, he was never far from the action. Ever cool and always composed, Bradford was seen, by his friend Sam Fleming, as someone who "doesn't ever get stampeded on things."

In 1971 J. C. Bradford & Company was one of 188 members of the 577-member New York Stock Exchange that were headquartered outside of New York. The company did many of the same things that the big New York wire houses did, except that it usually focused its activity in the Southeast. One of the best of the regional firms, J. C. Bradford & Company had a firm understanding of its customers and the companies in its area. The company's gross income for 1971 was running at an $18 million annual rate—the best in the company's history.

Bradford's business philosophy was simple: "Every person, every office must pay. If it doesn't, it goes. That's it." That year, the company had twenty-five branches, most in the Southeast. In 1974, the company hit a bump in the road by suffering its first unprofitable year since 1933. The company recovered and, a few years later, had more than $50 million in assets and thirty offices from Gulfport to Boston. The area of corporate finance was important in those years. Between 1970 and 1977, J. C. Bradford & Company managed or co-managed over $400 million for corporations in the Southeast. During the same time frame, the brokerage house managed or placed industrial revenue issues totaling over $400 million.

Bradford named his son, Jimmy, managing partner in 1976 when Einer Nielsen, who had been managing partner since about 1947, retired. The junior Bradford explained, "I think my father saw that Luke [Simons] and I weathered the market downturn [1974] without losing our heads, so he figured I was worthy of the position." Jimmy had been working for J. C.

Bradford since 1959. Before that, he had worked for Lehman Brothers on Wall Street since his graduation from Princeton in 1955.

After J. C. Bradford's death in December 1981, at age eighty-nine, Jimmy succeeded him as senior partner, and Luke Simons became managing partner. In the 1980s and 1990s, Bradford, Simons, and their management team grew the company from a few hundred employees to twenty-four hundred people.

In 1986 the company moved from its building at Fourth and Church to a new building at 330 Commerce Street. J. C. Bradford was a Southeastern financial powerhouse and a source of pride to Nashvillians. J. C. Bradford Jr. served on the board of directors of the New York Stock Exchange and as chairman of the NYSE Nominating Committee.

By the 1990s, J. C. Bradford & Company had grown to over eighty-six offices in fifteen states and was, in 1996, one of the largest privately owned brokerage firms in the southeastern United States.

In June 2000, in a changed business environment that materialized quickly, J. C. Bradford & Company was purchased by the New York–based Paine-Webber Group Inc. for $620 million. As a result, hundreds of former J. C. Bradford employees scattered among competing firms. Nashville's last homegrown financial institution was gone. At the time of the sale, J. C. Bradford & Company employed some 950 brokers and approximately twenty-five hundred people in eighty branches. About one thousand of them worked in Nashville.

CALDWELL & COMPANY was created when Rogers Caldwell obtained a charter from the State of Tennessee in 1917 to create "a body politic and corporate for the purpose of dealing in, buying and selling securities, stocks, and bonds." The original incorporators and directors of Caldwell & Company where Rogers; his three brothers, Dandridge, Meredith, and C. W. Caldwell; and L. J. Trousdale, a relative by marriage. Their initial capital stock was $100,000.

At the first meeting of stockholders, Rogers Caldwell was elected president and treasurer, and Dandridge Caldwell was elected vice president. In 1918 Caldwell & Company invested in the stock of the Fourth & First National Bank where his father, James E. Caldwell, was president. Rogers was elected to the bank board.

Rogers Caldwell, a financial genius, would become the most "talked about" man in the South during the 1920s. The company's first offices were at 205 Third Avenue near Union Street. An early step was to establish the Bank of Tennessee, wholly owned by Caldwell & Company. It had a capital of $200,000.

Young, aggressive, and ambitious, Rogers Caldwell intended to grow the company rapidly. *Meteoric* would be a better term. In 1923 Caldwell & Company bought controlling interest in Cotton States Life Insurance Company of Memphis. Afterwards, the insurance company made a $40,000 unsecured loan to Caldwell & Company. A year later, Caldwell &

Caldwell & Company Building under construction, June 1, 1923. *Collection of Kermit C. Stengel Jr. Estate.*

Company purchased the North American National Life Insurance Company of Omaha. Headquarters of both life insurance companies were moved to Nashville.

Beginning in 1923, Caldwell & Company entered the real estate bond field to finance construction across the country. During the 1926–29 period, Caldwell & Company originated and underwrote bond issues for twenty-four companies. Among the companies acquired by Caldwell & Company were the Kentucky Rock Asphalt Company and the Nashville Baseball Association, a member of the Southern Association. In 1926 Caldwell negotiated with the head of a much larger insurance company, Missouri State Life Insurance Company, to buy controlling interest in it.

By 1929 Caldwell & Company had invested $8.35 million in eight different insurance companies. To gain control of these companies, Caldwell & Company had assumed a large amount of debt. To pay these debts, Caldwell & Company depended on the marketing of the stock of these companies and a continuation of a bull market.

The widening scope of Caldwell & Company's influence in the insurance industry was paralleled by similar penetrations into the banking and newspaper businesses. The company continued to rely on the Fourth & First National Bank for funds.

In 1927 Rogers Caldwell and his business partner, Col. Luke Lea, borrowed money to purchase shares of Holston-Union National Bank, Knoxville's largest. The bank became unofficially known the "Colonel's baby."

Caldwell entered the Memphis market in 1928 when he, Lea, and Edward Potter Jr., for the Commerce Union, bought a 51 percent interest in the Manhattan Savings Bank and Trust Company.

Late in 1928 the Union & Planters Bank, one of the three largest in Memphis, suffered a run. Knowing of its vulnerable situation, the same men who bought the Manhattan Savings Bank, and some others, including James E. Caldwell, reorganized the bank and made the Manhattan Savings Bank an affiliate.

Soon, Caldwell saw to it that the Union & Planters Bank reward the Bank of Tennessee by making a deposit there of $500,000. Caldwell & Company also purchased considerable stock in as many as seventy other banks, including the Central Bank and Trust Company of Asheville. Caldwell saw this as an opportunity to expand his influence in North Carolina. Caldwell's new eight-story home office on Union Street prompted many to call Union Street "the Wall Street of the South."

Caldwell's association with Col. Luke Lea, whose political power rested partially on his ownership of the *Nashville Tennessean*, led to these two men purchasing the *Memphis Commercial Appeal* and the *Knoxville Journal*, and to attempt to purchase the *Atlanta Constitution*. Late in the 1920s, Lee and Caldwell came to be regarded as politicians as well as powerful businessmen. They supported Henry Horton in his campaign for reelection and heavily influenced his actions to benefit themselves. The *Nashville Banner* called Horton "governor-in-name" and Lea "governor-in-fact." Horton was reelected, and, as one would imagine, deposits of the state were put in the Bank of Tennessee. Many Tennesseans felt that with Henry Horton in the clutches of Lea and Caldwell, the state's finances were in danger of being unwisely if not dishonestly managed.

By 1930 Caldwell & Company operations in the bond field had expanded to every Southern state. When Caldwell & Company purchased municipal bonds, it did so on the condition that funds payable to the communities were deposited in banks chosen by Caldwell & Company.

When the Depression hit, Caldwell & Company's total assets, approximately $19 million, were extremely nonliquid. The company was fast becoming financially crippled. Internally, there was laxness in the accounting office and stockholders' meetings were never held. Auditors found a complete disregard for internal efficiency.

By 1928 $36.229 million of Caldwell & Company's real estate bonds were in default. By 1933 this number grew to $995.017 million. The companies' policies were described as exceedingly questionable.

In a bull market everything worked, but when the crash of 1929 came, Caldwell & Company was hard put to meet its obligations. Violations of trusts came about because of the company's lack of collateral. A relaxation of prudent safety standards occurred.

To avoid disaster, Rogers Caldwell and James B. Brown, chief executive officer of Banco-Kentucky Company, arranged for a merger of their respective companies. Later, it became clear to many that Rogers

Caldwell obtained his interest in Banco-Kentucky Company by grossly misrepresenting the true condition of his company, which may have been insolvent at the time of the merger.

Despite the merger, Caldwell was in the fight of his life in 1930 to stave off insolvency. A problem of violated trusts and a lack of cash also endangered the Bank of Tennessee. By various devices, Caldwell looted the portfolio of at least one of his life insurance companies. Unsound loans were made from the National Bank of Kentucky, the Fourth & First National Bank, and other banks under the control of Caldwell & Company. He also turned to the Central Bank and Trust Company of Asheville for financial assistance. All these efforts failed.

Morale at Caldwell & Company plummeted, and there was internal conflict. Throughout 1930 there was a steady and mounting withdrawal of funds from both Caldwell & Company and the Bank of Tennessee. The Fourth & First National Bank was also subjected to a heavy run and would have failed had not the American National Bank stepped in and bought it.

The receivership of Caldwell & Company was announced on November 14, 1930. A week earlier the Bank of Tennessee failed. The opponents of the Caldwell-Lea-Horton regime had a field day. Caldwell, Lea, and Horton were looked on as men who had robbed and cheated the taxpayers of Tennessee. Anti-Horton forces tried to impeach him. Blunders were made but Horton escaped. The *Nashville Banner* devoted many editorials to demanding that Lea and Caldwell be prosecuted.

The collapse of the Central Bank and Trust Company of Asheville led to the indictments against Lea; his son, Luke Lea Jr.; and Caldwell. Despite fruitless appeals to the Supreme Courts of North Carolina, Tennessee, and the United States, they were found guilty and imprisoned in North Carolina. A few months later, Luke Lea Jr. was paroled and, in May 1936, two years after his imprisonment, Luke Lea Sr. was given parole. In 1937 both men were given pardons.

After a number of civil actions against Rogers Caldwell, the State of Tennessee took possession of his home in Brentwood. Caldwell & Company, the Bank of Tennessee, and other banks affiliated with Caldwell & Company were liquidated, their creditors bearing tremendous losses. Rogers Caldwell was totally discredited, and the Depression in the

Midsouth was worsened by the failure of his empire. Caldwell retired to a house he bought in Franklin with very little evidence of being bitter about what had happened to his company. Instead, he kept abreast of everything that was going on and hosted frequent luncheons at his home on Bridge Street for former associates and friends.

Equitable Securities Corporation was formed on December 7, 1930, with an announcement stating that it had been chartered as an investment banking firm with Brownlee O. Currey as president, George Bullard as vice president, Ralph "Peck" Owen as secretary-treasurer, and Stuart Booker, Caleb P. "Cale" Haun, and Laird Smith as associates.

In 1927, Brownlee O. Currey, a fourth-generation Nashvillian and a Vanderbilt graduate in the class of 1923, opened a bond department at Fourth & First National Bank in Nashville. Over the next few years, he assembled a talented group that included George Bullard, Cale Haun, Peck Owen, and Laird Smith. In 1930, as the grip of the recession tightened, the management of Fourth & First directed Currey to close the department.

Family lore is that, after firing his friends and closing the department, Currey resigned and went down to Union Street where Bullard, Haun, Owen, and Smith were waiting for him. Currey then invited his former associates to join him in a new venture to be known as Equitable Securities Corporation, an investment banking firm to trade and underwrite high-grade industrial, municipal, railroad, and utility bonds. The new company was initially located in the Harry Nichol Building at 400 Union Street.

These young and ambitious men had all attended Vanderbilt. Three of them, Currey in the class of 1923, and Haun and Smith in the class of 1927, were graduates. Each invested the money he had, all together $47,262, in the new company. Currey, then thirty, became their leader, visionary, and deal maker. Owen, Currey's future brother-in-law by way of marrying sisters, was a cautious conservative who brought an element of stability to the company. Bullard was a thorough student of municipal finance and had more financial resources backing him than the others. Haun was a hard worker who had gained sales experience as the manager of the *Commodore* yearbook his senior year at Vanderbilt. Smith was likeable and outgoing and known for his integrity. He was also a natural salesman.

In 1931 William "Bill" Hendrix, Frank Burkholder, and Ewing L. "Commodore" Bradford joined the firm as salesmen. The following year, William J. Anderson Jr. joined the company. Barlow Henderson, with a background in project finance with a federal agency, and Thomas W. Goodloe joined soon thereafter in municipal and corporate finance.

In 1931 the Depression worsened, and bonds sold at deeper and deeper discounts. Despite this, Equitable opened an office in Knoxville, and Haun moved to Chattanooga in 1932 to open an office there. Offices were opened in Memphis in 1932 and in Birmingham, Alabama, in 1934. In 1935, Equitable moved to a three-story building at 404 Union Street.

More significant, the same year, Equitable stretched its geographical reach and influence by hiring E. Norman Peterson, a specialist in municipal bonds at Chemical Bank, to open an office in New York. Peterson was named first vice president and elected to the board of directors. Peterson was also successful in establishing offices in Boston, Hartford, and Philadelphia.

The year 1940 was a milestone for Equitable. The company purchased a four-story building at 322 Union Street for its home office. Nashville architect A. Herbert Rodgers redesigned and furnished the building in art deco style, said by many after completion to compare favorably with the finest addresses on Wall Street. The same year, Equitable moved its New York operations to the prestigious address of Two Wall Street.

Expansion was brought to a halt by World War II. Then, in 1946, Thomas B. Walker Jr., a Nashville native and Vanderbilt graduate who had worked a short time in the Memphis office, opened an office in Dallas, Texas. That office proved to be a fountain of corporate deals and underwritings for the company. It was about this time that the firm began to acquire equity positions for its own account in Trailways Bus System, Nashville Gas Company, and Continental Baking Company of Dallas.

All these transactions were dwarfed, however, by the acquisition in 1949 of a 9 percent interest in the common stock of the American Express Company, a story in itself. That same year, Equitable purchased the fifteen-story American Trust Company building at Third Avenue North and Union Street in Nashville for approximately $500,000. In 1950, Equitable acquired a further interest in American Express, giving Equitable the largest single block of ownership in the company and effective control. Currey became a member of the American Express board of directors.

Brownlee O. Currey, director of multiple public companies, a member of the Vanderbilt board of trust since 1947, chairman of the Montgomery Bell Academy board of trust, a vestryman and junior warden of St. George's Episcopal Church, died on February 21, 1952. He was only fifty-one years old. Currey was described by a friend as "a study in contradictions—this ruddy-faced, energetic investment banker who yet possessed the warm greeting faculty and the easy affability of the true Southerner." When Currey died, Equitable's net worth was $8 million.

Many who knew Currey well speculated that had he not died, he would have sold Equitable's stake in American Express. With Currey gone, the more cautious and deliberate Peck Owen, then president of the company, decided to hold the stock of a worldwide company he viewed as having a great future. The decision paid off handsomely as stock of American Express advanced steadily, resulting in Equitable's net worth skyrocketing.

With Currey's death in 1952, and Owen being elected president of Equitable, William Anderson was elected first vice president, succeeding Norman Peterson, who was elected executive vice president. That same year, Owen persuaded George Bullard, who had retired before Currey's death, to return to Equitable. Bullard's presence would be short lived, however, as he died in February 1953. Cale Haun had left the company in 1950 to pursue his own business interests and, in 1952, sold his entire interest in Equitable to a group of younger Equitable officers.

In March 1953, Equitable Securities Corporation and R. S. Dickson & Company, the latter a prominent investment house in Charlotte, North Carolina, co-managed a syndicate of investment houses to purchase and reoffer as a public offering 60 percent of the stock of Gulf Life Insurance Company of Jacksonville, Florida. This was the first of a number of transactions in stocks of life insurance companies for which Equitable was to gain wide recognition, including purchasing controlling interest in Missouri Insurance Company in 1954. Gus Halliburton, who had earlier come to Equitable from J. C. Bradford & Company, as vice president and head of corporate syndicate, was instrumental in the transaction.

By 1955, Equitable Securities Corporation had become the South's largest investment banking concern. *Finance* magazine, in its May 1955 issue, noted that Equitable had participated as an underwriter in $5.313 billion, or 31.5 percent of all new securities offered in the nation in 1954. The article went on to say that Nashville as a finance center occupied an unchallenged first place among Southern cities. Only 10 of the 159 investment houses in the country having at least $1 million of capital were in the South, and three of those—Equitable Securities Corporation, J. C. Bradford & Company, and Jack M. Bass & Company—were in Nashville.

Holiday Inns of America went public in 1958 with Equitable managing the underwriting. Holiday Inns became one of the largest and most successful motel chains in the world. Equitable investment banker Lem Clymer became a member of the Holiday Inns board. Clymer later became president of Holiday Inns, which blossomed into a worldwide lodging and entertainment company.

Brownlee O. Currey Jr. joined Equitable Securities Corporation in 1951 after graduation from Vanderbilt. He left for active service as a pilot in the Air Force Reserve and rejoined Equitable in 1954 in sales. In 1957 Currey took a position in sales in Equitable's New York office, where he later became manager of the firm's New York corporate syndicate department.

Many of Equitable's senior officers and major shareholders had, by 1968, reached or passed retirement age, and there were problems and concerns of illiquid estates to be resolved.

Equitable Securities Corporation agreed to merge into American Express by an exchange of stock. The transaction provided shareholders of Equitable with the liquidity of a publicly traded stock, and American Express dispersed the largest single block of its stock among a number of stockholders.

Ralph Owen retired from Equitable at the time of the merger and also retired from the board of American Express, where he served as chairman. Laird Smith had died only a few months before the merger while still active at Equitable. Currey Sr., Bullard, and Haun had all died, leaving Owen as the only founder who survived to see the merger. With the merger with American Express, Equitable's investment business was combined with that of the investment banking subsidiary of American Express, W. H. Morton & Company, and the business was operated as Equitable Securities Morton & Company.

By 1970 all of Equitable's branches, except Nashville, were closed. Ralph Owen, after guiding Equitable through a period of growth in standing, profitability and net worth, and an attractive merger for Equitable's shareholders, died in November 1983.

Equitable Securities Corporation was reestablished in 1972 as an independent firm in Nashville. William H. Cammack, who had joined Equitable in 1955 and had become a senior vice president and director of Equitable Securities Morton & Company, headed a group that acquired the business of the Nashville office and associated goodwill from American Express. Equitable Securities Corporation was merged with SunTrust Banks in 1998.

Thomas M. "Tom" Hudson, a vice president of Equitable in sales, and who had been appointed director of sales for the company's Southern Division in April 1965 following the death of William Anderson Jr., reflected on what Equitable had meant to him, saying that he would never forget the day, when he started at Equitable, that Owen and Currey stopped by his office to wish him the best of luck. Hudson told them his good luck had already come to pass just by his being asked to join the firm.

JEWELRY STORES

HAROLD L. SHYER JEWELER INC. began in 1916, when Harold Shyer started his own jewelry company at 627 Church Street. As a young man, he had been a salesman for his father's Nathan B. Shyer Jewelry Company, that was established in 1885. In the middle years of the twentieth century, Harold L. Shyer became one of the city's best-known jewelry stores. My wife's grandmother, Irene (Mrs. William C.) Weaver, bought a coin silver service from him.

The company always showcased Shyer as its central figure. During the 1940s through the 1960s, having an instinct for advertising, Shyer was continually heard on the radio waves advertising his jewelry business. In addition to selling jewelry in 1949, Shyer also sold smart, new Emerson radios. He always ended his advertisements by saying, "If you don't know diamonds, know your jeweler," and, "If Harold says it's so, it's so."

Shyer even distributed postcards of himself and professional wrestler Jackie Fargo, "the Fabulous One," promoting Shyer's store. Wrestling promoter Nick Gulas also promoted Shyer's diamonds, watches, and jewelry.

By 1960 Gil Green and Jack Simpson were assisting Shyer in managing Harold L. Shyer. By 1973 Sidney Polly had replaced Shyer as manager. His assistant was William F. Carpenter, who was secretary-treasurer. The jewelry company closed soon thereafter.

JENSEN, HERZER & JECK COMPANY was a jewelry store at 402 Union Street in 1907. In 1910 or 1911 the firm had moved to 602–604 Church Street. Later, the company moved for a final time to a handsome building on the south side of Sixth Avenue North, across the street from Stief's Jewelry Company. In about 1918 the company's name changed to Jensen &

Jensen, Herzer & Jeck.
Collection of Ridley Wills II.

Jeck. The company's officers in the early 1920s were M. C. Jensen, Charles N. Rolfe, J. H. Jeck, and William W. Benz. Rolfe, who began work as a watch repairman, rose to the presidency of the company.

In the late 1930s and early 1940s, Rolfe and several close friends, including Jack Norman and Norfleet Allen, would go down to Jensen & Jeck on Sunday mornings to have coffee and talk. Occasionally, Rolfe would take his young grandson, Charles N. Rolfe III, with him.

When Rolfe Sr. died later in the decade, his son, Charles N. Rolfe Jr., became president. The younger Rolfe held that position until the company was sold about 1950. He never had an office at Jensen & Jeck, however, as he was president of Capitol Chevrolet Company, a firm he actively managed at 510 Broadway.

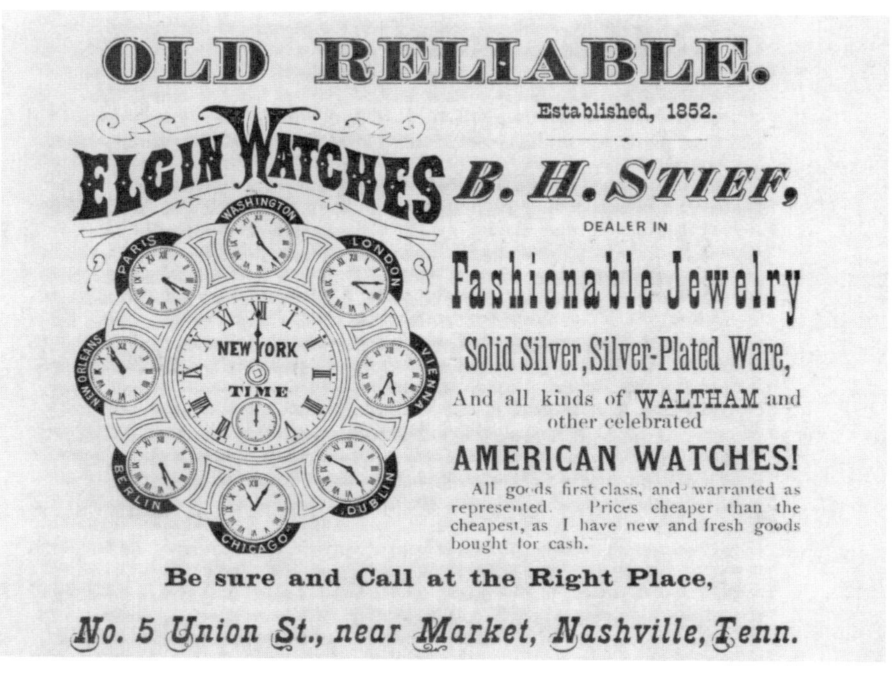

B. F. Stief Advertisement, 5 Union Street, 1880s.
Collection of Ridley Wills II.

B. H. STIEF JEWELRY COMPANY was established in 1858 by T. G. Goltz and his assistant, Bruno H. Stief. Goltz left Nashville in 1861, leaving the store in the hands of Stief, who kept it open during the Civil War. Goltz came back after the war only to sell the store to Stief, who slowly built the business.

After being at 5 Union Street for many years, the store was, in 1896, located at 208–210 Union Street, with James B. Carr as the manager. That summer, Stief had a full-page advertisement in the July edition of the *Confederate Veteran* magazine. It included an invitation "to one and all of the Veterans when they meet in Nashville next year to call on us that we may prove all statements we make in this publication." In 1900 B. H. Stief, then at 410 Union Street, called itself "Nashville's prettiest store," with customers in six states.

George Fox bought the store in 1918 and retained the name. After a spell on Church Street at Capitol Boulevard, the upscale store moved to 214 Sixth Avenue North, then Nashville's most fashionable retail street. When Fox died in 1942, the business was sold.

In the 1940s and 1950s, my grandmother, Jessie (Mrs. Ridley) Wills, who never learned to drive a gasoline-powered automobile, would, on special occasions, have her chauffeur drive her to Stief's. There, a saleswoman who knew her tastes would bring out several pieces of silver from which she could choose for wedding presents.

For years, the Stief windows displayed German-made clocks with animated figures that would march out at intervals and dance in time with the music. When I was engaged to Irene Jackson in 1962, she picked out her silver pattern at Stief's from Mary Elizabeth Cayce, who was president of the store from 1945 until 1970.

In 1970 Cayce sold the company to Jaccards Jewelry Company. Jaccards kept the store on Sixth Avenue North and opened a second store, Stief-Jaccards Jewelry Company at 719 Thompson Lane in 100 Oaks. The store at 214 Sixth Avenue North closed in about 1972.

LAUNDRIES

WHITE WAY LAUNDRY was a "family laundry service" established in 1931 by Wade Hampton Elam and his two sons, Ira Frank Elam and Nelson Crawford Elam, at the corner of Edgehill Avenue and Villa Place. When the company began, most Nashville laundries made home deliveries. Instead, the Elams offered cash and carry drive-in service at a 15 percent discount. The concept was very successful and spread across the country.

In the 1940s, White Way Laundry, as an additional service, added a modern dry cleaning facility at their plant. The advent of the home clothes dryer after World War II hurt the commercial laundry business, but dry cleaning sales continued to rise.

When Wade Elam died in 1951, his two sons took over the business. Fourteen years later, in 1965, Ira sold his interest to Nelson, who ran the company until April 19, 1973, when he sold it to his son, Wade H. Elam II, who had worked there since 1960.

Wade H. Elam II changed the name of the company from White Way Laundry to White Way Cleaners to emphasize its two services of laundry and dry cleaning. He also established six satellite stores. As White Way's customer base continued to move farther away, primarily to the south and west, Elam resumed offering home delivery service in 1988. In 1995 White Way Cleaners was recognized by the Varsity International Group as being one of the twenty "best dry cleaners in the world." Elam was personally honored that year by being elected president of the International Fabricare Institute, the worldwide Association of Drycleaners and Launderers.

Elam sold his company in 1999, ending a sixty-eight-year-long run of a well-known and respected Nashville company. The White Way building, on the corner of Villa and Edgehill, is today a "mixed-use" facility developed by Wade H. Elam II.

LAW FIRMS

TRABUE & STURDIVANT was formed by Charles C. Trabue Jr. and Robert W. "Bob" Sturdivant. After Trabue had received BA and LLB degrees from Vanderbilt University, he joined his father's law firm, Trabue, Hume and Armistead. In 1947 the junior Trabue left to begin Trabue & Sturdivant.

When Bob Sturdivant graduated from Vanderbilt Law School in 1937, he was awarded the Founder's Medal for scholarship, standing first in his class. He accomplished this despite having to work at WSM to pay his way through school.

After working as an associate in the law firm of Manier & Crouch, and later as a deputy clerk and master of the chancery court, Bob served as an officer in the US Navy on destroyers both in the Atlantic and Pacific theaters. After his release from the Navy, he took a graduate course in taxation at Harvard Law School. In 1947 Bob and his friend, Charlie Trabue, began their law practice in the Nashville Trust building. In 1950 they were joined by W. J. "Bill" Harbison, who had just graduated from Vanderbilt Law School as Founder's Medalist. Ward DeWitt Jr. joined the firm in 1955, several years before Bob Taylor joined.

After the Life and Casualty Tower opened in 1956, Trabue & Sturdivant moved to its twenty-sixth floor, two floors below where Life and Casualty's board chairman, Paul Montcastle, and company president, Guilford Dudley Jr., had their offices. The insurance company was a client of Trabue & Sturdivant. The same year, the law firm changed its name to Trabue, Sturdivant and Harbison.

Norman Mimmick, a veteran Nashville attorney, joined the firm in 1960, bringing with him two important clients, Werthan Bag Company and Commerce Union Bank. The bank also had a relationship with Dearborn & Ewing. Trabue, Sturdivant and Harbison changed its name again to Trabue, Mimmick, Harbison, and Sturdivant. When Mimmick retired in 1973, the law firm went back to its earlier name, Trabue, Sturdivant and Harbison. During these years, one of Bob Sturdivant's principal clients was Shoney's. Bob gained the relationship because he got along well with Ray Danner, Shoney's chief executive officer. Bob also had his cousin Jesse Wills and Jesse's family as clients.

When Harbison was named to the Tennessee Supreme Court in 1974, he resigned from the law firm, which then changed its name to Trabue, Sturdivant and DeWitt, the name it would use until the firm was acquired by Miller & Martin, of Chattanooga, in 1988. That was the year Bob Sturdivant died. He had been sick since his retirement in 1984. Charles Trabue Jr. practiced law almost until his death in 1992 at age ninety-one.

Four years before Charlie Trabue Jr. retired, Trabue, Sturdivant and DeWitt moved to the Nashville City Center. By then the law firm employed more than forty lawyers and had an outstanding list of clients, including a large number of casualty insurance companies.

LIFE INSURANCE COMPANIES

Life and Casualty Insurance Company of Tennessee was founded in 1903 by twenty-four-year-old Andrew Mizell Burton, with the help of Helena Haralson and investors J. C. Franklin, Guilford Dudley, and Pat M. Estes. Burton was a man of very strong religious faith but with a limited education. He was also smart and built the company.

In 1920 Life and Casualty wrote health and accident insurance with weekly benefits from $1.00 to $7.50; also industrial life policies with death benefits ranging from $20 to $1,000; and all forms of ordinary insurance from $1,000 to $100,000. The company's premium income for 1920 was $45,084,095.07, an increase of $1,493,728.59 over 1919.

Although Burton at one time owned almost 50 percent of Life and Casualty stock, he was always giving it away. He kept in his desk certificates in his name for one hundred shares each, and when Church of Christ preachers came around asking for money, he would pull out a one-hundred-share certificate, endorse it, and give it to them. He once told J. C. Bradford that he had no interest in accumulating money but "just wanted to service it."

In 1934 the Tennessee insurance commissioner became concerned over the state of Life and Casualty's assets and threatened to ask for receivorship. Friends of the company went to the governor and persauded him to call off the commissioner's efforts. The commissioner agreed on the condition that the company set up a voting trust and put control

Aerial photograph by Bill Lafevor of downtown Nashville, September 1983 when the thirty-one-story Life and Casualty Tower dominated the skyline. *Collection of Kermit C. Stengel Jr. Estate.*

of the company in the hands of a group of experienced businessmen. They included J. C. Bradford, chairman of J. C. Bradford & Company; Charles Nelson, president of the Nashville Trust Company; Charles McCabe, collector of Internal Revenue in Nashville; Burton; and Mr. E. E. Young, who had married the widow of Life and Casualty founder Dr. J. C. Franklin. Under their leadership, the company recovered and came out of the recession in good shape. Bradford, however, remained as chairman of Life and Casualty's board from 1934 until 1951.

In 1952 Guilford Dudley Jr., who had started with the company as an agent in 1931, was elected president, a position he held until 1969, when he resigned to accept the ambassadorship to Denmark tendered him by President Richard Nixon. He and his wife, Jane, returned to Nashville in 1971, and, the next year, he was named chairman of the board of Life and Casualty. Under his leadership, Life and Casualty grew into a multibillion-dollar company. In 1956, the company built a thirty-one-story tower on the southwest corner of Church Street and Fourth Avenue North. At the time, it was the tallest building in the Southeastern United States.

Dudley sold his controlling interest in Life and Casualty in 1958 but remained at the company's helm for several more years. Life and Casualty was acquired by the American General Corporation (AG) in 1967. Dudley was succeeded as chief executive officer by Allen Steele, whose Life and Casualty career had begun in 1946 as an attorney in the legal department. Steele was elected board chairman in March 1980. He retired in August 1982, when he reached mandatory retirement age of sixty-five. American General sold the Life and Casualty Tower to a group of investors that included Dudley in 1984. After National Life's parent company, NLT Corporation, was acquired by American General in 1982, AG merged National Life and Life and Casualty into the American General Life Insurance Company of Tennessee. Although the Life and Casualty Tower was renamed the Landmark Center, many Nashvillians still refer to it as the L&C Tower.

National Life and Accident Insurance Company began on December 27, 1901, when a group consisting of C. A. Craig, C. J. Hebert, and Thomas J. Tyne, of Nashville; Newton H. White, of Pulaski, Tennessee; and Ridley Wills, a native of Brownsville, Tennessee, purchased controlling interest in the National Sick and Accident Association at an auction sale at the south door of the Davidson County Courthouse.

At the first meeting of the stockholders on January 3, 1902, the new owners elected five board members: Craig, Wills, Tyne, White, and Hebert. The new board then elected as officers: C. A. Craig, president; Ridley Wills, secretary and treasurer; Thomas J. Tyne, general counsel; and C. Runcie Clements, assistant secretary and assistant treasurer. On January 20, Dr. Rufus E. Fort, of Nashville, one of the original stockholders in the National Sick and Accident Association, was named medical director.

In June 1902 the stockholders authorized the directors to amend the charter to change the company's name to the National Life and Accident Insurance Company. The new company initially sold health and accident policies with small death benefits. Sales of the policies, called industrial insurance, went well in 1902. That same year, company bylaws were amended to increase the number of directors from five to seven. Craig,

White, Tyne, and Wills were re-elected. C. J. Hebert, who was never active in the company, was not re-elected, and three new directors were added to the board: E. B. Craig, Dr. Rufus E. Fort, and Runcie Clements.

In the company's early years, C. A. "Neely" Craig and Ridley Wills, the company's two senior officers, worked closely together, devoting much of their time to directing the field force and developing new territories. Often, they would be visiting district offices during the week. Meanwhile Runcie Clements, a future National Life president, was in Nashville managing internal operations.

By early 1917 the company was doing business in fifteen states. Two years later, the company entered the field of life insurance and established an Ordinary Department. Its first manager was Edwin W. Craig, son of company founder, C. A. Craig, and a future National Life board chairman. With the introduction of Ordinary insurance, there was a need for a full-time medical director, so Fort disposed of his infirmary and private practice and came to the home office on a full-time basis. In 1921 the company introduced a full line of life policies in the Industrial Department. A new five-story home office building was completed in 1923.

On October 5, 1925, at the urging of Edwin W. Craig, the company started radio station WSM, which stood for "We Shield Millions." WSM became the number-one affiliate of NBC, and the proud sponsor of the world-famous Grand Ole Opry. The station became known as the "air castle of the South."

National Life went public in 1928 when 25 percent of the company stock was sold and it weathered the Depression well. The company's total life insurance in force increased 27.8 percent between the end of 1929 and the end of 1934, whereas the total life insurance in force in the United States, as reported in trade publications, was still less on December 31, 1934, than it had been at the start of 1930. During the Depression not one National Life agent was discharged, except when some act of his own made his continued employment inadvisable.

In 1931 Mr. Craig relinquished the position of company president to his closest associate and best friend, Ridley Wills, and assumed the new position of board chairman. A year later WSM completed its 878-foot-high radio tower south of Brentwood—the tallest radio tower in America. Wills remained president until 1938 when poor health forced him to resign. He was replacd by C. Runcie Clements, who was president from 1938 until 1943.

In 1937 the Mississippi and Ohio River valleys were hit by the worst flood in the country's history. The city of Louisville was hit extremely hard by the flood, with much of the city underwater and all electricity cut off. National Life responded by placing the entire facilities of its radio station, WSM, at the disposal of its sister station in Louisville, WHAS.

In 1943, Edwin Craig was elected president and Runcie Clements became board chairman. Ten years later, Eldon Stevenson Jr. became the first non-family member to be elected president. He succeeded his former Vanderbilt classmate, Edwin Craig, who became board chairman. Stevenson became vice-chairman in 1963 when Jesse Wills, Ridley's son, became president. Two years later, when Messers Craig and Stevenson retired, Jesse Wills became board chairman.

For many years National Life was viewed as the city's most high profile company and, perhaps, its most benevolent one. National Life became the largest debit life insurance company in the South. The fast-growing company built an eleven-story addition to its home office in 1941. Seven years later, having run out of space, National Life purchased the YMHA Building on Union Steet for use as a cafeteria, and recreational space and the upper floors for office space. The company grew especially fast during the 1950s, achieving a goal of having five billion dollars of life insurance in force in June 1958.

G. Dan Brooks, who was married to Runcie Clements's daughter, Julia, was named president and chief executive officer in 1965. When Jesse Wills retired in 1967, Brooks became board chairman. As chief executive officer, he saw the contract awarded to Henry C. Beck Company for construction of a thirty-one-story tower, encompassing the entire block between Charlotte Avenue and Union Street and between Seventh Avenue North and Eighth Avenue North. The new home office was completed in 1970. That same year, while Brooks was still board chairman ground was broken on Opryland.

On December 31, 1968 NLT was organized as a holding company to own the National Life and Accident Insurance Company, Third National Bank, and WSM Incorporated. Sam M. Fleming, of Third National, was elected president of NLT and Dan Brooks was named board chairman. NLT instantly became the largest financial institution in the South. However, stringent Federal legislation quickly threatened to severely restrict one-bank holding companies, such as NLT. Accordingly, NLT spun off Third National in 1970. Fleming remained as presient of NLT until his reitrement in 1973. Brooks retired a year earlier.

National Life and Accident Insurance Company home office, 1924, showing vice president Ridley Wills and "welcome home" cards welcoming him after an illness forced him to miss the dedication of the new home office building.
Collection of Ridley Wills II.

C. Runcie Clements Jr., who replaced Brooks as National Life president in 1967, retired in 1969. He was replaced by William C. Weaver Jr. who had come up through the Real Estate and Mortgage Loan Depatment. Weaver, whose wife was the former Elizabeth Craig, held that position until 1972 when he was promoted to board chairman on the retirement of Dan Brooks. At that time, R. L. "Rusty" Wagner, formerly chief actuary, was promoted to president of National Life.

In 1977 Wagner was promoted to chairman of the board of NLT, replacing Weaver. Wagner's position as president of NLT was taken by Walter M. Robinson Jr., who had been head of National Life's Legal Department and was the husband of Edwin and Elizabeth Craig's younger daughter, Margaret Ann.

Wagner would serve as NLT board chairman until his retirement in 1981. He was succeeded as president of National Life by John H. Tipton Jr., who had been manager of the Real Estate and Mortgage Loan Department. Tipton held the position from 1977 until 1980 when he was named vice chairman and chief financial officer of NLT. Also in 1980 Fred W. "Ted" Lazenby, who had come up through the Agency Department, replaced Tipton as National Life's president. In the same year C. A. "Neil" Craig became the third Craig to hold the position of board chairman at National Life.

In 1982 National Life's parent company, National Life Third (NLT), was acquired in a hostile takeover by American General Corporation of Houston, Texas. National Life and Accident Insurance Company that had created and owned radio station WSM, the Grand Ole Opry, Opryland Hotel, Opryland USA, and WSM-TV was no longer locally owned. This marked the end of an era in Nashville. On January 3, 1994, Nashville's tallest building was sold by American General to the State of Tennessee, and American General moved to new headquarters in Brentwood, Tennessee.

SOUTHLIFE HOLDING COMPANY was founded on September 30, 1983, by F. W. "Ted" Lazenby, former president of the National Life and Accident Insurance Company, with the help of Edward G. Nelson, then chairman and chief executive officer of Commerce Union Bank. Lazenby and Nelson went to Jack Massey and Lucius Burch, of Massey Burch Investment Group, with the concept of starting a debit life insurance company. Massey Burch agreed to contribute $500,000 of the initial $1 million initial capital.

The next year, Southlife, with loans from a number of banks, bought Public Savings Life Insurance Company for $18 million. The company, headquartered in Charleston, South Carolina, had $33 million in assets and $12 million in capital and surplus with branch offices in South Carolina and Georgia. Shortly thereafter, Southlife Holding Company, with headquarters at One Commerce Place in Nashville, acquired the assets and insurance in force of Coastal States Life Insurance Company, of Atlanta, Georgia. Combined, these two companies had $80 million in assets, $33 million in total revenue, and $4.5 million in annual income.

Southlife Holding Company went public in 1986 with Alex Brown & Sons, of Baltimore, the lead underwriter. One of the other underwriters was J. C. Bradford & Company, of Nashville.

In 1987 Southlife grew again through the acquisition of Security Trust Life Insurance Company, a subsidiary of ICH Corporation of Louisville. This company was acquired for $100 million. Southlife was then a company with $300 million in assets and $112 million in revenue, with over fifteen hundred employees in eighty-seven branch offices scattered from Virginia to Florida.

In 1990 Southlife merged into Capital Holding Company for $160 million. Southlife shareholders received Capital Holding Company stock that over ten years grew eight times. Lazenby stayed chairman of Southlife until 1994, when the company ceased to exist. Jack Massey thought his investment in Southlife was one of the best he ever made.

LUMBER COMPANIES

PRUITT, SPURR, AND COMPANY supplied much of the lumber used during Nashville's building boom in 1878. This lumber company was established in 1866 on the east bank of the Cumberland River opposite the Nashville warf. The company, that employed 125 men and boys, consisted of three kilns and a bucket factory, planing mill, sawmill, varnish room, and warehouse. Pruitt, Spurr, and Company produced ashware, lumber buckets, and churns.

Along the east bank, anchored to the shore, were log rafts that had been floated down the Cumberland from the upper river, the Caney Fork, and the Obey. An expert riverman on a "good tide" could pilot a log raft 220 miles from Celina, at the mouth of the Obey, to Nashville in five days. The logs remained in the water until needed, when they were hoisted one log at a time into the mill yard. Tom Webb, who grew up in Nashville in the 1890s once told me that, at the height of the season, the line of log rafts extended upriver beyond today's Shelby Park. Pruitt, Spurr, and Company stood about where LP Field is today.

FARRIS HARDWOOD LUMBER COMPANY came into being around 1913 or 1914, as an evolution of the lumber business Willis M. Farris Sr. had begun in the 1890s. Initially, Farris and H. J. Shafer owned Hilham Lumber Company in Hilham, Tennessee, and operated circular sawmills. Their lumber was shipped by steamboat or rafts to Nashville from Butler's Landing.

By 1904 or 1905 Farris was manager of Central Lumber Company, whose president was George W. Gilliland. The business was located on the west bank of the Cumberland River at Jefferson Street. When the property was condemned in 1905 for the construction of the Jefferson Street Bridge, the corporation was dissolved.

Farris and three of his sons then organized the Cherokee Lumber Company in 1906. Willis M. Farris Sr. was president, Lee Farris was vice president, Willis M. Farris Jr. was secretary-treasurer, and Alfred Farris was manager. The company was located on Monroe Street. Cherokee had sawmills in White Bluff, Tennessee, and in Colbert County, Alabama, and sold a lot of quartersawn red oak to Cumberland Telephone & Telegraph Company for telephone boxes.

In 1910 Willis M. Farris Sr. bought a four-acre tract in East Nashville between Oldham Street and the Jefferson Street Bridge from the Indiana Lumber Company. Three or four years later, he changed the name of Cherokee Lumber Company to the Farris Hardwood Lumber Company. He later purchased fifteen acres north of the Jefferson Street Bridge from Ransom & Killebrew. For some time, a neighbor and friend, Harmon J. Shafer, held an interest in the Farris Hardwood Lumber Company. During this time, Willis M. Farris Sr.'s son Frank was employed as an assistant cashier of State Trust Company. His other three sons continued in the family lumber business.

On July 9, 1918, Willis M. Farris Sr. boarded the Nashville, Chattanooga and St. Louis Railway train no. 4 at Union Station to go to Kingston Springs, Tennessee, to sell some lumber. Unable to find a seat, he was standing in the back of the train, when a friend gave him a seat in the smoker car. About five miles out of town, as the train reached Dutchman's Curve, near what is now the walking bridge immediately east of the White Bridge Road Bridge, there was a terrific collision between train no. 4 and eastbound train no. 1 coming from Memphis. When the collision occurred, the car in front of the smoker car on train no. 4 telescoped. There were numerous fatalities, including the elderly Willis M. Farris Sr. The crash was the deadliest in American railroad history.

After their father's unexpected death, Alfred, Lee, and Willis Jr. ran Farris Hardwood Lumber Company, then a corporation. Alfred was president, Lee was vice president, and Willis Jr. was secretary-treasurer. Frank was not involved, as he was assistant cashier at Cumberland Valley National Bank in 1920. In 1926 the company officers were Alfred C. Farris, president; Lee H. Farris, vice president; and Willis M. Farris Jr., secretary-treasurer.

Farris Hardwood Lumber Company's greatest challenge in the 1920s was a devastating flood. On Christmas Eve 1926 heavy rains pummeled the area. By Christmas morning, the Cumberland River was rising rapidly and would soon be out of its banks. Alfred, Lee, and Willis assembled their entire staff—Jim Scott, Jack Ellis, Joe Stevens, some raftsmen (sometimes called river rats), Burrell Ball, and the rest of the office staff—and went to the lumber yard to start securing the lumber.

The river crested at 56.2 feet, the official record high, on January 1, 1927. Burrell Ball managed to reach the office in a canoe. Finding the building under six feet of water, he opened the safe that was underwater and removed its contents.

Farris Hardwood Lumber Company suffered flood damages estimated at between $40,000 and $50,000, however, no lumber floated away.

The next spring, a Mississippi River flood created such a shortage of lumber, particularly in Mississippi and Arkansas, that Farris Hardwood Lumber Company was more than compensated for its losses the previous winter.

In 1927 Frank Farris resigned from the American National Bank, where he was cashier, to open his own bank. He and Walter J. Diehl founded Third National Bank on July 18, 1927. Farris used his own savings, what he received from selling his interest in the lumber company to his brothers, and his share of the proceeds from a life insurance policy on his father's life to help capitalize Third National at $300,000. He invited all Farris Hardwood Lumber Company employees to invest in the bank. Frank Farris was the driving force behind the bank until he turned over the presidency to Sam Fleming three weeks before his death in 1950 at age fifty-nine.

For many years, Farris Hardwood Lumber Company owned Central Oak Products Company, a West Nashville business that made hardwood flooring and manufactured barrel staves for the Jack Daniel's Distillery. The company was later located at Twenty-Fourth Avenue North and Clifton Avenue. During the Depression, the two companies provided quite a few jobs in a beleaguered Nashville. A Central Oak Products Company sawmill burned in 1938, but it was rebuilt and the company remained viable until it was liquidated in 1971, when Willis M. Farris Jr. was its president.

Willis Farris Jr.'s daughter, Rachel, began working at Central Oak Products Company in 1949. Seven years later, her brother, Alfred C.

Lee Farris of the Farris Hardwood Lumber Company, during the January 1927 flood. *Collection of Alfred C. Farris III*

Farris III, joined Farris Hardwood Lumber Company. He left in 1971 to pursue farming and mission work in Uganda. Rachel also left to pursue family affairs and volunteer work.

When Alfred C. Farris died in 1958, Willis Farris Jr. succeeded his brother as company president. The company's motto in the 1950s and 1960s was "Anything in Hardwood."

During the 1970s, Farris Hardwood Lumber Company, then a limited partnership, began selling off parts of its property, including a 6.45-acre tract to Alley-Cassetty Coal Company in April 1973. On June 19, 1974, the company's large sawmill burned again. Carpet companies, most located in or near Dalton, Georgia, were encroaching on the flooring market and Farris Hardwood Lumber Company felt the competition.

Willis M. Farris Jr. died on September 27, 1986, at age ninety-eight. He worked at his office the day before he died. His obituary said that the Farris Hardwood Lumber Company once had as many as seven sawmills in three states, and that he had been president of the Nashville Lumbermen's Association and a former member of the National Oak Flooring Manufacturers Association.

In about 1990 Farris Hardwood Lumber Company closed. The lumber business then was far different and far less lucrative in the 1980s than it had been one hundred years earlier when there were twenty lumber and wood products mills in Nashville manufacturing more than eighty-six million board feet of lumber.

JOHN B. RANSOM & COMPANY began in Murfreesboro, Tennessee, as a business venture of John B. Ransom and Dr. J. O. Kirkpatrick. The business grew so fast that, in 1889, its headquarters were moved to Nashville. In 1897 the partnership with Kirkpatrick was discontinued, and Ransom was joined in the company by his half brother, Arthur B. Ransom (who had also been in the lumber business in Murfreesboro); John W. Love; and M. F. Greene. Love and Greene left the partnership a year later.

In 1906 John and Arthur Ransom were manufacturers of lumber and boxes on Nineteenth Avenue North, where the Nashville, Chattanooga & St. Louis Railway crossed. Three years later, John B. Ransom & Company was handling between fifty million and sixty million feet of hardwood timber, earning the distinction of having the largest hardwood lumber business in the South.

John Ransom was also president of the Nashville Hardwood Flooring Company; the Conasauga Lumber Company in Conasauga, Tennessee; and the Gayoso Lumber Company of Memphis. He was also vice president and a large stockholder in the W. J. Cude Land and Lumber Company,

Plant of John B. Ransom & Company, manufacturers and wholesale dealers in lumber, showing Fisk Memorial Chapel and Jubilee Hall in the distance.
Nashville Public Library, Special Collections.

which had branches in Kimmins, Tennessee, and Cude, Mississippi. In 1908 he was elected president of the Hardwood Manufacturer's Association of the United States, the largest organization of lumbermen in the hardwood trade in America.

When he died on January 5, 1910, at age forty-nine, his friends were stunned, and the Nashville community suffered a huge loss. He had been a member of the Vanderbilt Board of Trust, on the YMCA committee that raised the money to build the new YMCA building on Seventh Avenue North, and a leading member of West End United Methodist Church.

Arthur Ransom succeeded John as president of John B. Ransom & Company, and Marvin M. Ransom was named treasurer. In 1921 Arthur B. Ransom was still president, John B. Ransom Jr. and R. T. Wilson were vice presidents, Marvin M. Ransom was secretary, and J. M. Ransom was treasurer. The company specialized, during this period, in providing their customers with quality millwork and hardwood floors. Their lumber yard was for many years at 700 Nineteenth Avenue North. The company also had a sawmill at the end of Fifty-Fourth Avenue North next to the Cumberland River. The company slogan in 1925 was "Everything in Lumber."

By 1937 Arthur Ransom had changed the name of the company to Ransom Lumber Company, and moved it to 212–18 Shelby Avenue. Kath D. Swartz was secretary at that time.

The 1943 city directory lists Arthur B. Ransom as president, with his office located on the fifth floor of a building at 150 Fourth Avenue North. This seems a clear indication that he had greatly downsized company operations. The Ransom Lumber Company closed around 1943 or 1944.

MANUFACTURING COMPANIES

Aladdin Industries LLC was a vendor of lunch boxes, kerosene lamps, stoves, and thermal food storage containers. Its predecessor company was Western Lighting Company, founded in 1907 by Victor S. Johnson Sr., and incorporated in 1908 as the Mantle Lamp Company of America. Its purpose was to provide superior kerosene lighting to rural America. A 1912 company advertisement heralded the lamp as "the best rural home lamp in the world."

Aladdin Industries began in 1914 as a subsidiary of Mantle Lamp Company for the purpose of manufacturing vacuum bottles. Under Johnson's leadership, Aladdin expanded its product line and, in 1933, made the first character lunch box, using images of Hopalong Cassidy.

Before his sudden death in 1943, Victor Johnson had encouraged Wade V. Thompson in his efforts to bring natural gas to Nashville. He told Thompson that if that project succeeded, he would consider moving his company to Nashville.

On his father's death, Victor Johnson Jr., who had received a law degree from Yale in 1941, assumed the position of interim president of Mantle Lamp Company of America. In 1946, upon completion of his military obligation, Johnson entered the family business on a full-time basis at its headquarters in Chicago, Illinois.

In 1949, after Nashville received natural gas, he decided to move both the executive offices and the manufacturing facilities to a 130,000-square-foot plant the company built in Nashville on Murfreesboro Road. This was the first post–World War II industrial plant built in the city. Later named Aladdin Industries LLC, Victor Johnson Jr. led the company as its chief executive officer and board chairman for the next thirty-five years. Under his leadership, Aladdin modified its product line to manufacture thermos bottles, school lunch boxes, electronic components, food-service systems, and real estate development. Aladdin became one of Nashville's largest privately held businesses, selling its products worldwide. Johnson was a hands-on manager known for frequently walking the plant floor and talking with his employees.

Victor Johnson Jr. made as big an imprint on Nashville personally as did his company. He served as president of the Nashville Area Chamber of Commerce in 1956. He was a member of the Metropolitan Charter Commission for Nashville and Davidson County in 1957–58 and again in 1961–62, and was a leader in the successful move to adopt a metropolitan form of government for the city and county. A progressive, he was proud to serve as chairman of the Meharry Medical College board from 1955 until 1983. He was a director of the Nashville Branch of the Federal Reserve Bank of Atlanta and a member of the board of trustees for George Peabody College For Teachers.

In 1971 Johnson became a partner in a massive real estate development project that converted 850 acres of Cumberland River floodplain in North Nashville into MetroCenter, one of the city's premier business parks. Johnson was also an influential force behind the effort to create the Tennessee Performing Arts Center and was credited with proposing to Governor Ned McWherter the idea of the State of Tennessee buying land behind the State Capitol and placing the Tennessee Bicentennial Mall there.

I knew Victor Johnson Jr., as we were both Presbyterians and members of The Roundtable, a Nashville literary club. He was a delightful member of The Roundtable, both interesting and visionary, even in his late eighties. He seemed to personally know half of the most important people in America and was interested in the personal lives of his fellow members, most of whom were a generation younger than he was.

In 1985 Johnson retired as chairman of the board of Aladdin Industries LLC, by then a company that had manufacturing plants, sales operations, licensees, and joint venture companies in over sixteen countries outside the United States. In 2000, when he was well in his eighties, Victor Johnson Jr. chaired the Citizens Goal 2000 Committee, which sought ways to preserve the quality of life in Nashville for all its citizens. He died on January 19, 2008, at age ninety-one.

The headline of the *Tennessean* on December 21, 2001, was shocking. It read, "Aladdin Sale May Close Plant Here." The article said that Aladdin Industries LLC planned to sell its Aladdin and Stanley lines of thermos bottles and insulated products to a Seattle Company, leaving the fate of the fifty-two-year-old Nashville plant and its 550 employees up in the air. The sale did materialize, and today Aladdin Industries is an arm of privately held Pacific Market International (PMI), headquartered in Seattle, Washington, with offices in Asia, Australia, and Europe. Aladdin Industries LLC produced its last thermal bottle in Nashville in July 2002, closing its plant on Murfreesboro Road that had meant so much to the Nashville community.

DAVIS CABINET COMPANY began as a sawmill on the north bank of the Cumberland River that produced lumber from logs rafted down the river. The mill owners saw an opportunity to maximize their business by forming a subsidiary company to manufacture veneered bedroom suites and sewing machine cabinets. They named the company Standard Furniture Company.

In 1921 Lipscomb "Lip" Davis, an East Nashville native who had been educated at Hume Fogg High School and Vanderbilt, joined Standard Furniture Company. He had dropped out of Vanderbilt to enter World War I, later becoming a traveling manager-secretary for World War I hero Alvin York. He also worked briefly for Volunteer Manufacturing Company that made overalls.

By 1926 Davis had worked his way up to plant superintendent at Standard. Davis began to formulate his own ideas about the furniture business. He wanted to start his own company to produce high-quality furniture at marketable prices. An opportunity to do so came in July 1929, when the Norman Davidson family decided to sell Standard Furniture Company.

Immediately interested, Davis asked Frank Farris, the founder of Third National Bank, and his brothers, Willis and Alfred Farris, both in the lumber business, to underwrite his venture. With their loan, Davis bought the factory on his twenty-ninth birthday, July 15, 1929. The company's balance sheet as of November 30, 1929, showed assets of $341,091.26.

Davis acquired Standard Furniture Company at a discount because its factory had suffered devastating damage when the Cumberland River rose sixteen feet above flood level on New Year's Day 1927 and had covered the first floor of the warehouse with four feet of water.

If Davis was fortunate in being able to purchase the company at a discount, he was unlucky in that the devastating stock market crash on October 29, 1929, brought on the Great Depression that lasted until World War II. With his buildings and equipment in poor state of repair, production was almost halted. During the bleak days of 1930–32, Davis had to go to Third National Bank on "many a Friday" and ask Farris to advance additional money. To keep his business afloat, Davis also sold a one-third

Davis Cabinet Company, 1950s.
Collection of Lipscomb Davis Jr. Estate

interest in Davis Cabinet Company to the Morrison family and a like amount to Edmund W. Turnley. Business gradually improved after 1932. Turnley became secretary and treasurer of Davis Cabinet Company in 1933.

The Lillian Russell line of fine furniture, primarily made of cherry wood, was Davis's best seller and would remain so throughout the history of the company. Davis employed three salesmen in the 1930s.

During World War II, Davis converted his factory to manufacturing gunstocks from solid walnut for the M1 Garand and the M1 Carbine. When the war ended in 1945, Davis Cabinet Company had a surplus of gunstocks so he formed the Morrison Novelty Company to manufacture wooden toy guns that were sold primarily to Sears and Montgomery Ward. Interestingly, this company was owned by the wives of the three owners: Adelaide Davis, Louise Morrison, and Lula Troop Turnley.

With the war over, Davis Cabinet Company resumed production of high-quality bedroom furniture made of cherry, walnut, mahogany, maple, pine, pecan, and ash. On the company's twenty-fifth anniversary, Davis Cabinet Company had five hundred employees and was shipping furniture to forty-six of the forty-eight states.

In about 1952 the J. W. Rowland family, who owned Bradford Furniture Company on Third Avenue, asked Lip Davis if he would purchase 20 percent of the company to help finance their move to Hillsboro Road in Green Hills. He agreed to do so and found that he enjoyed going by Bradford's on Saturday afternoons, often giving up golf to do so. Bill Rowland and Joe Murphy helped him by critiquing designs for Davis Cabinet Company from 1950 to 1985.

At Thanksgiving 1953 President Dwight D. Eisenhower hosted a small party at Augusta National Golf Club. That evening Sam Fleming, an Augusta National member, told the Eisenhowers about his Nashville friend, Lip Davis, who owned a furniture manufacturing plant. Somehow, Sam arranged for bedroom pieces made by Davis Cabinet Company to go in the Eisenhower cottage at Augusta National and in Mrs. Eisenhower's bedroom at Camp David.

In June 1954 Nathan Craig, Sam Fleming, Stewart Campbell, and Lip Davis established a private venture capital corporation known as Hillsboro Enterprises. Three decades later, Hillsboro Enterprises would buy a substantial interest in Davis Cabinet Company.

Also in 1954 the United Furniture Workers of American gained enough support among the Davis Cabinet Company's employees to unionize the plant. This was a huge disappointment to Davis, who had voluntarily put in a profit-sharing plan for his employees. It also drove a wedge between management and the workers.

The next year, Lipscomb "Buzz" Davis Jr. joined the company. In 1958 an attempt to renegotiate the labor contract led to a five-and-a-half-month strike that closed the plant for two months. There was considerable violence and the company suffered both financially and in the quality of its furniture, as two hundred replacement employees had to be hired.

Despite the labor turmoil, Davis Cabinet Company opened a second plant in Portland, Tennessee, in 1959, and Lip Davis gradually bought out the Turnley interest. By 1960, the Davises and the Morrisons owned all the Davis Cabinet Company stock. Davis would eventually buy out the Morrison interest.

The United Brotherhood of Carpenters and Joiners replaced the United Furniture Workers of America in the mid-1960s. Their relationship with management was better and the contract signed satisfied both sides. The later 1960s were difficult: a fire destroyed the finishing room, there was another strike, and Metro Government put restrictions on the amount of sawdust a company could release in the air.

In 1970 the Simmons Company, of New York, approached Lip Davis about acquiring Davis Cabinet Company. The possible merger would involve an exchange of one hundred thousand outstanding shares of Davis Cabinet Company stock for fifty thousand shares of Simmons Company stock. At the time, the Davises were optimistic about their company's future, feeling that profitability was "just around the corner." Consequently, they decided not to accept the Simmons offer.

In 1973 Lip Davis's declining health led him into taking retirement. By then, Buzz Davis realized that they had made a mistake in not accepting the Simmons offer, as the furniture manufacturing business was steadily leaving the United States for China, South Korea, and other Asian countries. The same year, Davis Cabinet Company enlarged its Portland plant's manufacturing space by 40 percent.

Lip Davis died in April 1978 at age seventy-eight. He had served as president of Davis Cabinet Company from 1929 until 1965, when he became chairman. Under his leadership, the company he founded became one of the nation's outstanding furniture manufacturers. His son Buzz succeeded him as company chief executive officer.

Hillsboro Enterprises bought their interest in Davis Cabinet Company in 1982. At the time, the Davis family owned approximately 23 percent of Hillsboro Enterprises.

In the fall of 1983, Nat Ancell, who had founded Ethan Allen, approached Buzz Davis about buying Davis Cabinet Company. Buzz and Sam Fleming flew to New York and negotiated a sale to Ancell. Davis was inclined, either to sell the family business to Ancell, liquidate it, or reduce the company to a size of about $10 million in sales. By this time, however, Davis had stepped down as chief executive officer and was not inclined to tell his successor, Walt Campbell, what to do. In January 1984 Sam Fleming wrote his grandson Fleming Wilt, saying, "It looks like we have been successful in disposing of Davis Cabinet Company." He added that the company had been a real problem for a long time. The sale to Ethan Allen never materialized.

After two or three more years of losing money, Toby Wilt, acting for Hillsboro Enterprises, sold Davis Cabinet Company to Unique, a North Carolina furniture maker, in 1986. Unique tried to make veneer and solid furniture in the same plant but was unsuccessful. Two years later, Unique went bankrupt. Adelaide (Mrs. Lip) Davis, Buzz Davis, Stewart Campbell, and Sam Fleming liquidated Hillsboro Enterprises in 1986 and distributed the assets to the partners.

FORD GLASS PLANT's introduction to Nashville was on July 14, 1955, when Ford Motor Company announced that it was building a $10-million glass plant that would employ twenty-five hundred people. In 1966, Ford reported the addition of a "float process" furnace at its Nashville glass plant. Mr. L. O. Seltz, plant manager, said that "since the plant was built, nearly 800,000 square feet have been added to the plant in six expansions." In 1965, the glass plant's payroll was $21 million. In 1966, employment reached 3,000.

After decades of supplying windshields and windows for some very popular American light vehicles, including the Ford F-150 pickup and the Escape SUV, Nashville's Ford Glass Plant found itself unneeded. At the end of the 1990s, the parent company spun off its huge parts operations, including the Nashville glass plant, into an independent publically traded entity, Delphi Corporation. Delphi went public in 1999 but soon collapsed, filing for Chapter 11 bankruptcy in 2005. Two of the three towers were taken out of operation. Inside heavy machinery sat idle.

Zeledyne LLC took over in 2008. Zeledyne and the rest of the US auto industry were hammered by the recession. By 2010 Zeledyne management put the plant up for sale.

After having five different owners in twelve years, Carlex Glass America, the US subsidiary of Japan's Central Glass Company, took over. The company found the employees in Nashville a little jaded and uncertain about the new owners. The State of Tennessee helped by paying for the retraining of 450 employees. Carlex announced that it was investing $100 million to clean up the plant, modernize its equipment, and boost its capacity. The company relied on new technology, including a modern process called press-form that permitted greater manipulation of glass and the ability to handle more creative vehicle designs. One of the goals was to produce thinner glass that would mean less weight and would improve fuel economy. Carlex continues to operate the massive plant in 2013.

Gray & Dudley Company was started by two brothers, Houston and Guilford Dudley, who grew up in Tennessee. They arrived in Nashville soon after the Federal occupation in 1862. Not long after opening a hardware store on Market Street, they discovered that, in the middle of the Civil War, they could not find enough suppliers to meet their growing needs. So, they built their own foundry at the same location.

In 1895 they merged their company, Dudley Brothers Hardware, with a Chattanooga firm, Gray, Fall & Company. The newly incorporated company was named Gray & Dudley. The two Dudley brothers headed the firm, while John M. Gray was listed as a founder, and his son, John M. Gray Jr., was named vice president. Four years later, the four senior officers were Houston Dudley, president; John M. Gray Jr., vice president; J. T. Jenkins, treasurer; and Houston Dudley Jr., secretary.

In 1900 Gray & Dudley Company occupied an impressive six-story Chicago-style building at 222–24 North Market Street in Nashville. Constructed entirely of steel, pressed brick, and stone, the massive building was described as "the largest business house ever constructed in the city."

By this time, Gray & Dudley had twenty-five salesmen "on the road" across the Midsouth. Its warehouses were on Chestnut Street and on the Louisville & Nashville Railroad line in West Nashville. The company's 1900 catalogue was three inches thick, advertising metal products in eleven categories, including wagon and buggy hardware; farming implements and agricultural tools; and guns, ammunition and sporting goods.

Gray & Dudley was on a roll. In 1905, the company built a two-story warehouse at 2300 Clifton Road, where they manufactured iron ranges and stoves. The company also had a harness factory at the State Prison that moved to Clifton Road sometime between 1910 and 1920.

As Nashville headquarters for athletic and sporting goods, Gray & Dudley had an ad in the 1915 *Commodore* that read, "All Vanderbilt

Teams Are Equipped By Us." By 1922 the company's assets had grown to $3,359,768.76.

Gray & Dudley sold its hardware department in 1925 to concentrate exclusively on the manufacture of stoves, ranges, heaters, and hollowware, being ranked as one of the largest manufacturing entities in the country.

In 1927 Houston Dudley Jr., who had been general manager of the company for twenty-five years, bought a majority interest in Gray & Dudley for approximately $1 million. The transaction, paid for in cash, was said to be one of the most important business deals that had taken place in Nashville for many years. The sellers were Joe B. Palmer and the John M. Gray Jr. and B. F. Wilson families. (The Wilsons were the parents of Mrs. John M. Gray Jr.) The new officers were Houston Dudley Jr., president; Foskett Brown, vice president; James C. Lauderdale, secretary; and Ernest Baldwin, superintendent of the factory. Foskett Brown was Dudley's son-in-law. At this time, John M. Gray Jr. retired due to poor health.

Times were changing. A rapid decrease in the cost of electricity and the extensive highway and railroad distribution systems that were crisscrossing the United States in the second half of the 1920s did much to popularize electric cooking in the country and diminish the market for wood- and coal-burning stoves, such as Gray & Dudley's wood-burning Washington Home Furnace. Gray & Dudley was on the crest of the wave. In about 1929 or 1930 the company introduced its Washington brand of electric ranges. Its salesmen initially encountered resistance because of the comparative high cost of electric ranges and their slowness in cooking.

By 1932 new and improved burners proved to be both economical and fast. That year, there were an estimated one million electric ranges in use in the United States, and that total would skyrocket.

Later in the 1930s, when it was becoming increasingly clear that electric and gas ranges were going to make wood- or coal-burning cast-iron ranges obsolete, Gray & Dudley introduced their Martha Washington line of gas and electric ranges. Gray & Dudley's balance sheet for the year ending December 31, 1936, showed the company's net worth to be $1,671,181.35. At the time, the company employed twelve hundred people.

To maintain good employee relations, Gray & Dudley fielded an amateur baseball team that won the Dixie League championship in 1936. Gray &

Dudley supplied all the necessary equipment for the team that typically played before anywhere from three thousand to six thousand people.

Houston Dudley Jr. died on March 18, 1938, at age sixty-eight. An editorial in the *Nashville Banner* read: "He was a man of public spirit, keenly alive to enterprises that promised public benefits, and had been always active in the affairs of business organizations and civic bodies. . . . Mr. Dudley measured fully to the responsibilities of life in every domain in the circle of family and friends, in social relations, as a churchman and in business; and his demise is a positive loss to our community."

Foskett Brown succeeded his father-in-law as president of Gray & Dudley. Other officers were J. B. Duke, vice president, and James C. Lauderdale, secretary-treasurer.

During World War II, Gray & Dudley retooled its plant on Clifton Avenue to manufacture no. 1 army heaters, no. 5 army ranges, and cast-iron griddles for the US Army. This was difficult because of the shortage of materials, supplies, and, above all, labor.

After the war, Gray & Dudley went back to producing stoves, ranges, and heaters. As late as 1947, there were still shortages of sheet metal and pig iron that slowed down production. There was also more competition from such national companies as General Electric and Westinghouse. Gray & Dudley's corporate offices were then at 2300 Clifton Road, where the company already had its factory and sales room.

Gray & Dudley Company, 1930s.
Collection of Lemuel B. Stevens Jr.

In 1954 the company was the second or the third manufacturer to introduce electric built-in wall ovens and later introduced its gas built-in wall oven, a first in the industry. In 1963 Gray & Dudley pioneered the field of low-temperature oven cleaning by introducing its continuous cleaning oven. Gray & Dudley had as many as 350 employees during these years.

In the late 1950s, Lemuel B. Stevens bought the company and became chairman of the board. Louis B. Carroll was president and chief executive officer. In 1962 Ross I. Evans, owner of the Chattanooga Royal Manufacturing Company, became a substantial owner of Gray & Dudley. Although his relationship with Gray & Dudley only lasted about a year, Evans brought with him the brand name Royal Chef, which Gray & Dudley adopted, replacing its Martha Washington brand.

In 1966 Lemuel B. "Lem" Stevens Jr., a Vanderbilt graduate, was named president. During the 1970s, Gray & Dudley purchased the tooling of Crown Stove Company of Chicago and began producing Crown free-standing gas ranges. American Crown was added as an additional brand name to Royal Chef. When Lem Jr.'s father died in 1977, he became board chairman.

John F. Sorey became president in 1979, succeeding Lem Stevens Jr., and served for about four years. In the early 1980s, a firm headquartered in California began to acquire an interest in Gray & Dudley. Just when it looked like the acquisition would be completed, an industrial accident in the Gray & Dudley fabrication building in 1986 caused the roof of the aged building to partially collapse. This ended further negotiations for new ownership. When Gray & Dudley finally reached a settlement with the insurance company, the amount the company received was not sufficient to reopen the plant, and the company that had been a major appliance manufacturer with a national reputation for the quality of its products was forced to close.

HORACE SMALL MANUFACTURING COMPANY was founded in 1937 by Horace Small. Under the leadership of three generations of the Small family, it grew to become one of the nation's largest manufacturers and distributors of uniforms for law enforcement and commercial use.

During World War II, Horace Small made uniforms for US military forces. From 1937 until 1990, Horace Small Manufacturing Company was privately held by the Small family.

In 1972 Horace Small established a subsidiary company, R&R Uniforms, to manufacture uniforms for federal, state, and local law officials. R&R Uniforms was located in an eighty-six-thousand-square-foot facility on Freeman Station Road in MetroCenter. At the same time, the corporate offices and sales and distributions were relocated from Charlotte Avenue to the Fairway Center in MetroCenter. Robert W. Gates Jr., president of R&R Uniforms, said "the move to MetroCenter will streamline operations by bringing divisions together as well as offering space for expansion."

In 1990, Horace Small Manufacturing Company went public with a $60 million initial offering. The proceeds were used to pay down debt incurred during a 1987 buyout of the company from Small family members. In a reverse takeover, the company ended up in the hands of institutional British investors including Drayton Consolidated Trust. In its first year as a public company, Horace Small showed profits and expanded its manufacturing facilities. That year, Horace Small employed about five hundred workers at the company's Twenty-Eighth Avenue North plant, two hundred workers at a plant in Mt. Pleasant, Tennessee, and another one hundred at a plant in Guthrie, Kentucky. In addition to manufacturing employees, the company had about one hundred people at its distribution center in MetroCenter, where it moved in 1990. "The hourly work force was primarily female and the average seniority was about fifteen years," said company president Doug Small.

In fiscal year 1995, Horace Small reported sales of $126 million, up 11 percent from 1994. Earnings also rose to $6 million, up 15 percent from fiscal 1994. In 1996 Doug Small, grandson of the founder, stepped down from his position as chief executive, leaving the company without a Small family member at the helm since the company was founded in 1937.

KUSAN INC. was a plastics manufacturing company founded in 1946 by William R. "Bill" McLain and Earl Horton. McClain, a chemical engineering graduate and a Navy veteran, had been a roommate of Horton's at Georgia Tech. McClain chose the name "Kusan" (the name of an ancient American Indian tribe in Oregon) from an encyclopedia.

For the first two or three years, Kusan exclusively made plastic toys, the most successful of which was a plastic block with five clear sides and a solid, colored base. Inside the block was a small pellet so that the toy rattled when you shook it. Kusan won a Modern Plastics Award in 1947 for the toy. It also brought financial stability to the company whose workers gained valuable experience in molding plastics.

In 1948 McLain and Horton decided to establish a second plant in Nashville just north of Madison. A year later, they moved the company's headquarters from Henderson, Kentucky, to leased space over the Chocolate Shop at 2716 Franklin Road in Nashville. In 1952 the Madison plant was destroyed by a fire, causing Kusan to relocate to a building at 2001 Nolensville Road.

In 1954 Kusan's officers were Bill McLain, president, and Earl Horton, vice president. Cornelius A. Horton, who had been vice president, was then secretary-treasurer, while Charles M. Anderson was a vice president. That year, Kusan was busy making plastic injection molds for industry manufacturers, producing plastic trays, and colorful plastic toys, including a derringer replica cap gun and a pop gun that would fire Ping-Pong balls.

In 1959 Kusan moved its corporate headquarters to 3206 Belmont Boulevard. By this time Kusan had three manufacturing facilities in Nashville, the original one in Henderson, Kentucky, and one in Franklin, Tennessee. The Franklin plant had between two hundred and three hundred employees.

Bob Chickey, who joined the company in 1958 as a sales engineer, moved to Greenville, South Carolina, in 1967 as president of Kusan's newly acquired Southeastern-Kusan Inc. Kusan had also acquired Nichols-Kusan Inc. in Jacksonville, Texas; J. Halpern Company in Pittsburgh, Pennsylvania; Schaper Manufacturing Company in Minneapolis, Minnesota; and Elastics in Atlanta, Georgia.

Kusan, in turn, was acquired by Bethlehem Steel Corporation in February 1970 in an exchange of stock worth an estimated $20 million. The company then had sales of about $20 million.

Bob Chickey returned from Greenville in 1974 to become president and chief operating officer of Kusan. By 1979, Kusan, as a division of Bethlehem Steel, had between 325 and 375 employees at their Nashville plant, then on Massman Drive, where plastic components were made for Ford, General Motors, Whirlpool, and others. Kusan had more than 3,000 employees in Georgia, Indiana, Minnesota, South Carolina, and Texas plants, where PVC siding, textiles, furniture components, toys, and games were produced. This growth was fueled primarily by acquisitions.

L. P. "Bill" Brittain, of Nashville, who recruited Bob Chickey in 1958, worked for Kusan for thirty-eight years. His last assignment, before his retirement in 1985, was as president of Kusan's Southeast Plastics Division in Greenville. Bill recalled in 2012 that, when he retired, Kusan had sixteen plants and that its corporate offices were in Maryland Farms in Brentwood, Tennessee.

In 1986 members of senior management at Bethlehem Steel and some Bethlehem investors bought the Kusan Division from Bethlehem Steel in a leveraged buyout. The group, called KAC Inc., then sold the separate parts individually to various companies and investment groups, thus ending Kusan's existence of more than forty years. Bethlehem Steel filed for bankruptcy in 2001 and was liquidated and its assets sold in 2003.

MAY HOSIERY MILLS was founded in 1896 by Jacob May, a native of Hoechst, Germany, who had come to Nashville from New Hampshire when he read in a Boston newspaper that the State of Tennessee was taking bids for the hiring of convict labor. When his bid to hire fifty convicts was accepted, he moved to Nashville with his wife and two sons, Mortimer and Abraham.

His home at 113 Belmont Avenue was within walking distance of the prison. When the state prison moved to Cockrill Bend in 1896, May rode a train from Union Station to the prison, where his factory, Rock City Hosiery Mills, was housed in a three-story building in the northeast corner of the prison yard. There, using prison labor, May's company manufactured socks.

In 1898 a third son, Dan, was born. Three years later, Jacob bought out his partner. In 1907, with the company quite profitable, Jacob took his family to see the town in Germany where he was born, and where his family had lived for hundreds of years. The same year, his second son, Abe, died of meningitis.

In 1908 Jacob lost the contract with the state. Discouraged, the Mays moved to New York City, although Jacob kept up with friends in Nashville. Soon, he reentered the hosiery business with two Nashville partners. The

May Hosiery Mills' receiving and shipping dock on Brown Street in South Nashville, 1918.
Collection of Joseph L. "Jack" May.

three men sold socks, primarily, to the large jobbing houses of the Midwest but also to Nashville wholesale houses clustered around the public square.

The company, then renamed May Hosiery Mills, prospered during the Great War. After a new DuPont rayon factory opened in 1925 in Old Hickory, May Hosiery Mills began making socks with the rayon. The mill had earlier used cotton, wool, and silk. Jacob May and his third son, Dan, who had entered the business earlier in the decade, took full control of the company that was located at 450 Houston Street in South Nashville.

Although the 1930s brought hard times for the hosiery industry, May Hosiery Mills developed some important new customers, including the Boy Scouts of America, Montgomery Ward, and Walt Disney. They also moved their entrance to the other side of the building. Henceforth, the company's address would be 425 Chestnut Street.

Business improved after America entered World War II. During the war, May Hosiery Mills used all of its available yarn to make socks for the armed forces. The company also became a prime contractor on mortar fuses. At its war-time peak, the mill employed twelve hundred people.

During the 1950s and 1960s, May Hosiery Mills was making approximately one million socks a week. By then the company had expanded its customer base to include the Girl Scouts of America and Sears Roebuck. Dan's son, Joseph "Jack" May, became president in the 1960s, succeeding Shep Schwartz.

In 1965 May Hosiery Mills was bought by Wayne Knitting Mills, of Humboldt, Tennessee. Jack May stayed on to run the local mills that became a division of Wayne. The 1970s saw the May Hosiery Mills Division still expanding, with two locations in Nashville and one in Athens, Tennessee; employing about one thousand workers; occupying over 300,000 square feet of floor space; and shipping almost one million socks each week. May Hosiery Mills even had a contract with NASA. (All the socks worn by the astronauts who went to the moon were made in South Nashville.)

When Wayne Knitting Mills sold its May Hosiery Mills Division to a competitor, Renfro Hosiery Mills, of Mt. Airy, North Carolina, Jack May retired. Renfro found it too difficult to operate a plant so far from their Mt. Airy headquarters, and closed the Nashville division in 1983, after moving its equipment to North Carolina. The buildings on Chestnut Street were sold to Bobby Moore, of Franklin, and Earl Beasley, of Nashville, who still own the sprawling complex in 2013, leasing it as rental property.

NASHVILLE BRIDGE COMPANY was founded in 1902 by Arthur J. Dyer, an 1891 graduate of Vanderbilt Engineering School, when he bought out his partner H. T. Sinnot and renamed their firm the Nashville Bridge and Construction Company. A year or two later, Dyer reorganized the company and named it the Nashville Bridge Company. The company built a slender six-story building on the east bank of the Cumberland River a short distance upstream from the foot of Broadway.

Nashville Bridge Company, 1956.
Metropolitan Nashville Archives.

The firm soon became recognized for building bridges in the Southeast as well as in Central and South America. When standardized bridge designs became common in 1916, Nashville Bridge Company adapted by shifting from bridge construction to the marine field. In 1922 and 1923, the company built a new plant in Bessemer, Alabama. In 1927, Dyer's son Harry assumed responsibility for the marine department. He began building barges at the Nashville plant, sliding them in the Cumberland River from pivoted arms, a technique developed by Nashville Bridge Company. The production of barges became very lucrative. This business and other marine projects allowed the company to survive the Depression.

Early in World War II, the US Navy hired the company to build dozens of vessels, including mine sweepers. Nashville Bridge prospered and expanded its East Nashville plant, where Nashvillians enjoyed watching the boats slide down a ramp to the river, making an enormous splash.

During the 1950s, Nashville Bridge Company identified its products as buildings, bridges, steel barges, boats, and galvanized structures. One barge, launched in September 1963, was twelve feet deep, fifty feet wide, two hundred feet long, and could carry twenty-eight thousand barrels of petroleum products.

In 1968 the Dyer family sold the company to Whale Inc. When Whale declared bankruptcy several years later, Nashville Bridge was taken over by a bank that sold it to American Ship Building Company. By the 1980s, Nashville Bridge, with an infusion of new money, became the largest builder of inland barges in the country.

Trinity Marine was the owner in 1988. They moved the company from their location in Nashville downstream to a less expensive site a short distance upstream from Ashland City.

In 2011 and 2012 the Nashville Bridge Company building next to LP Field on one side and a new waterfront park on the other side, was enlarged and completely renovated by the Nashville Park System. Its first tenant was the Cumberland River Compact that leased the third floor, which has a breathtaking view of downtown Nashville.

National Casket Company, 1960s.
Metropolitan Nashville Archives.

National Casket Company was a burial case manufacturing company that began about 1900 at 128 South Front Street. Frank C. Guthrie, the manager, remained in that position through World War II. In 1902, the company moved to 102–116 South Front Street before constructing its own four-story brick building at 121 Bridge Avenue (later Woodland Street) in 1903. The building, that was on the trolley line and had a round horse watering trough in the street, was an East Nashville landmark for decades. In about 1946, W. Hardin Guthrie became manager. In 1969 C. H. Swift was manager for manufacturing, and J. B. Folkes was district supervisor. In 1972 Folkes's title was district sales manager. In about 1975 the company moved to 708 North First Street. It had closed by 1980.

Old Hickory Powder Plant was an $87 million plant built in 1918 by E. I. du Pont de Nemours and Company for the US government. The plant, located in the Jones Bend of the Cumberland River, made smokeless gunpowder for the American Army in World War I and was, at the time, the world's largest munitions plant.

DuPont built more than a plant; it built an entire company town, complete with churches, a hospital, housing for workers, restaurants, and a school. At its peak of production, the company employed over fifty thousand workers, more than ten thousand of whom were women. My aunt, Mary Harding Buckner, then about twenty years old, rode the train from Union Station five days a week to Old Hickory to work as a volunteer at the powder plant.

When the armistice was announced on November 11, 1918, the plant, despite being only 75 percent complete, was producing 750,000 pounds of powder every twenty-four hours. Nashvillians were extremely proud of it. As an example, all postcards of Nashville produced in 1918 had a small caption that read, "Nashville, Powder City of the World." The Old Hickory Powder Plant closed in January 1919.

Phillips & Buttorff Manufacturing Company began around 1881 as an incorporation of businesses owned by H. W. Buttorff and W. P. Phillips. As a teenager, Buttorff worked for four years as a sheet metal worker in Carlisle, Pennsylvania, before heading to the South in 1858 as an industrious and bright twenty-one-year-old. With considerable difficulty, he reached Greensburg, Kentucky, penniless. From there, he walked all the way to Nashville.

Relying on his work experience back home, he got a job with J. W. Wilson & Company, a tinner on College Street. Buttorff's first job was to put a roof on a house built by Samuel Watkins. A year or two later, he became foreman and later a partner in J. W. Wilson & Company.

Following the Civil War, Buttorff resigned from his position and bought an interest in Phillips & Ashley, a roofing company on Market Street. The business moved to 10 College Street in 1870. The next year, Buttorff bought J. W. Wilson & Company and moved his combined companies to a building on the corner of College Street and Bank Alley. There, in 1881, he and W. P. Phillips organized a new company to manufacture and sell wholesale stoves, tinware, and house-furnishing goods. Shortly afterward, Buttorff's wholesale business and Phillips's retail business were incorporated as Phillips & Buttorff Manufacturing Company, with Buttorff as president. The company was located at 24 and 26 College Street (later, Third Avenue North).

After the turn of the century, Phillips & Buttorff sold Enterprise stoves, ranges, heaters, and furnaces. The company also made or distributed, through their retail store at 217–23 Third Avenue North, fine china, glassware, homeware, and ranges. The company was also a large shipper on the Cumberland River. When famed steamboat captain Tom Ryman died in 1904, one of the five steamboats he then owned was the

"H. W. Buttorff," named for his friend. By 1909 Phillips & Buttorff's factory covered six acres.

Possessed of a sterling character, integrity, and tireless energy, Buttorff was, during his business career, extremely active in his industry and in Nashville. He was the first president of the Nashville Builders' Exchange and on the boards of the Fourth & First National Bank; the Nashville, Chattanooga & St. Louis Railway (NC&StL); the Ryman Steamboat Line, where he was president; and the Nashville Woolen Mills. He was also vice president of the Indiana Manufacturing Company and of the Nashville Sheet Metal Roofing Company. He was a trustee of Roger Williams University and the Masonic Widows' and Orphans' Home. It was not surprising, therefore, that, in 1905, Buttorff was elected president of the Nashville Chamber of Commerce. He was also a member of Edgefield Baptist Church, where he was superintendent of the Sunday school, and a member of the Nashville Golf and Country Club.

Even at age seventy, Buttorff was the first person to open the company's mail each morning. He said that it was no more difficult to manage five hundred people at Phillips & Buttorff than it was to manage when the company had only ten employees.

Buttorff remained president of Phillips & Buttorff until the day of his death on September 16, 1915, at age seventy-eight. The *Nashville Banner*'s obituary said of him, "He was widely known and loved in this city, where he had grown from young manhood to a ripe age." The board of the Nashville Commercial Club hailed Buttorff, at his death, with this comment: "Our Merchant Prince Is Dead."

Buttorff was succeeded by B. E. McCarthy as president. The company was still at 217–23 Third Avenue North, with its warehouse on Church Street and its foundry in North Nashville by the NC&StL railroad tracks.

In 1927 Douglas W. Binns was elected president of Phillips & Buttorff. The company had by then expanded its products to include stoves, ranges, warm-air furnaces, hollowware, metalware, and glassware.

In about 1930 the company's retail store, which had started on North College Street in 1856, moved to 705 Church Street. Hundreds of young Nashville women had their bridal registries at Phillips & Buttorff. Before

Phillips & Buttorff Manufacturing Company letterhead, 1930.
Collection of Betty (Mrs. James R.) Stadler.

the days of catalogue showrooms, the store was the largest distributor of china and crystal in the southeast. It also was the largest Lenox china dealer in the region.

Binns remained president until July 1956, when he was succeeded by W. R. Lawrence Jr., who had formerly been the manager and vice president of Avco's Nashville plant. That year, the company's main office and sales department were still on Third Avenue North, the wholesale department and warehouse were at 210–212 Second Avenue North, and the foundry was still on Twelfth Avenue North. The company also had a shipping department at 801 Twelfth Avenue North, an enameling department on Herman Street, and sheet metal and furnace departments at 813 Twelfth Avenue North.

In 1956 the new management team of president W. R. Lawrence Jr. and board chairman Bert R. Prall instituted badly needed but sweeping and expensive changes. They upgrading the machinery and property, the retail store was modernized and decorated, and additional lines of merchandise were added. A modern accounting system was also installed. Net sales for the year ending June 30, 1956, were $5,126,288. Net profit "approximated the amount paid in dividends on the common stock."

In his annual report, Lawrence was cautious about the prospects for 1957 because of necessary wage and salary increases, the high cost of rehabilitating the plant, high maintenance, and other non-recurring expenses. At the company's annual meeting on Janaury 15, 1957, the stockholders approved changing the company's name from Phillips & Buttorff Manufacturing Company to Phillips & Buttorff Corporation, which seemed more appropriate for the changed business environment the company faced.

The changes instituted by the new management team may not have worked as, in 1958, Phillips & Buttorff sold its retail and wholesale store to the Nashville Bank & Trust Company for between $250,000 and $300,000. After the sale, Phillips & Buttorff opened a new retail store, called The House of Treasured Gifts, at 705 Church Street. It featured a complete selection of fine china, silver, crystal and gifts, "the most beautiful, modern and unique store of its kind in the South."

Phillips & Buttorff remained at 705 Church Street, offering china crockery, and earthware, for many years. In 1977 Earl W. Flynn, executive vice president, announced the closure of its aging plant on Twelfth Avenue North where about 150 people were still employed making gas and electric ranges. The plant could not meet strict environmental and safety regulations. Flynn announced that the company was discontinuing its manufacturing operations.

In 1985 Marshall S. Whitney was president of what had been, since 1970, Whitney's Phillips & Buttorff Jewelers. When he died in 1989, his son, Guy, closed the downtown store and moved to the Belle Meade Galleria.

Whitney's Phillips & Buttorff Jewelers closed in February 1995, ending a history that began 137 years earlier when twenty-one-year-old H. W. Buttorff arrived in Nashville.

SOUTHERN PUMP COMPANY was organized in 1873 by E. P. Smith, R. M. Lafferty, and S. W. Freeman to manufacture wood pumps. In 1874 George W. Bliss and Henry L. Hall became associated with the company. Early in 1875, having enjoyed rapid growth, the company built a combined factory and sawmill on fourteen acres of land on the east bank of the Cumberland River immediately downstream from the Louisville & Nashville Railroad bridge. Their address was North First Street. The company additionally built a two-story building measuring 106 by 112 feet, a boiler room, an engine room, a machine shop, and a store room. They also had a three-hundred-horse-power engine, three circular sawmills, and four Wyckoff patent pump augers.

The logs that the company used to stock their mills were either white wood or yellow wood trees, many of which grew in the Cumberland Mountains above Cumberland Falls, four hundred miles upstream from Nashville. Below the falls, the logs were caught in booms at Isabel Point, Kentucky, and rafted down to Nashville. Until Southern Pump Company did this, the idea of floating logs to Nashville from above Cumberland Falls was thought to be impossible.

On January 1, 1880, four co-owners, Smith, Lafferty, Bliss, and Hall, bought out the interest of Freeman and incorporated Southern Pump Company. Smith was president and Bliss was secretary. That year, the company had broadened its products to include pumps, tubing, sash, doors, blinds, molding, picture frames, and wooden boxes. These products were shipped by rail to every state in the Union. The company ran their factory twenty-four hours a day and employed about two hundred men. Had not electric lights been installed, this would have been impossible. The company produced, on average, one pump every two minutes.

By 1885, company ownership had changed considerably. E. P. Smith had been succeeded as president by John M. Thompson and had become sales manager, while there was a new vice president, J. P. Prutzman. The next year, Southern Pump Company moved its executive office to 40½ North College Street.

The company disappeared from the *Nashville City Directory* in 1887. One wonders if Southern Pump Company was bought out by a competitor, possibly Prewitt, Spurr & Company. George Bliss, one of the founders, was listed in the 1887 city directory as being in the lumber business at the corner of Spring and North Third Street.

TENNESSEE ENAMEL MANUFACTURING COMPANY INC. (TEMCO) was founded in September 1921 by Malvern H. Wright and W. Bratten Evans. The company did custom porcelain enameling and had a small custom metal stamping operation. Less than a month after the

Tennessee Enamel Manufacturing Company Inc., 1961.
Collection of Ridley Wills II.

company was organized, a devastating fire destroyed their building and almost caused the new business to fail. Wright saved the day by getting a $3,000 loan from a local bank to meet his payroll.

The company moved to a new 65-by-180-foot building on Park Avenue on April 1, 1924. In 1932, in the middle of the Depression, company officials decided to build a finished product and named the company Temco. Their Coca-Cola sign, produced in 1933, is now a collector's item. The management team at that time consisted of Wright and Evans, Robert G. Calton, C. F. Bauman, and Robert N. Smith.

Temco was Nashville's first small-business success of World War II. Bratten Evans, the company president, designed and built a prototype bomb in mid-1941 and flew with it to Washington, DC, to convince government purchasing agents that his small company could reliably produce bombs in meaningful quantities.

Hopeful of a contract, Temco began retooling their plant late in 1941 to produce aircraft bombs. By March 1942, after a private investment of $135,000, Temco received the job they were waiting for—a $4 million contract to produce bombs. The company delivered one million bombs every three months. Its workforce, which had been three hundred in 1941, more than doubled to nearly seven hundred in 1943. By then, Temco had received another $8 million in bomb manufacturing contracts.

Forty or more Nashville companies received government contracts during World War II, totaling more than $226 million. The three largest were Vultee, Nashville Bridge, and Temco, collectively accounting for over 80 percent of the total. For its outstanding contribution to the war effort, Temco received the Army-Navy "E" Award, also known as the Army-Navy Production Award. In 1944, the company officers were W. Bratten Evans, president; Robert G. Calton, vice president; and Robert N. Smith, secretary-treasurer.

After the war, Temco sold porcelain and enamel parts for both Phillips & Buttorff and Gray & Dudley, and explosive shells. In the 1960s, when Donald Hart was president, space heaters were added to the company's line.

On April 18, 1968, Whale Electronics Corporation bought Temco for an estimated $4 million. Whale later leveraged Temco's assets to purchase other companies. By the summer of 1969, Whale's stock was in steep decline and soon became worthless. When Whale filed for bankruptcy in 1970, Temco had only about seventy employees, only 10 percent of what it had in its glory days during World War II.

Vultee Aircraft Plant was the first major industrial plant to be built in Nashville since the black powder plant opened in Old Hickory in 1918. It was built in 1939 by the Aviation Manufacturing Corporation and subsequently bought by Vultee Aircraft in 1940. On May 4, 1941, former Republican presidential candidate Wendell Willkie dedicated the plant to the "Defense of the Democracies." During World War II, Vultee employed seven thousand workers, most of whom were women. Located adjacent to Berry Field, east of Murfreesboro Pike, Vultee produced dive bombers, fighters, observation planes, and other military aircraft. In 1949, the plant became the Nashville Division of Avco Corporation.

Washington Manufacturing Company was started in 1914 by Robert Wirt Comer and a friend named Dodd. Originally, the modest company was called Dodd-Comer Manufacturing Company and operated out of an old house in West Nashville with four sewing machines and fourteen employees. The company made handkerchiefs, garters, suspenders, and a devise called a "shirgar" (shirt garter) that attached a man's socks to his shirttail. Dodd was never active in the company, which in 1916 changed its name to Washington Manufacturing Company with Robert Wirt Comer as president.

Wirt Comer's sons, Guy L. and Mont, came to work for the company in 1918. That January, Guy showed a guest through the plant located at 218–220 Second Avenue North. Down in the shop, the visitor saw that Washington Manufacturing Company made nothing but work shorts, garters, suspenders, and handkerchiefs. At this task, the company employed 225 girls and "about a score of traveling men" and occupied all the floor space in the five-story building that dominated the 200 block of Nashville's Second Avenue North. Even then, the company sold goods in all parts of the United States, Canada, and Mexico.

Washington Manufacturing Company prospered during the 1920s and suffered during the Depression. A Nashville banker, familiar with the company, said that Washington was one of the few clothing manufacturers that kept all its contractual commitments to the textile mills during the 1930s.

The company's growth accelerated after World War II. By then, Guy Comer had succeeded his father as president and chief executive officer. He held those positions for about twenty-five years. During that time, the company expanded enormously, ultimately having twenty thousand employees in twenty-six plants scattered across the Southeastern United States.

In 1953 the company manufactured casual wear, work wear, and men's and women's sportswear. Some of their most familiar brand names were "Dee Cee" shirts, "Deer Creek," and "Guymont" sports shirts and "Happy Jack" and "Happy Jill" dungarees. Washington Manufacturing later owned the National Stores, a chain of clothing retail stores founded in 1962 in Los Angeles, California. Guy Comer was succeeded by his son, Thomas W. "Wick" Comer, in about 1968.

In the early 1970s, Washington Manufacturing was one of the ten top companies in the US apparel industry and doubtless the largest privately owned company in that group. In addition to apparel manufacturing, Washington's extensive business interests included an automobile agency, apartments, banks, farms, a fire and casualty insurance company, grocery companies, hosiery manufacturing, real estate, retail stores, and wholesale textile houses.

Bitter infighting among Washington's management team in the early 1970s led to two lawsuits and to Wick Comer and E. H. Hatcher, president and vice president, respectively, resigning in 1976. Following the power struggle, Paul Hargis became president. He had been treasurer under Wick Comer in 1975. The other officers who survived the transition were R. Hix Clark, who was secretary under both Comer and Hargis; and R. H. Dawson and R. Hatfield, both vice presidents. Soon, Washington Manufacturing Company liquidated its assets and closed. By September 1985 the seven-story Washington Manufacturing Company building had been rehabilitated into a $25 million Washington Square complex, covering one and one-half blocks of Second Avenue North.

MEATPACKING COMPANIES

NEUHOFF PACKING COMPANY was established in 1906 by Henry Neuhoff. He was a German immigrant who, with his brothers, started a meatpacking plant in St. Louis before coming to Nashville in 1897. Henry and his wife, Emma, initially lived at 1326 North Market Street where he and his brother John sold boneless boiled hams. Neuhoff incorporated Henry Neuhoff & Company in 1906, the same year he built the initial section of his packing plant, that would continue expanding until 1950, when it included 700,000 square feet and sprawled over fourteen acres. The company prospered, becoming a well-known Nashville institution.

In 1920 Henry Neuhoff was president, Lorenz Neuhoff was treasurer and general manager, and E. J. Koehn was sales manager. That year, the company address was 1308–1312 Adams Street, with a retail store at 13 Market House in the public square. One of the company's specialties was Hampshire brand hams.

Neuhoff Packing Company, 1950s.
Metropolitan Nashville Archives.

In 1930 Neuhoff Packing Company expanded with a plant in Dallas, Texas, on the site of the present-day American Airlines Center, the home of the Dallas Mavericks.

On New Year's Day 1931 Henry Neuhoff sold Neuhoff Packing Company to Swift & Company for a reported $2.5 million plus inventory. Swift & Company, founded in 1855 in Chicago, kept the Neuhoff name since the company had such a strong reputation.

In the 1940s and 1950s, my parents always served "spice round" from Neuhoff Packing Company at Christmas dinner. I still miss not having it.

Neuhoff's last general manager was L. T. Bott. Swift & Company closed its Nashville plant in 1977, thirteen years after Henry Neuhoff died in Dallas, Texas, and the same year that Swift & Company closed several other plants across the country.

MOTELS

Belle Meade Motel started out as a tourist camp, run in 1940 by Anne M. Bomar. (In the 1930s and early 1940s motels were called tourist camps.) In 1942 John R. Bomar Jr. was the manager. He was followed by B. H. Alexander and, in about 1946, by Clyde and Ruth Stamper, who lived in the motel that was at 5133 Harding Road. By 1950, when Lloyd Holden was manager, the motel's name had been changed from Belle Meade Tourist Camp to Belle Meade Motel.

In about 1950 Betty Sue Jackson, of Birmingham, came to Nashville to visit her Mount Vernon Junior College roommate, Betty Bullard. Betty arranged a blind date for Betty Sue with Craig Parrish. After dinner, when the four young people were pondering what to do next, Craig said, "Let's go to the Belle Meade Motel." Not having any idea that the motel was primarily a restaurant, popular with young people, Betty Sue cringed and tried to make herself as inconspicuous as possible. They had fun at the motel, and no one misbehaved.

During the 1960s and 1970s, the twenty-five-room motel was closed and in the hands of a receiver. In 1981 Gary Lee Smith bought the motel from the First American National Bank and operated it until 1986. Among Gary Smith's employees were Paul Holden, the brother of previous owner Lloyd Holden. He worked for Gary Smith after he retired from Paul's Barbeque as did Hugh Cooksey, after a long career at Burruss & Webber Cafeteria. Both men were instrumental in the success of the motel in the 1980s. During the five years that Smith ran the restaurant, his specialties were fried chicken and steak and biscuits. Also popular were bacon and eggs, turnip greens, Reelfoot Lake crappie, and wild game. Smith's primary focus was on the restaurant, but there were still overnight guests at the motel.

Some of Smith's most faithful customers were John Eddie Cain; John Bransford Jr.; Neil Cargile Jr.; the Wallace brothers, Hamilton and J. Bransford "Jake"; and the Cunningham brothers, Bud and John. From the start, John Eddie Cain was unofficial chairman of the board. If customers wanted to register complaints or make changes, Smith referred

1947 photograph of Harding Road showing the Belle Meade Motel.
Collection of Grannis Photography.

them to John Eddie, who had a strong voice and was willing to use it to maintain proper order. Other honorary board members were Skipper Donnelly, Ham Wallace, and John U. Wilson.

Mr. and Mrs. Cohen T. Williams were regular customers. When Tennessee Ernie Ford was in town for the Grand Ole Opry or to film a commercial for Martha White Flour, the Williams would often take him to the motel for dinner and conversation. One night, when the three of them were there for a long evening, Mrs. Williams said that she was ready to go home. Williams and Ford didn't want to leave, so Williams suggested that his wife drive the car home and that he and Ford would get Smith to take them home when he closed for the night.

After she left, Williams and Ford got into a heated discussion about who could make the best biscuits. To settle the affair, they asked Smith if they could go in the kitchen when the motel closed and make biscuits. He agreed, and they made biscuits, using the motel's Martha White Flour, until Smith told them the sun was coming up and he needed to take them home so he could come back and open the restaurant. Smith never figured out which man made the best biscuits.

During Vanderbilt basketball season, in the 1980s, Mr. and Mrs. Horace G. Hill Jr. always sat at a table in the back room on game nights. If anyone wanted to sit there earlier, they could with the understanding that they would have to move when the Hills came in. Upon their arrival, Smith would turn off the jukebox, and the Hills, often with friends, would listen to the games on H. G. Hill Jr.'s transistor radio.

One afternoon, Hill called to ask how often Robert Hunter, longtime manager of H. G. Hill's Belle Meade store, was there, and whether or not he brought employees with him. Smith was guarded in his reply because he didn't want to get Hunter, a good customer, in trouble with his boss. So, he told Hill that Hunter came in occasionally, mostly on Saturday nights.

The next day, at lunch, Hunter appeared with a large group of H. G. Hill employees. Obviously nervous, he told the waitress he needed to talk to Smith. When Smith came over, Hunter said that he had received a call from Hill the day before stating that he did not patronize the motel enough and that he needed to go more often and take other employees. Hunter wanted to be sure Smith reported to Mr. Hill that he was there with a large group.

The Belle Meade Motel closed in 1986 because the owner of the property, First American National Bank, sold it to Lon Raby. The building was torn down, and the site is now occupied by the Belle Meade Galleria.

NEWSPAPERS

N*ASHVILLE AMERICAN* newspaper opened on September 1, 1875. In the early 1900s, the American Building was on Cherry Street (later renamed Fourth Avenue North), three doors down from Church Street. On September 16, 1910, the *American* was purchased by and merged with the *Nashville Tennessean* to form the *Nashville Tennessean* and the *Nashville American* (which existed from September 1910 to January 1920). The merged newspaper moved its offices into the American Building at 160

Fourth Avenue North. On January 18, 1920, the newspaper was renamed the *Nashville Tennessean*. In 1973 the newspaper's name was changed to the *Tennessean*, the name it carries today.

NASHVILLE BANNER was a daily afternoon newspaper that opened on February 10, 1876. For more than nine decades, the newspaper carried the stamp of the Stahlman family. This started in 1891 when Maj. Edward Bushrod Stahlman acquired an interest in the paper. He assumed sole ownership in 1893 and ran the newspaper until his death in 1930. Leadership then passed to his grandson, James Geddes "Jimmy" Stahlman, who became sole owner in 1955.

In the 1950s, the *Banner* touted its sports section as "The South's Most Interesting." Its staff that year included Fred Russell, George Leonard, Dudley "Waxo" Green, Edgar Allen, Bill Roberts, Bob Witt, John Steen, and Ed Given. Russell wrote a wildly popular "Sidelines" column for many years.

In June 1972 Stahlman, who was a passionate and outspoken conservative, retired, six months after selling his newspaper to Gannett Company.

Gannett Company sold the newspaper to Brownlee O. Currey Jr., John Jay Hooker Jr., and Irby C. Simpkins Jr. in 1979 and bought the *Tennessean*. Currey and Simpkins bought Hooker's interest of the *Banner* in 1981.

During its existence, the *Nashville Banner* had such journalism stars as Ralph McGill and Fred Russell. United States Senator Lamar Alexander worked for the *Banner* as a correspondent while attending Vanderbilt. Although circulation slowly but steadily declined in the 1980s and 1990s, the newspaper and its staff continued to win journalism awards, including being named the top newspaper in the state in 1992 and 1993. On February 16, 1998, *Banner* publisher Irby C. Simpkins Jr. and chairman Brownlee O. Currey Jr. announced its closure.

NASHVILLE GLOBE was founded in 1906. This weekly African American newspaper promoted self-reliance and racial solidarity as the best way for Nashville's African American community to survive and prosper within the restrictions of the "Jim Crow" South. Its founders, who were

The *Nashville American*, circa 1905.
Collection of Ridley Wills II.

incensed by a legislative action on April 4, 1905, that mandated segregation on streetcars, were Richard Henry Boyd, Charles A. Burrell, Dock A. Hart, and Evans Tyree.

From 1910 to 1930, the *Globe* had the largest circulation of any black newspaper in Tennessee. At its peak in 1921, the circulation was estimated at about twenty-four thousand. The financial backing of Richard Boyd, founder and secretary of the National Baptist Publishing Board, and a banker, preacher, and entrepreneur, was key to the newspaper's success.

Following his death in 1922, his son, Henry Allen Boyd, who controlled the newspaper's strong editorial content, was equally important. He used the newspaper to promote a successful campaign to establish a state normal school for blacks in North Nashville (now Tennessee State University).

The newspaper promoted racial pride and promoted black businesses. The *Globe* was published weekly from its office on Fourth Avenue North in the heart of Nashville's "Black Wall Street."

In the late 1930s, L. D. Williams was the editor. Offices were then at 403 Charlotte Avenue. About that time, the newspaper merged with the *Nashville Independent* to become the *Globe-Independent*. The newspaper ceased publication in 1960, soon after Henry Boyd's death. Dr. Theophilus Boyd Jr., his nephew, made the decision to close. He cited high production costs and declining sales as the major factors.

NIGHTCLUBS & SALOONS

AUTOMOBILE BUSINESS CLUB was a well-known club on Hamilton Road in Bordeaux. It was run by "Big Al" Allesio, an Italian-American, and Jake Markel, a third-generation Nashville Jew. Also known as the ABC Club, it lasted for thirty-five years, beginning in the heart of the Depression. Markel and Alessio paid for police protection, which made their customers comfortable that they could gamble safely and eat great food. Steaks were a specialty, as was the famous house dish, Pepper Pot Soup.

To enter the Automobile Business Club, one had to ring the doorbell. A sliding door would open, and the security man would allow the patron to enter if he recognized him. Inside, there were roulette, craps tables, and slot machines for the men and Bingo games for the ladies.

If the ABC Club was going to be raided, someone from the police station downtown would call the club and warn them. Alessio and Markel would have plenty of time to hide the gambling apparatus, and when they arrived, the police would find only patrons enjoying dinner with no alcohol. An anonymous source said, "Half the Woodmont Country Club and many of the Nashville socialites and Tennessee legislators could be found there on weekend nights."

Alessio had a soft side. Each Christmas, he made a point of buying clothes for the needy and toys for their children. In the great flood of 1937, he helped rescue families stranded by the record-high water. He and a close friend, Nashville gambler Jimmy Washer, who owned the Uptown Club, both had arrangements with Garner Robinson, an East Nashville political figure and owner of Phillips-Robinson Funeral Home on Gallatin Pike, that they would anonymously cover the costs of funerals for families who could not afford to do so.

In the 1960s, the Automobile Club received some unwanted publicity from an article in *Time* magazine that may have prompted the federal government to put Markel and Alessio out of business. During the trial, an aging, arthritic, wheelchair-bound Catholic priest testified that the ten thousand poker chips held in evidence by the prosecution were, in fact,

Christmas presents for the Men's Club of St. Pius Church and the Knights of Columbus. Many Nashvillians were disappointed when their favorite place to drink, dine, and play closed.

Climax Saloon was an Italianate-style building at 210 Cherry Street that was built by V. E. Schwab in 1887. The Climax was more ornate, sordid, and successful than its neighbor, the Southern Turf, built in 1895. It featured a first-floor theater with resident cancan dancers. Visiting actors performed there. "Spot" McCarthy, a dice dealer, "held court" on the second floor where there was a bar, as well as billiard and gaming tables. On the third floor, there were elaborately decorated bedrooms. The women in residence would take their places on the stairway from the second to the third floor, enticing the men to choose them as evening partners. The proprietor even had a false wall that the women could open if there was a police raid. A room behind the wall had a bench on which they could sit until all was clear.

Throughout the 1890s, Nashville newspapers treated the "Men's Quarter" as a necessary evil. However, after 1902, reformists began to put the squeeze on the Climax and the other saloons. Public opinion, influenced by the temperance movement, began to swing away from those who supported the status quo for the Men's Quarter. The passage of a prohibition bill in 1909 and a Nuisance Act in 1913 finally did the trick. The Climax was forced to close in 1914. The building still stands today as a reminder of the glory days of the Men's Quarter.

Club Plantation, on Murfreesboro Road, was the most exclusive of the many supper clubs that flourished in Nashville from the 1930s until the 1960s, when liquor-by-the-drink became legal. Many nationally known performers such as Gene Austin, Jimmy Dorsey, Andy Griffith, and Woody Herman came to Nashville to perform in the Plantation's one-thousand-seat ballroom, known as the "Murfreesboro Road Branch of the State Legislature" because of the large number of state legislators who showed up there regularly for the 10:00 p.m. or 1:00 a.m. shows. In January 1949 William O. "Bill" Daugherty became manager of Club

Plantation. He had formerly managed both the Belle Meade Country Club and the Colonial Dinner Club. In 1952 Club Plantation offered a Sunday evening smorgasbord for three dollars, which entitled patrons to "all you can eat with dancing and floor show." The club called itself "The Showplace of the South."

COLONIAL DINNER CLUB opened on May 18, 1940. It was advertised as being "across from the old Wagon Wheel," which burned down the previous July. Located at the split of Highways 70 and 100, the Colonial stood where A-1 Appliance Company was in 2013. Les W. Woolridge, a well-known Nashville restaurateur, owned and managed the club that had good food and entertainment. The club closed on December 2, 1942, the day after war-time gasoline rationing went into effect.

After Woolridge died in June 1943, his widow sold the property to Stanley C. "Slick" McDonald, who reopened the club on October 1, 1943, under the management of Jack C. DeBell. The dinner club advertised itself as "Nashville's finest—on Harding Road." The next eight months were difficult as the club was raided several times, with McDonald being found guilty of tippling and gaming.

A 1944 advertisement in the city directory touted the club's entrées of Southern-style steak, chicken, and country ham dinners and the fact that the club was available on Monday and Tuesday nights for special parties and banquets. Wednesday through Sunday nights, Bob "Hamp" Young and his orchestra played. By mid-July 1944 Robert E. Miller became manager.

William O. "Bill" Daugherty, a former manager of the Belle Meade Country Club, became a partner of McDonald's and assumed active management of the club on November 1, 1945. He had a reputation of being able to bring in big-name bands and first-class entertainment. The Colonial then advertised itself as having the "South's finest steaks" and claimed that it served "food cooked right, served right." One person, who must have believed that, was H. G. Hill Jr., who ate a steak there almost every night, often with his girlfriend, Edith Caldwell, whom he married in 1961.

On October 22, 1946, at about 2:00 a.m., the club burned to the ground. On that tragic morning, the Francis Craig Orchestra, that had played at the club that night, lost almost all of their musical arrangements. A. B. Anderson, then the club's manager, and his wife escaped from their apartment in the back of the building.

The fire did not end the Colonial Dinner Club story as, on January 23, 1948, Daugherty opened a new "Colonial Club" in a modern, fireproof building on Harding Road near Leake Avenue. By January 20, 1949, Daugherty had moved on to the Club Plantation on Murfreesboro Pike, which he advertised as the "Showplace of the South."

Several months later, Jimmy Dubois assumed control of the Colonial Club business and, on July 8, 1949, closed it and opened a new club there named The Tropics with a South Pacific theme. It advertised itself as "Nashville's Most Romantic Dinner Club" with good food and dancing.

The Copia was another Harding Road favorite. On the site of the old Colonial Dinner Club, The Copia opened June 19, 1947, and was owned and managed by Mike Rose. Associated with Rose in the business was Fred Horn. J. Boyle Sanders, who went there frequently, said, "The food was incredible as long as you didn't look in the kitchen." The Copia had a dance floor surrounded by booths. In the back, there was a card room. Sanders said parties at The Copia often got wild, describing the roadhouse as "a den of iniquity."

Chloe and Dick Lenderman, Margie and Bill Brooks, and Tupper and Lola Saussy were regular Copia patrons. I went to The Copia occasionally. Pretty quickly, I realized that one of the more popular waiters there was an African American man whose first name was Ridley. When asked if I was kin to him, I said "no" and added that "I am also not kin to all the Ridleys in Maury County."

Mike Rose eventually sold The Copia to Jimmy DuBois and, relying on his own salad dressings, went on to form his own company, Mike Rose Foods. The Copia closed March 1, 1968.

Hettie Ray's Dinner Club was a West Nashville fixture for many years. It opened in 1936 on Nine-Mile Hill, where the Wessex Towers Condominium stands today. Hettie Ray's had a dance floor surrounded by two-tiered seating. Down the hill, there was an open-air pavilion, where young people danced and drank beer. Hettie Ray, who knew practically everyone who came in her place, sometimes would intervene when she thought some young person had too much to drink.

A tragedy occurred in August 1939 when Walter Tanksley was up there with some of his Montgomery Bell Academy friends, including Lewis Lyne. On his way home, Tanksley crashed while driving too fast down Nine-Mile Hill and was killed. A 1939 All-City tackle, Tanksley had planned to play football at Vanderbilt that fall.

Hettie Ray's Dinner Club closed at the end of 1942 because of gasoline rationing. As Ray still owned a restaurant at 1303 Twenty-First Avenue South, she encouraged her dinner club customers to go there. In May 1944 Ray reopened her dinner club on Nine-Mile Hill and operated it until 1946 when Jimmy Kelly opened the Biltmore Club there. After the Biltmore club closed in 1958, Ray, once again reopened her dinner club, doing so on June 19, 1959. This time, the venture was short lived, as that October Nick Varallo purchased the property from Hettie and her husband Carroll Reed. Varallo got a permit to operate a restaurant there, but it never materialized. The building burned down in April 1962.

RAINBOW ROOM fronted on both Fourth Avenue North and Printer's Alley. It was run by David "Skull" Shulman for forty years and was a favorite tourist spot. Shulman's first Alley ventures are thought to have been gambling related. About two o'clock one Sunday morning in 1953, Metro police raided the packed Rainbow club when there were about 175 to 200 people there, drinking and dancing. The dance floor was so crowded that the vice squad had trouble clearing out the place and making arrests on tippling charges.

In the 1980s and 1990s, Shulman could be seen daily walking with his white poodle, Sweetie, along Fourth Avenue North, dressed in his bib overalls. The unofficial mayor of Printer's Alley was ruthlessly murdered by a robber in 1998 just before his nightclub was set to open. He was eighty-three years old. His departure from the scene removed one of the city's most colorful characters. With Skull gone, there was no way for the Rainbow Room to survive.

SILVER DOLLAR SALOON was housed in a unique three-story Victorian structure during the "Gay Nineties" that still stands at the northeast corner of Broad and Second Avenue North. The building was designed by architect J. G. Zwicker, who later in the decade was a partner in Thompson & Zwicker, Architects. It was constructed not long after the property was purchased by V. E. "Manny" Schwab's wife in 1892.

Schwab, a German immigrant, was in business with George A. Dickel, his sister-in-law's husband. Dickel and, later, Schwab ran the George A. Dickel Company at the corner of Church and Market Streets. Their business was selling "wines, liquors, cigars, etc."

The Silver Dollar Saloon building was completed by 1895, when its assessed value rose sharply.

From its opening until 1901, the Silver Dollar Saloon's proprietor was W. W. Parminter, a steamboat captain, who attracted many river men to his "high-class" saloon. To make access more inviting, the main entrance was a swinging door. Upon entering, customers immediately noticed that every other floor tile had a silver dollar imbedded in it. At the front of the bar there was a large glass case containing all kinds of smoking tobacco. There was also a gas-burning pipe from which patrons could light their cigars.

In 1901 the saloon was acquired by Liggett and Camp, and then by William Bass. When prohibition came in 1919, the saloon closed.

SOUTHERN TURF opened in the fall of 1895 at 222 Cherry Street. Built by Marcus Cartwright, one of Nashville's most famous and successful bookmakers, the club was located in the heart of the men's district of Nashville, known as the "Men's Quarter," across the street from the Maxwell House Hotel. Initially, Ike Johnson tended bar downstairs while Felix Zollicoffer "Zol" Cartwright, Marcus's son, ran the gaming operation on the second floor.

In deference to the Tennessee Centennial tourist trade, city officials mounted no raids on the Southern Turf during the Centennial Celebration in 1897. After 1902 with reform in the air, the police put increasing pressure on the Southern Turf and other saloons to stop ignoring gambling statutes. The saloons fought back and stayed open. The Men's Quarter saloons were finally pressured into closing in June 1914 when the Anti-Saloon League brought a large number of injunction law suits in the Circuit Court. That month, gambling tables and bars were dismantled and moved.

Ike Johnson had suffered enough. In February 1916 he put a pistol to his head and pulled the trigger. Johnson died in his third-floor apartment above the Southern Turf. An era had ended. Respectable women could once again walk the 200 block of Fourth Avenue North.

In July 1991 the law firm Doramus and Trauger bought the seventeen-thousand-square-foot building at 222 Fourth Avenue North and renovated it for their law offices.

WAGON WHEEL was a Harding Road nightclub that opened in 1934 near the Highways 70 and 100 split. John C. "Chet" Eakle was manager in 1937. The club boasted of having Nashville's largest dance floor, accommodating five hundred customers.

Elizabeth Proctor remembered it well. When she was a teenager, her father, Edwin Craig, would never allow her to go there. There was one exception. It came when Eddie Dutchin brought his nationally acclaimed orchestra to perform one weekend at the Wagon Wheel. Since Mr. and Mrs. Dutchin were houseguests of the Craigs, Elizabeth was told she could take several friends to see his performance.

Popular with Vanderbilt students, the club often hosted Vanderbilt football post-game parties. Three local bands that performed there regularly were Jimmy Gallagher's orchestra, which played on opening night; Francis Craig and his orchestra; and Beasley Smith's band, whose performances there were sometimes broadcast over WLAC.

Other nationally known bands that performed at the Wagon Wheel included Ozzie Nelson and his orchestra who were there August 7, 1935 with their vocalist Harriet Hillard. Ozzie and Harriet married later that year. Jackie Coogin and his fourteen melodymen came on September 11, 1937. His vocalist was Lila Lee, a former silent film star.

The weekend cover charge in 1937 was fifty cents. A bouncer met you at the door, collected your money, and stamped your hand after making sure you were appropriately attired.

Once inside, male customers immediately noticed the attractive cigarette/concession girls walking around with straps around their necks holding drink trays out front. When the girls bent over to serve drinks or offer Lucky Strike cigarettes, the men rewarded them with tips that often increased depending on how far the girls bent.

The Wagon Wheel building, owned by Howard Werthan, burned to the ground on July 19, 1939, when Jack Price Jones was club manager.

OIL COMPANIES

RED ACE PETROLEUM COMPANY, founded by James W. Perkins in 1934, was to become a marketer of gasoline as a low-price, private-brand company. As was the case with most businesses in those days, the company struggled during the Depression.

By 1940, Red Ace had opened approximately thirty locations around Nashville and Middle Tennessee. That September, Perkins was inducted into the US Army with the Tennessee National Guard. From then until the end of the World War II, Red Ace Petroleum was practically dormant with gas rationing in effect.

Following the war, gasoline became available, and Red Ace, located at 5 Main Street, began to expand. By the 1950s, it was operating some fifty oil and gas outlets around Middle Tennessee, Southern Kentucky, and Northern Alabama.

Red Ace continued a steady growth pattern during the 1960s and 1970s. When Perkins passed away in 1970, his son, James W. "Jimmie" Perkins Jr., became company president.

The big energy crunch came in 1972, and Red Ace had an opportunity to merge with a larger public company, Earth Resources, of Dallas, Texas. That company owned Delta Refining Company of Memphis and operated a sixty-thousand-barrels-a-day refinery on the bank of the Mississippi River. One reason the merger was attractive was that, by merging with Earth Resources, Red Ace was assured of having a continuous supply of gasoline.

Red Ace retained its name following the merger and began expanding its operations in the states of Alabama, Arkansas, Georgia, Louisiana, and Mississippi. The Red Ace brand also continued in Nashville and Middle Tennessee.

In the 1970s, Red Ace was renamed Gasoline Marketers Inc. and grew quite rapidly to 250 outlets in the Southeast. By 1978, Gasoline Marketers Inc. was operating gasoline stations under the names Red Ace, Western, and Delta.

In 1980 the parent company, Earth Resources, was merged into MAPCO, of Tulsa, Oklahoma, and eventually all locations were changed to the MAPCO name that continues today.

SPUR DISTRIBUTION COMPANY was founded in 1928 by J. Mason Houghland, a native Texan who spent his adult life in Nashville and became one of the leading fox hunters in the state of Tennessee. Spur Distribution Company began with one filling station in Old Hickory, Tennessee, that Houghland built on land leased from a railroad. By leasing land on railroad rights-of-way, Houghland's land costs were well under those of his competition.

At the first station, Spur employees literally pumped gas directly from a tank car to their customers' automobiles. Under Houghland's adroit guidance, Spur Distribution Company grew to become the largest independent retail gasoline distributing company in the world.

By 1949 Spur Distribution Company, headquartered at 2300 Franklin Pike, had a chain of 243 stations in twenty states in the South and Midwest. Earnings for the year, after taxes, were $787,780.

In 1957 Houghland, president of Spur Distribution Company, owned about 45 percent of the stock of the company. The other 55 percent was owned by Fritz von Opel, a German whose stock had been seized by the US government as enemy alien property during World War II. Houghland's fight to acquire the stock owned by von Opel had taken thirteen years and had gone to the Supreme Court three times before the sale to him was finally approved in 1958. That February, the government accepted a $5,038,103 bid from Houghland, for 55.5 percent of the company stock.

On December 4, 1958, the directors of Spur Distribution Company voted to call a stockholders' meeting on December 15 to consider a proposal by Equitable Securities, of Nashville, to buy the assets of Spur. The directors' recommendation also included consideration of liquidating the Spur Distribution Company and the sale of its assets to a new company named Spur Oil Company of Delaware. At this time, Spur had 316 stations in twenty-one states.

Ralph Owen, president of Equitable, explained that stockholder approval was considered routine, in that 90 percent of the 131,600 shares were owned by Houghland. Owen said the purpose of the transaction, approved on December 15, was to change Spur from a mostly family-owned firm to a publicly held one. The net cash offer was for $18,197,400.

The negotiations with Equitable Securities was considered the high point in the life of a rugged individualist who was an astute businessman and a nationally recognized historian, horseman, and devotee of steeple chasing. Houghland lived at Green Pastures, a handsome Georgian house, built in 1840 on the Franklin Pike, that he restored and where he maintained a large kennel of foxhounds and a stable of thoroughbreds. Houghland was one of the founders of the Iroquois Memorial Steeplechase in Percy Warner Park.

In an editorial at the time of the sale, the *Nashville Banner* congratulated "Mr. Houghland, to whose labor, vision, and business genius the 30-year record of Spur Distributing Company bears witness."

On April 25, 1959, Houghland died at Green Pastures. The following September, he was named a charter member of the National Petroleum

News' Oil Hall of Fame. Following Houghland's death, his longtime associate H. D. Hines became president and chief executive officer of Spur Oil, still headquartered in Nashville. The following April, Hines moved up to board chairman, and Paul Banks Jr. became president.

In 1960 Spur Oil Company merged with Murphy Corporation, an El Dorado, Arkansas, petroleum and natural gas production company. Murphy reportedly issued seven hundred thousand new shares and exchanged them for Spur's one million outstanding shares. The market value was about $13.5 million, with Murphy assuming all Spur liabilities. This brought the approximate amount involved to about $18.5 million.

PHOTOGRAPHIC STUDIOS

CALVERT BROTHERS STUDIO was originally called Taylor Brothers Studio until Peter and Ebenezer Calvert purchased the business in 1896. Originally from England, the Calverts were both portrait painters. Their business was initially located at Fourth and Union Street. Thirty years later, Calvert's moved to the corner of Sixth Avenue North and Church Street. Finally, in 1955, the company moved to its final Nashville address at 2110 Twenty-First Avenue South.

In 1964 Bob and Doris White bought the company. Bob White did the lab work; Doris White touched up photographs and did the framing. Most of their business involved portraits and wedding pictures, with 90 percent of their portrait subjects being children. In 1980 the Whites estimated that they had about 525 sittings per year. Doris White said that "people come from Alabama, Georgia, North Dakota, and Texas. We do a lot of families from generation to generation. Grandmothers think they've got to have a Calvert picture."

Early in 1980 Calvert's, one of the city's oldest and best-known photography studios, moved to Burns, Tennessee, because of lease problems. Shortly after the move, they said, "We haven't noticed any change in business at all." Calvert's is still a viable business in Burns today.

PIANO COMPANIES

Jesse French Piano and Organ Company, at 240–42 North Summer Street, was one of the largest companies of its kind in the United States in 1890. Jesse French, the company president, started in the music business in 1872. Three years later, he branched out into the piano business. That year, he published the "Centennial National Song" for the 1876 Centennial International Exposition in Philadelphia. The company's phone number in 1884 was 38.

Jesse French Piano and Organ Company incorporated in 1887. By then, the company was a giant retailer of pianos and organs. Based in Nashville, it had branches in Birmingham, Dallas, Little Rock, Memphis, Montgomery, and St. Louis, with a force of one hundred traveling salesmen.

In the 1870s, the Nashville office was on Union Street. By 1890 it had moved to a new five-story brick building with the largest plate glass window in Nashville. Each floor, serviced by an elevator, contained 15,750 square feet and was finished with hardwood floors.

Jesse French Piano and Organ Company handled all the standard makes of pianos and organs. In the Nashville store the stock, all first class, consisted of two hundred instruments, including Chickering & Sons, Hardman, New England, Steinway and Sons, and Vose & Sons pianos, and Jesse French, Mason & Hamlin, Packard, and Storey & Clark organs. Mr. French's senior management team included John Lumsden, vice president, and O. A. Field, secretary-treasurer, both residing in St. Louis.

By the 1890s, the company had grown large enough that it decided to manufacture its own line of pianos. John Lumsden of the James M. Starr and Company of Richmond, Indiana, probably introduced French to James Starr, head of the company. As a result, merger negotiations were begun in 1892 and completed on April 7, 1893. At that time, French; his brother-in-law, Oscar Addison Field; and the stockholders of the Jesse French Piano and Organ Company bought controlling interest in Starr's piano factory in New Castle, Indiana. The pianos manufactured there became known for their fine musical qualities and their remarkably beautiful case designs. They gained visibility as a result of being on display at the Chicago Columbian

Exposition in 1893. French's name soon became a household word in homes across the country where his pianos graced parlors and sitting rooms.

French understood the important link between the sale of ragtime sheet music and piano sales, both of which reached their peak during the ragtime era from about 1897 to 1917. In the interest of Jesse French Piano and Organ Company, French involved himself indirectly with the publication of key Mississippi Valley ragtime composers. Jesse's son, H. A. French, published various ragtime songs beginning with "A Tennessee Tantalizer" in 1900. He followed up by publishing two of Charles H. Hunter's works in 1901, "Possum and Taters" and "Queen of Love—Two Step."

Claude P. Street was manager of the Jesse French Piano and Organ Company during the first eleven or so years of the twentieth century. In about 1915 he went on to establish his own company, the Claude P. Street Piano Company. This was several years after the Jesse French Piano and Organ Company closed its Nashville office. Claude P. Street Piano Company would operate for many decades at 164–66 Eighth Avenue North.

Jesse French's nephew, O. K. Houch, would also establish a Nashville piano company. As a teenager, he worked in one of his uncle's stores during vacations and after school. Houch later traveled across the country selling pianos and organs. At age twenty-one, he and his father entered the piano business in Memphis. By 1911 they had opened a branch in Nashville at 531–33 Church Street in competition with his uncle's famous but fading company.

PLUMBING & HEATING COMPANIES

Kane and Murray Plumbing and Heating was established by Martin T. Kane in the late 1880s. Located at 905 Church Street, Kane ran the business until 1907, when one of his sons, John Bernard Kane, took over, forming a partnership with Edward J. Murray. At this time, the company was at 1513 Church Street.

When John Kane died in 1943, his son, Ward Randolph Kane, became the firm's sole owner. Ward Kane had a fleet of trucks, each one of which had

"Kane and Murray Plumbing and Heating" posted on the back windows. Below the back windows was the word "Dependable."

Kane's best plumber was Willie Hawkins, who first came to work as a twelve-year-old boy willing to do anything. Kane paid him a dime for sweeping the floor. The young boy kept coming back and, in time, became a beloved part of the Kane family. When Ward Kane died in 1965, his sons were too young to run the company. Consequently, the company closed that year.

PRINTING COMPANIES

Baird-Ward Printing Company was founded in 1910 by A. J. "Little Man" Baird and William E. "Pops" Ward, who bought the assets of the Cumberland Presbyterian Church Printing House, where they had worked as shop foreman and salesman, respectively. The new company was located in the Cumberland Presbyterian building at 150–54 Fourth Avenue North. Baird-Ward continued to print literature for the Cumberland Presbyterian Church as well as telephone directories for Southern Bell.

A breakthrough occurred in 1936 when the company successfully bid on Sunday school literature for the Southern Baptist Sunday School Board. As part of the contract, the company moved to 910 Commerce Street.

In the 1930s, both Baird and Ward died, to be succeeded by their sons, A. J. Baird Jr. and William E. Ward Jr. In the same period, Robert E. McNeilly was employed as financial officer. Baird-Ward weathered the Depression, thanks in large part to the acquisition of the Baptist Sunday School Board contract.

In 1952, unable to expand on Commerce Street, Baird-Ward moved to their new plant at 50 Thompson Lane. By this time, Baird-Ward had diversified into magazine printing in addition to their Sunday school literature and telephone directories. Another breakthrough took place with the acquisition of a contract to print five large magazines for Parents Magazines Inc. This required the building of another plant further east on Thompson Lane. In rapid succession, other magazine titles were added:

Field and Stream, *Southern Living*, *Changing Times*, *Leatherneck*, and *American Rifleman*.

In 1966 a third-generation family member, William E. Ward III, became president. By then, the company was the second largest printing company in Tennessee, and one of the largest in the South. In 1976 Baird-Ward was acquired by Arcata National Corporation of Menlo Park, California.

BENSON PRINTING COMPANY was established around 1910 by John T. Benson, William A. Benson, and Robert C. Benson. In 1907 John Benson was treasurer and business manager of the Pentecostal Mission Publishing Company at 125 Fourth Avenue North. Three years later, he held the same positions but had also started a small printing business two doors up the street at 129 Fourth Avenue North. By 1914 the three Bensons had moved to 136 Fourth Avenue North.

The Benson Printing Company job was a part-time one for John Benson as, in 1918, he was also president at the Pentecostal Mission Publishing Company. He must have resigned a year or two later because, by 1922, he was listed in the city directory only as an officer of Benson Printing Company.

The company called itself “College Annual Headquarters” because, in 1922, more than ninety colleges, schools, and universities in the South favored the company with their printing contracts. Their dominance of the school market continued for several decades. As an example, in 1928, Benson printed the Vanderbilt *Masquerader*.

By 1940 John’s son, John T. Benson Jr., had replaced his father in the company (by then renamed the John T. Benson Publishing Company). The 1949 and 1950 *Commodore*s, printed by Benson, were the recipients of the “Highest Awards of Merit in Printing Exhibits of the Southern Graphic Arts Association for Excellence.” In 1951 John T. Benson Jr. was both president and general manager of the company that was still located downtown. In the 1950s Benson was printing booklets, catalogs, cloth-bound books, large catalogues, sales promotion pieces, and college and high school annuals.

By 1968 Charles G. "Pirk" Pirkle was president, and William A. Benson Jr. was vice president. Early in the 1970s, Pirkle became chairman of the board, and W. H. McMillan was president. In 1977 the company was no longer listed in the city directory.

Brandau Craig Dickerson Company was founded in 1912 when A. G. Brandau left Brandon Printing Company with two associates, W. Ezell Craig and C. S. Dickerson, to acquire the ownership of Standard Printing Company at 309 Fifth Avenue North.

The business became Brandau Craig Dickerson Company and, as is true with all long-standing firms, began to evolve and find new niches. From the hand-set type and the letterpress process and offset lithography with images stored on Bavarian sandstone blocks, it moved into large format sheet-fed lithography using glass negatives, later film negatives, and then digital sources.

From printing corporate stationery, railroad schedules, and insurance policies, Brandau Craig Dickerson moved into producing color labels for fruit and vegetable crates shipped from across the South. Seven staff artists provided the designs, drawing on an overlay for each of the colors making up the life-like illustrations.

In 1926 the company moved to a custom-designed building at 304 Tenth Avenue South that was designed by Donald Southgate, a well-known Nashville architect. When Brandau died in 1931, W. Ezell Craig succeeded him as president. During the Depression, the company produced millions of dollars of script in one-, five-, ten-, and twenty-dollar denominations for the Nashville banks, who used them in lieu of currency. The factory that produced the script was guarded twenty-four hours a day against theft. The quality was flawless, and there was never a complaint.

During World War II, the company printed army field manuals and maps. After the war, its jar and can labels were seen nationally in grocery stores, on Noxema skin cream jars, on Aladdin thermos bottles after 1949, and, for years, on Jack Daniel whiskey bottle labels. For the music industry, the company produced life-size standing cut-outs of country music stars.

In 1950 Seawell Brandau, Chester A. Roberts, and Thomas B. Walker purchased W. Ezell Craig's interest. Brandau became president, Roberts was vice president, and Walker was secretary-treasurer.

In 1979 Roberts became chairman of the board, while Brandau remained president and chief executive officer. Their sons, Seawell J. Brandau and Allen Roberts, became executive vice president and vice president, respectively. In 1989, after sixty-three years of active service, Seawell Brandau retired and Seawell J. Brandau became chief executive officer.

In 1994 the company relocated to a custom-designed building at 575 Brick Church Park Drive and changed its name to Brandau Printing Company to more accurately reflect its industry.

In 2000 the family sold the company to W. Hayne Hamilton Jr., who kept the company for a few years before selling it to the Lewisburg Printing Company. They moved most of the equipment to Lewisburg and discontinued the use of the Brandau Printing Company name.

BRANDON PRINTING COMPANY began in 1885 at 41 North Market Street. In 1882 Charles A. Brandon had been superintendent of the Cumberland Presbyterian Publishing House, but by 1885, he was manager of the new Brandon Printing Company. Two years later, J. N. Brooks was president of the company, and H. A. Meyers was secretary-treasurer. In 1892 the company advertised itself as lithographers, printers, and blank book manufacturers in a new six-story building at 228 North Market Street.

By 1896 Brandon was treasurer of the company and became president by 1898. Over the next ten years, Brandon Printing Company purchased two adjoining buildings, first one at 226 and, in 1907, one at 224 North Market.

According to Mrs. R. H. Tudor, who had been a summer employee at Brandon Printing Company, Brandon ran the business almost by himself. This seems amazing, as the company grew to be one of the largest printing houses in the South. She said that, after Brandon died in the 1920s, $40,000 was found in a safe in the basement of his home at 512 Woodland Street.

The firm was still operational at 224–28 Second Avenue North in 1935, when F. W. Washington was president and L. L. Gambill was vice president.

Brandon Printing Company.
Collection of Ridley Wills II.

In 1937 Henry F. Armstrong was listed as trustee of the company, which suggests that the company had closed. In 1939, Washington Manufacturing Company took over the Richardsonian-style building. Washington Square Management occupies the building today.

PROFESSIONAL SPORTS

Dixie Flyers was Nashville's first professional hockey franchise beginning in 1962, when David Patterson, a Nashville businessman, became the principal owner. Playing in Municipal Auditorium, the Dixie Flyers won championship titles in the Eastern Hockey League in 1965–66 and 1966–67 and were instrumental in establishing a loyal fan base for professional hockey in Nashville. The team's first captain was Ken "Red" Murphy, who became a fan favorite for his aggressive play. The franchise also took the lead in developing the city's junior hockey program.

After the team folded in 1971, one of the players, "Flo" Pilote, a French-Canadian, opened a restaurant in the Hermitage community called The Penalty Box.

NASHVILLE ELITE GIANTS had its beginnings in 1920, when Thomas T. Wilson, an African American businessman and sportsman, received a charter for the Nashville Standard Giants, an all-black semi-professional baseball team. His team played all comers, including white-only teams.

In 1921, the team changed its name to the Nashville Elite Giants and became a power in the Negro Southern League that consisted of teams in Atlanta, Birmingham, Memphis, Montgomery, Nashville, and New Orleans.

Wilson served as secretary and president of the league. He built an eight-thousand-seat stadium in North Nashville that years later was torn down to be replaced by the Paradise Ballroom.

Two of the Elite Giants stars were Eddie Noel, a pitcher in 1921, and Norman "Turkey" Stearnes, who began his career with the Elite Giants in 1921 and later played ten years for the Detroit Stars in the Negro National League. A prolific hitter, Stearnes was inducted into the Baseball Hall of Fame in 2000.

In 1931 the Nashville Elite Giants team was accepted into the Negro National League. When the league disbanded later that year due to the Great Depression, the Elite Giants rejoined the Negro Southern League. When the Negro National League was resurrected in 1933, the Elite Giants rejoined it. At that time Wilson was vice chairman, treasurer, and president of the Negro National League.

In the 1920s and early 1930s, the Elite Giants often played the Nashville Vols in preseason, either at Sulphur Dell or at Tom Wilson Park.

Due to a declining economy, Wilson moved his team to Columbus, Ohio, following the 1934 season, then subsequently to Washington, DC, and Baltimore. In his autobiography, *It's Good to be Alive*, Roy Campanella wrote this about the Elite Giants:

> Training in Nashville, or anyplace else with the Elites, was nothing like my Dodger days at Vero Beach. In the

> big leagues the first week and more is spent pretty much just loosening the winter kinks and getting your arms and legs in shape. But that's not how it was, ever, in the Negro Leagues. No sooner did you pull on your uniform than you were in a game, playing before paying customers.

NASHVILLE VOLS, along with the Nashville Elite Giants and many amateur teams, played baseball over many decades in Sulphur Dell, once known as "Baseball's Most Historic Park."

Union soldiers, camped near the Cumberland River, are said to have brought the sport of baseball to Nashville. The city's first professional team, the Nashville Americans, was organized in 1885 to join the newly founded Southern League. At that time the diamond where they played was known as the Athletic Park. Earlier, the area was known as Sulphur Springs Bottom. Amateur baseball was played there as early as 1866.

In 1887, two years after professional baseball made its debut in Nashville, the name of the team was changed to the Nashville Blues. The team had financial troubles and dropped out of the league in August 1887. In July 1889 the Southern League folded.

In 1901 Nashville again fielded a team in the newly reorganized Southern League. Grantland Rice, a 1901 graduate of Vanderbilt, wanted to play for the Nashville team, but his father wouldn't let him. Instead, Rice became a sportswriter for the *Nashville Daily News* and later the *Nashville Tennessean*. In 1908 Rice held a contest to give the Nashville baseball team an official name. Voters chose to name the team the Nashville Volunteers, quickly shortened to "Vols." Rice also began referring to the Athletic Park field as Sulphur Dell.

Many Nashville men remembered going to Sulphur Dell as boys with their fathers on Sunday afternoons to watch the Vols play. They would ride downtown on the streetcar and get off at the transfer station, where they would catch the baseball car, often standing on the running board for the short ride to the park. If they were early, they might see the fife and drum corps. Bringing up the rear would be a man carrying a huge banner announcing the time of the game and who the Vols were playing.

Sulphur Dell, April 5, 1953.
Collection of Grannis Photography.

In 1927 the old grandstand was demolished, and the playing field was turned around so that the setting sun would not be in the eyes of the batters. The new concrete and steel grandstand had a seating capacity of seven thousand. In 1938 the capacity was increased to eighty-five hundred. Sulphur Dell was bordered by Fourth Avenue North, Jackson Street, Fifth Avenue North, and a spur railroad track.

In 1949 the Nashville Baseball Club, owners of the Nashville Vols, had Theo L. Murray as president, Larry Gilbert as vice president, and J. M. Flanigen as treasurer.

One of the largest crowds at Sulphur Dell during the early 1950s came on Sunday afternoon, April 5, 1953, when 12,059 fans, including hundreds of African Americans who sat in the outfield, watched an exhibition game in which the Brooklyn Dodgers defeated the Milwaukee Braves 3–1. Nashville native Junior Gilliam, who played second base for the Dodgers, had two hits as did Brooklyn first baseman Jackie Robinson. A third African American, Roy Campanella, caught for the Dodgers.

The Nashville Vols continued to play at Sulphur Dell until 1963, when the organization failed, leaving the city without professional baseball. Sulphur Dell was torn down, and the area is now a parking lot.

Professional baseball was resurrected in Nashville in 1978 by a group of local investors led by Larry Schmittou. In 2005 the AAA Nashville Sounds won the Pacific Coast League championship. The Sounds play in Herschel Greer Stadium, built at the foot of Fort Negley in South Nashville. Greer, an avid baseball fan, who died in 1976, had been the first president of Vols Inc., the organization established to bring professional baseball back to Nashville.

PUBLISHING HOUSES

Acuff-Rose Music Inc. was a music publishing business founded by country music star Roy Acuff and Fred Rose in 1942. Acuff wanted to start the company to supplement his income from performances and approached Rose about his plan.

Rose, a pop music songwriter, had been in Hollywood since 1938, writing songs for Gene Autry cowboy movies. When Autry joined the Army Air Corps as a pilot in 1942, Rose returned to Nashville, where he had hosted a popular radio show on WSM and where he had so many contacts. With sterling reputations, Rose and Acuff were determined not to take advantage of country music stars who were not well educated. Rose, an excellent talent scout, was in a position to blend the pop music with country music and do much to make Acuff-Rose the success it became.

In September 1946 Acuff-Rose signed songwriter Hank Williams to a contract on their Starling label. The songs of this troubled musician became the cornerstone for the Acuff-Rose catalogue, even though Williams later left for MGM. Some of the great Hank Williams songs recorded by Acuff-Rose were "I Can't Help It If I'm Still in Love With You," "Your Cheating Heart," "Jambalaya," "I'm So Lonesome I Could Cry," and "Hey, Good Looking." Acuff-Rose's first pop hit was Patti Page's "Tennessee Waltz" in 1950.

When Fred Rose died in 1954, his son, Wesley Rose, became president of Acuff-Rose, a position he would hold for thirty years. Wesley Rose deserves credit not only for the growth of Acuff-Rose but for the spread

Southern Publishing Association complex, 1950s.
Collection of Ridley Wills II.

of country music around the world. Acuff-Rose, located on Eighth Avenue South in the Nashville's Melrose district, was the first American publishing company to establish offices abroad.

From the 1950s to 1970s, Acuff-Rose published songs by the Everly Brothers, Don Gibson, Doug Kershaw, Pee Wee King, John D. Loudermilk, Roy Orbison, Marty Robbins, and others. The company also had a record label called Hickory Records.

In 1984 Roy Acuff, "The King of Country Music," was eighty-one years old and in failing health. Given that and the recent decline in the country music recording business, he suggested to Wesley Rose that it was time to sell Acuff-Rose. In May 1985 this materialized when Gaylord Entertainment Company purchased their catalogue.

For awhile, Acuff-Rose did well under the management of Music Row veterans Jerry Bradley and Troy Tomlinson. However, in 1992, Gaylord Entertainment sold Acuff-Rose to Sony/ATV Music Publishing Company, who had already acquired Tree International, Acuff-Rose's longtime Music

Row competitor. This led to the giant Sony/ATV Music Publishing Company dominating the industry.

SOUTHERN PUBLISHING ASSOCIATION was established in 1901 to produce Seventh-Day Adventist literature. Its headquarters and factory were located in North Nashville, with branches in Atlanta and Fort Worth.

In 1914 the company's logo was "The Home of the *Watchman*," a monthly magazine devoted to an intelligent study of world topics in the light of prophecy. The magazine sold for ten cents a copy or one dollar for a year's subscription. In the 1950s, the company published and printed *These Times*, *The Message Magazine*, *the MV Program Kit*, and *The Adventist Home and School*, as well as many other books, including high quality Bibles and cedar cases.

Located on Twenty-Fourth Avenue North for more than seventy years, the Seventh-Day Adventist Church sold the 100,000-square-foot building and 8.5 acres to a Bible publishing company, Memorial Bibles International Inc.

In 1984 the property was appraised at nearly $600,000. By the early 1990s, the value had dropped by more than half, and a building permit was issued to convert the property into the Music City Antique and Flea Market. This never materialized, and Keith Churn bought the property for $158,000. He had myriad legal problems, and the abandoned property quickly became an eyesore to the neighbors. To make matters worse, the building caught fire in 2010, sustaining extensive damage.

Finally, on February 22, 2012, the Metro Legal Department gave the go-ahead for the city to take over the property and begin demolition, which they did.

RACE TRACKS

CUMBERLAND PARK held its inaugural meet on October 20–24, 1891. The park was on the north side of Nolensville Pike, two and one-half miles from downtown Nashville. The owner was the Cumberland Park Fair and Racing Association. Officers were Godfrey M. Fogg, president; Van Leer Kirkman, first vice president; William Hicks Jackson, second vice president; Campbell Brown, third vice president; Matthew M. Gardner, fourth vice president; and John J. Carter, secretary-treasurer. Their initial ad in the *Turf, Field and Farm* newspaper announced that there would be $20,000 in stakes and purses, and that Cumberland Park had a new mile track, new grand stand, new stables, good water, and first-class hotel accommodations.

The association sponsored harness races there for three years. The greatest match in the park's history happened on October 21, 1891, when Direct, a California pacer, defeated Hal Pointer, the pride of Tennessee, in all three heats with a record time.

There were signs of trouble in 1895 when turfmen, long identified with racing in the South and West, predicted that race tracks there would soon be controlled by laws similar to those governing racing in New York. In Nashville, a more immediate concern was that the stands were not filled for the trotting horse races that fall.

When pari-mutuel betting was outlawed in 1906, Cumberland Park closed and was replaced by the new Tennessee State Fairgrounds.

NASHVILLE RACE COURSE, also called the Burns Island Track, was opened in 1828. It was a six-tenths-of-a-mile-long track on the west bank of the Cumberland River in today's North Nashville. On October 10, 1843, the $35,000 Peyton Stakes, then the richest race in the world, was held at the track. The winner, owned by Thomas Kirkman, was renamed Peytona. The sporting world's most prominent newspaper, the *Spirit of the Times*, regularly carried articles about Nashville race courses, including the Peyton Stakes. In its July 22, 1848, issue, the *Spirit of the Times* correspondent from Nashville wrote, "I can also affirm that at no time in the past twenty years has there been such a prospect of fine racing, for you must know that we have a new as well as an old race course, and clubs and stakes at both this fall."

The reporter went on to describe the new course: "The new course is laid off in a beautiful grove near the line, and just beyond the corporation limits; it is a fine, elastic sort, with undulating surface, and when, just in the right condition, there is reason to think it will be a quick track, but in wet weather it must be deep and heavy. This is a common feature of most of our western courses. The proprietor is Mr. Samuel Carter; as he is well-known to most of the western sportsmen, to them he requires no commendation. There is extensive stabling at each course. There are almost forty horses in preparation for these races."

On April 1, 1886, the *Nashville Banner* speculated that "The Nashville Horse Racing Association might move its racing operation from the Nashville Course nearly three miles below town on the south bank of the Cumberland River to the track at the Fairgrounds two miles west of town. The arguments given for such a move were the relative inaccessibility of the Nashville Race Course, which was not served by either the 'steam or horse cars.'" The article went on to say that, "during the racing season, the road to the track was usually very dusty, which was a particular annoyance to the ladies. Occasionally, the road to the track was very muddy. Conversely, the fairground was on the car line, which was not subject to flooding, and was closer to town." When this article was published, the Cumberland River was at flood stage in Nashville.

On April 3, 1886, the *Nashville Banner* reported that the lower end of the Nashville track was under water and that water was within one foot of the stables. That Cumberland River flood and another one a few years earlier when "many of the stables were washed away and the stand injured and fencing destroyed," caused the Nashville Blood Horse Association to close the Nashville Race Course.

Walnut Grove Race Track was built in 1848 by Samuel J. Carter on a 250-acre tract north of Nashville owned by Dr. David T. McGavock. Walnut Grove had a springy, if uneven, surface that was "deep and heavy" in wet weather but fast under ideal conditions. Gen. William G. Harding, of Belle Meade, raced his horses at the track each spring and fall.

On October 15, 1851, McGavock leased the course to the new Walnut Jockey Club for three years at $1,000 per year, renewable for three additional years. The agreement stipulated that he would have a well dug, would allow horse trainers to use any fallen dead wood that was on the premises, and that he would improve the track and make it exactly one-mile long. Harding, as president of the Walnut Jockey Club, signed the agreement with three other officers.

When the lease expired in 1854, the jockey club chose not to renew it and disbanded. A year later, on October 1–4, 1855, the biennial State Fair took place there. Samuel J. Carter, the owner at that time, gave the use of the course, which by then had extensive stabling. The course was located between present-day Monroe Street and Hadley Park.

WEST SIDE PARK was a handsome racing park with two tracks, a grandstand seating seven thousand spectators, and a clubhouse. Godfrey M. Fogg, a leading Nashville lawyer and businessman, was the park's guiding light. Located where Centennial Park is today, West Side Park opened in 1887 on the site of the "old Fair Grounds" where the Tennessee Agricultural Association had sponsored fairs in 1879 and 1884. Earlier, from 1869 through 1873, the Tennessee Agricultural and Mechanical Association had held fairs there.

The six-day opening meet at West Side Park, which began May 2, 1887, was held on what was called the "finest race course and grounds in the South or West." The park had a half-mile and a mile track, both running north and south. Along the tracks' west side was the new club house and the three-hundred-foot-long grandstand. Sixteen stables near the Nashville, Chattanooga & St. Louis Railway tracks held stalls for 320 horses.

On the Sunday before the opening, ten thousand people visited the park, mostly by streetcar or the railroad. Immediately upon arriving, they enjoyed band music. On opening day, tickets sold for one dollar, with two dollars charged if the customer wanted to visit the quarter stretch and the paddocks.

The great Belle Meade stallions—Enquirer, Iroquois, Bramble, Luke Blackburn, and others—were exhibited after the first race. The opening meet was attended by thirty-five thousand people. Fall and spring meets followed until 1891, when racing moved to Cumberland Park.

RAILROADS

Franklin Interurban Railroad made its first run on Christmas Eve 1908. In 1902 a group of Nashville business and political leaders met to organize two electric railroads connecting Nashville to the towns of Columbia and Gallatin. Each of the three towns—Franklin, Columbia, and Gallatin—to be served by the railroads had to grant a charter to the railroad. Franklin did so in November 1904.

It had taken nearly two years, as there was considerable opposition from Louisville & Nashville Railroad (L&N) officials; from businesses in Franklin, who were afraid they would lose business to larger Nashville stores; and from the owners of large estates along the line of the proposed railroad, who did not want trains running through their front yards. Still, the organizers, interested in the proposed rail line to Franklin, were determined.

In 1905 Henry Hunter Mayberry, a forty-four-year-old Franklin resident who had made a fortune selling steel nails forged in Birmingham, was named president. He luckily found two men, John H. Carpenter and J. W. Howard, both of the Tennessee Fertilizer Company, who agreed, along with Mayberry, to finance the railroad. Columbia and Gallatin had, by this time, dropped out of contention.

Mayberry determined that the Franklin Pike corridor would be the least costly route along which to build the railroad. He then hired surveying crews to lay out the proposed route and talked to each of the property owners through whose land the Interurban would pass. There turned out to be nineteen such families. Going from Nashville to Brentwood, the impacted estates were owned by the families of C. D. Berry, Joseph Vaulx, Oscar F. Noel, James E. Caldwell, John Thompson, Norman Kirkman, Jacob McGavock Dickinson, A. J. Phillips, and Ed Baxter. From Brentwood to Franklin, the railroad would go through the farms of the McGavock descendants at Midway, the farms of Oliver Bliss Hayes and the Andrew Mizells, and farms belonging to the Grissom, Moore, Poynter, Cook, Webb, Bowman, and Brown families. Most of these property owners were receptive to the railroad since it would enable them to get to Nashville more quickly and, just as important, to get their farm produce to market faster. Automobiles were a rarity in 1905 and the road from Nashville to Franklin was terrible.

Of the total roadway of 88,840 feet, more than 60,000 was donated, about 25,000 was purchased, and the rest was taken by condemnation. The 1,874 feet that passed in front of Longview, the Franklin Road estate of Nashville financier James E. Caldwell, was the most difficult to obtain. Caldwell tried to get the Interurban moved to the other side of Franklin Pike. The Interurban owners declined, arguing that to do so would require two grade-level crossings and create a bad curve.

A bitter lawsuit followed, with the case going to the Tennessee Supreme Court, which ruled in favor of the Interurban. The court ruled that Caldwell's carriageway would be an official stop, which meant that every train would have to stop there and the conductor would have to get off the train and flag the carriageway. For a number of years, the conductors also blew their high-pitched whistles every time they approached Longview. This infuriated Mr. and Mrs. Caldwell, who complained about the whistle and the loss of privacy.

The electric railway did not always parallel the Franklin Pike. At points, it temporarily veered away from the pike, only to return where the railway crossed the pike a number of times, dictated by the terrain. Today, there is still a Franklin Interurban stone bench in front of Franklin Road Academy on the east side of Franklin Pike.

Groundbreaking for the Interurban took place in May 1907. Construction took nearly eighteen months. On Christmas Eve 1908 thousands of people were in the public square at Franklin to see the first electric train brake to a stop at 2:30 in the afternoon. A giant welcome sign hung over the square where the electric cars made a loop around the Confederate Monument. Franklin's mayor, Edwin M. Perkins, drove a golden spike into the ground, and Mayberry was hailed a hero. He, in turn, gave credit to his board of directors.

The Franklin Interurban proved to be a big success. For the first week or so, the cars, designed to hold fifty passengers, were packed with people. The first car left Franklin at 6:00 a.m., and the last car from Nashville arrived at

11:30 p.m. A one-way trip cost ten cents, and a round-trip cost twenty cents. You could carry up to 150 pounds of baggage with no extra charge.

The railroad got a huge boost in 1911 when the Tennessee Fertilizer Company, still controlled by Carpenter and Howard, built a forty-one-mile-long steam engine line from Mt. Pleasant to Franklin. This meant that, all of a sudden, a large volume of freight from Hickman and Maury Counties was being transferred to the Franklin Interurban that had a baggage car on every train. There were four trains a day between Mt. Pleasant and Franklin. Each trip normally took one hour and fifty-five minutes.

The Franklin Interurban hauled freight, primarily phosphate, to its connection with the Tennessee Central belt line that encircled Nashville, giving the latter railroad a small measure of independence from the L&N. Coming the other way were dry goods, farm equipment, hardware, furniture, and barrels of fish and meat. All of this brought a rising prosperity to Franklin.

The Interurban from Franklin to Columbia never materialized, but work started on the Nashville-Gallatin Interurban in 1911. Electric trolley car service between those cities started in 1913 and lasted until the mid-1930s. One of the many challenges that both railroads faced was heavy snowfalls. In the winter of 1929, an Interurban car was stuck on West Main Street about one mile west of the Gallatin Public Square for some time.

After World War I, the increase in automobile traffic between Franklin and Nashville on both the Franklin and Hillsboro Pikes put pressure on both the Franklin Interurban and the Middle Tennessee Railroad. The railroad was losing money as the phosphate and fertilizer industries began to decline. On October 7, 1920, the Middle Tennessee Railroad closed, catching farmers and small businessmen by surprise. The Interurban reacted by leasing the Middle Tennessee Railroad's line in 1922 and providing service between Franklin and Mt. Pleasant with a gas electric car until 1927. That year, the Tennessee Railroad Commission gave the Middle Tennessee Railroad permission to abandon the line. The small depot at McKnight's Station, north of Fly, still stands.

The Interurban, while still profitable, saw its profits diminish in the 1920s. In 1925, the line cut back on night trips between Nashville and Franklin, and three years later, the company's bond holders took over the company. The Franklin Interurban got a reprieve in 1928, when the Franklin mayor and aldermen gave it the franchise to sell electricity to the city.

Overton Thompson Jr., who was born in 1915, grew up at Glen Leven, right across Franklin Pike from the Interurban. When he went to school at Robertson Academy, Overton would usually ride his pony. However, if the weather was bad, he would catch the Interurban. In a 1990 interview with his daughter, Ophelia Thompson Paine, Overton said, "Mr. Cotton would stop right in front of Glen Leven and pick me up. From time to time, he would let me sit in his lap and operate the Interurban."

By the mid to late 1930s, it was obvious that the Franklin Interurban was doomed to failure as automobiles became faster and more numerous and as roads improved. By the end of the decade, Hillsboro Road had been widened and graded for a few miles out of Franklin. Still, the Interurban maintained its hourly schedule to and from Franklin, except at eleven o'clock in the morning and at two o'clock in the afternoon. Freight still was handled, although usually in less than carload shipments. On the Middle Tennessee Railroad line, unused since 1928, the small railroad stations at the villages stood deserted. In Nashville, the city was tearing up old electric streetcar lines as the move toward motorized buses progressed. Soon, the Interurban would have to stop at the city's edge and transfer its passengers to buses. This led the owners of the Interurban to consider replacing the electric streetcars, which were still making money, with motorized buses. In November 1941 the last run of the old Franklin Interurban line was made.

The Public Utilities Commission had given the Interurban permission to make the change to buses, despite opposition from the bus transportation company Greyhound Lines. Buses were purchased, and the old electric streetcars were sold to an airplane plant in Marietta, Georgia.

For years to come, people driving down Highway 31 between Nashville and Franklin could see the outline of the electric car railroad. During World War II, the Interurban bus line advertised rates at "One Cent Per Mile," encouraging passengers to "Save Your Tires." The bus service lasted until 1969.

Louisville & Nashville Railroad (L&N) was granted a charter by the State of Kentucky on March 5, 1850. (A railroad between Louisville and Nashville had been wanted since the early 1830s.) In 1852 the State of Tennessee, jealous of Kentucky's control of the railroad, issued a less generous charter for the portion of the road that would be in Tennessee. Progress was slow, with only eight miles having been completed south of Louisville by 1855. Regularly scheduled trains began operating between Louisville and Nashville on Monday, October 21, 1859. The trip normally took nine hours.

The Civil War was extremely disruptive for the L&N. After Nashville fell in February 1862, the Union controlled the line which had been badly damaged by retreating Confederates. By March 1862 service of a sort had been reestablished. However, John Hunt Morgan, Nathan Bedford Forrest, and other Confederate cavalry leaders would continually disrupt the line though 1864.

By 1870 the L&N had established a line from Bowling Green, Kentucky, to Memphis, Tennessee; a line to East Kentucky to haul coal from coal mines there; a very short line to Glasgow, Kentucky; and one other short line in central Kentucky. In 1871 the L&N penetrated the deep South by acquiring a line extending 303 miles south of Nashville to Montgomery, Alabama. By 1880 the L&N had doubled its size by extending its reach to St. Louis and New Orleans. That year, the road owned and operated 1,839.95 miles of track in eight states. This didn't include 508 miles owned

"The Pan-American, deluxe train of the Louisville & Nashville Railroad. Daily between Cincinnati, Louisville and The Gulf Coast and New Orleans. *Collection of Ridley Wills II.*

by the Nashville, Chattanooga & St. Louis Railway (NC&StL), which the L&N controlled.

Magnificent Union Stations were built in Louisville in 1891 and in Nashville in 1900. During the early 1900s, the L&N was making money hauling steel from Birmingham, Alabama, to northern markets, enabling Tennessee Coal and Iron and Railroad Company (TCI) to compete with northern steel manufacturers. A continued expansion into the rich coal fields of East Kentucky led to the first passenger train reaching Harlan in 1911.

On December 28, 1917, the federal government assumed control of all transportation systems in the United States. This lasted until March 1, 1920. During this period, passenger traffic on the L&N reached an all-time high. Because so many troop trains came through Nashville, a Red Cross canteen was established on a twenty-four-hour basis in Union Station. My grandmother, Jessie (Mrs. Ridley) Wills was one of the Red Cross volunteers stationed there.

On the railroad's seventy-sixth birthday on March 5, 1926, the line, whose nickname was "Old Reliable," was in good financial condition. After expansions in the late 1920s, the line tightened its belt during the Depression years, abandoning branch lines, scrapping obsolete equipment, and consolidating divisions.

Beginning in the fall of 1933, WSM recorded the sounds of the crack L&N passenger train, the Pan-American, as it sped south past WSM's 878-foot-tall radio tower in Brentwood. WSM listeners would count on this every afternoon at five o'clock, so the microphone continued to capture the sound daily for more than ten years.

The railroad's next period of great prosperity was during World War II. Its passenger traffic grew from 3,589,198 in 1941 to 10,047,128 in 1945. During the same span of time, its freight tonnage grew from 58,504,412 to 70,235,764.

Dozens of Tennessee military camps were served directly by the L&N, including the Milan Ordnance Center in Milan, the Clinton Engineering Works in Oak Ridge, and the Barrage Balloon Training Center in Paris. The L&N also contributed to the war effort by demolishing some of its obsolete bridges and giving the metal to scrap drives.

After World War II, the earlier trend away from railroad passenger traffic to cars and airplanes accelerated. One of the modern lightweight trains put into service in 1946 to counteract the trend was The Humming Bird, which operated between Cincinnati and New Orleans through Nashville. An entirely new freight facility, Radnor Yards, was also built south of Nashville.

Between 1949 and 1958, more than $1 billion was spent by new industry locating on L&N tracks, making the railroad's traffic more diversified and traffic flow more balanced.

In 1957 the NC&StL was finally merged with the L&N. In the 1960s, acquisitions in Illinois enabled the L&N to achieve its long-sought entry into Chicago. Some of the remains of the L&N's old rival, the Tennessee Central, were also acquired.

Nashvillians were understandably upset when, in 1970, Nashville lost its last passenger service. In 1971 the Seaboard Coast Line Railroad (SCL) purchased enough additional shares of L&N stock to gain control of the company and make it a subsidiary. That same year, Amtrack, the government-formed railroad, took over the few remaining L&N passenger trains. By 1982 SCL had absorbed L&N entirely. Four years later, the SCL system was merged into the Chesapeake & Ohio Railway (C&O)/Baltimore & Ohio Railroad (B&O) combined system. This company became CSX Transportation, which has owned all the former L&N lines ever since.

NASHVILLE, CHATTANOOGA & ST. LOUIS RAILWAY (NC&STL) was originally the Nashville & Chattanooga Railroad, chartered in December 1845. The first stockholder meeting was held in Nashville in January 1848, and the road's first locomotive was delivered to Nashville by steamboat in December 1850. The first train ran south from Nashville nine miles to Antioch in April 1851. By then, a tunnel had been punched through the Cumberland Mountains near Cowan.

Upon completion of a long wooden bridge over the Tennessee River at Bridgeport, Alabama, train service to Chattanooga began in early 1854. The important connection with the Western & Atlantic Railroad at Chattanooga made it possible for Davidson County planters to ship their farm products all the way to Charleston, South Carolina.

The Nashville & Chattanooga was strategically important during the Civil War. The railroad served as the artery over which the Federal Army supplied Sherman's troops during the 1864 Atlanta campaign. Because of its importance, the Federal Army confiscated the railroad from 1863 until the end of the war.

The US Military Railroad also extended track on the Nashville & Northwest Railroad from Kingston Springs, twenty-three miles west of Nashville to Johnsonville in early 1864 so that supplies could be brought into Nashville during the months when the Cumberland River was too low to be navigated.

The Nashville & Chattanooga was badly battered by the war. Col. E. W. Cole, its president, deserves credit for restoring the line. He also wanted to extend the road to St. Louis, outflanking the Louisville & Nashville Railroad (L&N). Toward that end, the NC&StL laid track between Johnsonville and McKenzie in 1867–68.

In 1870 the NC&StL leased the Nashville & Northwest line (acquiring the line in 1872) and made arrangements with the L&N to use their track, and for the Nashville & Northwest to allow passengers to travel more directly from Nashville to Memphis.

During the 1880s and 1890s, the NC&StL, through acquisitions and track construction, acquired significant additional trackage, particularly in Tennessee and Northern Alabama. In 1892 the Dixie Flyer first ran over NC&StL tracks on its trips between St. Louis and Florida. Soon, the railroad began promoting itself as "the Lookout Mountain Route." The NC&StL and the L&N formed the Nashville Terminals Company to construct Union Station, that opened in Nashville in 1900. In 1919 the NC&StL renewed its lease of the Western & Atlantic track for fifty years.

Because of the number of major military institutions along its route and its strategic location, the NC&StL had unprecedented traffic, both passenger and freight, during both world wars. A modernization program in the 1940s led to trains called The Georgian and the City of Memphis going into service in 1946 and 1947 respectively.

The merger of the NC&StL and the L&N in 1957 was not unexpected. The two lines had worked closely together since well before the turn of the century. With the acquisition of the NC&StL, the L&N had some fifty-seven hundred miles of track, making it the third largest line in the South and the sixteenth largest in the country. Much of the NC&StL's former mileage is now part of the CSX Transportation system.

Nashville Railroad & Light Company had its beginning in 1900 when an agreement was filed with the Tennessee secretary of state consolidating, under the name Nashville Railway Company, three companies that had operated street railroads in Nashville. The three companies were Nashville Street Railway, Citizens Rapid Transit Company, and the Nashville and Southern Railway Company.

An ordinance authorizing the consolidation had been passed over the veto of Mayor James M. Head. The city sued the new company, alleging that the Nashville City Council had not consented to the transfer to Nashville Street Railway of franchises of the old United Electric Railroad purchased by the Nashville Street Railway at a foreclosure sale. The litigation with the city was settled by a consent decree entered in the Tennessee Supreme Court on October 2, 1902. The Nashville Street Railway Company's general manager, Percy Warner, was gratified with the settlement, saying, "It is a victory for each side and I am satisfied in every way with the result."

Following the settlement, Maj. Eugene E. Lewis, of the Louisville & Nashville Railroad (L&N), and Warner, son of wealthy iron magnate James C. Warner, reorganized the Nashville Railway Company under the name of Nashville Railroad & Light Company, purchasing the assets of the former company at a foreclosure sale.

Percy Warner became president of the new company. Among its incorporators were Warner, Lewis, Joseph Fall, A. M. Shook, Joseph H. Thompson, and Frank O. Watts. The new company issued stock valued at $6.5 million, at $100 per share, with four thousand common shares and twenty-five hundred preferred shares. The Nashville Railroad & Light Company had its offices in the Watkins Institute building on Church Street.

The Nashville Railroad & Light Company quickly built a transfer station, which opened on June 25, 1902. Nashville's modest version of "Grand Central Station" was located west of the public square, between Market (Third Avenue North) and Cherry (Fourth Avenue North) Streets and between Deaderick and Cedar Streets (Charlotte Avenue). Two tracks entered on Market Street and exited at Cherry Street. Both tracks curved north and south at each end, making a total of eight tracks that radiated to all sections of the city.

At the zenith of electric streetcar use, more than 2,200 cars daily passed through the tunnel-shaped transfer station. In the winter, the station was said to be the coldest spot in the city, as it had no heat. A concrete island separated the tracks and accommodated passengers, who found the building always brightly lit but also sooty and dingy. Nevertheless, passengers on the Nashville Railroad & Light Company or ones on the Franklin Interurban, after 1907, could spend their time waiting for their cars in a variety of ways. There was a penny arcade, a newsstand, a popcorn wagon, a barber shop and shoeshine stand, and the Sparkman Brothers Soda Fountain that sold hamburgers, hot dogs, cold drinks, and ice cream.

Streetcar transportation was comfortable and cheap. The cost to ride from one end of the city to the other was five cents. The Nashville Railroad & Light Company's president, Percy Warner, lived at his home, Renraw, three miles from town on Gallatin Pike and several blocks beyond Ordway Place. Naturally, the streetcar line stopped there as beyond Renraw the homes were spread out on farms.

Percy Warner agreed to extend the Nashville Railroad & Light Company's Broadway and West End line from its termination at Wilson's Switch four additional miles to what would later become the entrance to Percy Warner Park on Belle Meade Boulevard. Had he not agreed to this, the Nashville Golf and Country Club would not have moved to Belle Meade. Warner built the single-track line on the urging of his son-in-law, Luke Lea, who agreed to underwrite the entire cost as well as the cost of a macadamized boulevard on either side of the car line for the last three miles.

With public transportation assured and a promise of water lines, Lea offered the directors of the Nashville Golf and Country Club 140 acres in a remote section of the old Belle Meade Farm. They accepted and, in 1915, built a $50,000 clubhouse and finished a year later an eighteen-hole golf course designed by Herbert H. Barker. Of course, Lea knew that, with a

Transfer station, 1920s.
Collection of Kermit C. Stengel Jr. Estate.

new road, a streetcar line, and Nashville's most prestigious country club all in Belle Meade, wealthy club members would build homes on land his Belle Meade Company owned. Electric streetcars were also introduced out Charlotte Pike and Belmont Boulevard.

In January 1939 Mayor Thomas L. Cummings announced the creation of a municipal bus system. This was the death toll for electric streetcars. That same year, the Nashville Electric Service was formed out of the Nashville Railroad & Light Company. The last electric streetcar run in Nashville was on the Nolensville Pike line early in the morning of February 2, 1941. Earlier, in 1940, the Nashville Coach Company introduced 154 new forty-passenger gas-powered buses that would replace electric streetcars as Nashville's means of public transportation.

TENNESSEE CENTRAL RAILROAD (TC), an east-west line, was largely the creation of Nashvillian Jere Baxter, a spirited entrepreneur, who wholeheartedly believed in his railroad and its potential. Baxter's idea was to build a railroad from Knoxville to Nashville, and then on to the banks of the Tennessee River west of Nashville. He also envisioned building a magnificent terminal in Nashville on the south bank of the Cumberland River.

The Louisville & Nashville Railroad (L&N) and the Nashville, Chattanooga & St. Louis Railway (NC&StL), which was controlled by the L&N, were adamantly opposed to Baxter's plan, which would eliminate their monopoly on Nashville traffic. They decided to build their own terminal in Nashville, which was accomplished in 1900. Baxter failed in his attempt and was shut out from using the L&N and NC&StL terminal.

After many trials and tribulations, including losing control of the Tennessee Central, the situation brightened for Jere Baxter in 1901. Financial backers in St. Louis paid for the completion of the TC line from Monterey to Emory Gap, and promised to do so for the expansion of the railroad west into Nashville, and then north to Kentucky. A more modest passenger depot and freight house were built along Front Street and a freight yard constructed further east.

The TC finally began operations from Nashville east to South Harriman Gap across the Emory River from Harriman in 1902. Because ordinances passed by the Nashville City Council prevented Baxter from using downtown tracks as its major line, the Tennessee Central was forced to build a semicircular belt line west and south of the city.

Baxter also wanted to build a Western Division from Nashville to Hopkinsville, Kentucky, to provide a junction with the Illinois Central. He additionally had the idea of expanding his line north into the coal fields surrounding Madisonville. This would end the L&N monopoly there. The first train to enter Hopkinsville from Nashville arrived on October 20, 1903. The previous spring, Baxter had unexpectedly resigned as president of the Tennessee Central in hopes that the personal animosity that L&N officials had for him would not apply to his successor. In February 1904 he suddenly died at age fifty-four. His dream had only been partially fulfilled.

The Tennessee Central struggled from 1904 until 1922 with too much debt and too little income. In 1915 the line was in receivership but still running trains. The Nashville Special left Nashville at 10:40 p.m. and reached Knoxville the next morning at 7:00 a.m. It then continued on to Bristol, Roanoke, Washington, Philadelphia, and New York on other lines, arriving in New York City at 7:13 a.m. on the third day.

Potential buyers, the Illinois Central and the Southern, never exercised their options to purchase pieces of the Tennessee Central. A new railroad, also named the Tennessee Central, took over the line in 1922. It was profitable during the 1920s largely because of an increase in coal tonnage hauled. The new owners had their first deficit in 1932 as shippers cut back and fewer passengers rode the lines. The late 1930s was a period of moderate prosperity that was followed by a war-time boom with a dramatic increase in freight and passenger traffic, much of which came from Camp Campbell. (Note: Camp Campbell was constructed in 1942. In April 1950 the training camp became a permanent installation and was renamed Fort Campbell.)

The end of the war meant a temporary end to the Tennessee Central's prosperity. Ownership changed again when a Philadelphia syndicate purchased control. The arrival of diesel engines in 1949 helped the railroad return to profitability. The railroad then went through cycles of boom and bust in the 1950s.

Traffic fell in the mid-1960s when Interstate 40 was completed between Nashville and Knoxville. Meanwhile, the State Highway Department was pressuring the TC to give up part of its Nashville belt line for construction of Interstate 440. A deal was reached in 1965 for the TC to give up 3.85 miles of its belt line for $2.59 million. Still, at the beginning of 1967, the TC had only $327,009 in cash and nearly $6 million in outstanding loans. Derailments added to the line's misery.

After operating in the red for eight consecutive years and with no prospects of returning to profitability, the railroad filed for bankruptcy on December 14, 1967. Nashville businessman A. Battle Rodes was appointed receiver. Early in 1968, he filed for an abandonment petition with the Interstate Commerce Commission. Despite efforts to save the railroad, the

Tennessee Central ceased operations on August 31, 1968, and formally went out of business in 1970.

RESTAURANTS

BURRUSS & WEBBER CAFETERIA, or B & W as it was known to several generations of Nashvillians, was named for business partners Ernest H. Burruss and Fred R. Webber. Webber opened the cafeteria in the spring of 1930 at 222 Sixth Avenue North in Nashville. About the same time, a second B & W opened in Memphis. Webber, who had previously run a chain of cafeterias in North Carolina named S & W, ran the Nashville B & W while his partner Burruss, ran the Memphis cafeteria. Soon thereafter, Burruss died, and the Memphis B & W closed.

Fred Webber was president of the Nashville cafeteria until his retirement in about 1950. He was assisted for much of this time by his brother-in-law, Oscar Calvin Plaxico, who would get up at about 3:00 a.m. six days a week to go to the market before opening the cafeteria at 6:30 a.m.

B & W was a success from the very beginning, feeding an average of two thousand to twenty-two hundred meals each day, consisting of breakfast, lunch, and dinner. The food was both excellent and reasonable,

Burruss & Webber Cafeteria, 222 Sixth Avenue North.
Collection of Ridley Wills II.

which, in the hard times of the Depression, meant good business. Many local businessmen and state officials regularly ate breakfast or lunch there. With the State Capitol and state office buildings less than three blocks away, there was always good support from state employees.

Thursday night was traditionally "Family Night" at B & W. It attracted big crowds, enticed by lower prices and a wholesome atmosphere. Charlie Plaxico, O. C.'s teenage son, would often play the accordion on these nights. White table cloths and cotton napkins were standard fare. Dinners, which cost fifty cents, consisted of a choice between two meats, two vegetables, bread, coffee or tea, and dessert. Before the meals were served, waitresses would come by and offer complimentary small biscuits and extra iced tea or coffee. In 1950 the B & W was recommended by Duncan Hines and approved by the AAA.

In 1964 B & W had cafeterias at 222 Sixth Avenue North and at 3835 Green Hills Village Drive. The company slogan that year was "Every Night is Steak Night at B & W Cafeteria." In 1969 Paul Wiseman was manager of the Sixth Avenue B & W, while Tom Clancey managed the Green Hills location. Wiseman continued to manage the Sixth Avenue restaurant until it closed in 1977.

The Green Hills B & W was managed in the 1970s and 1980s by Bill McClain, Joe Donnell, and, finally, by Tom Griffin, who was manager in 1988. By then, B & W had moved to its final address of 3808 Cleghorn Avenue. The cafeteria closed in about 1990.

Brass Rail Stables was a restaurant and lounge that opened in 1930 in Printer's Alley, between Third and Fourth Avenues North. The restaurant, originally a hamburger joint, featured a dining room that supposedly was the carriage house where Andrew Jackson used to keep his horse and carriage. The restaurant's proprietor made the claim, which is strengthened by the fact that General Jackson's law office was just around the corner on Union Street. To emphasize the point, a subsequent Brass Rail Stables owner had an historic marker made and installed at the restaurant.

In the 1930s, Mr. and Mrs. Tom Forrester purchased the Brass Rail Stables. They enlarged it and began serving wholesome Southern food. In the late 1940s, Helen Nolan bought the restaurant and maintained the same historical atmosphere and the same quality of food. In 1950 the Brass Rail Stables featured steaks, chops, chicken, and seafood. The list of people who ate there included Eddy Arnold, Smiley Burnette, Tex Ritter, and Dinah Shore.

When the McGavock Block was demolished in 1971 to make way for a modern mid-rise office building, the seven tenants on the block, including the Brass Rail Stables, had to move. The new Brass Rail location was one door down from the back entrance to the old Noel Hotel in the boiler room of the former Utopia Hotel at 206.5 Printer's Alley. Lorell Moore, president of Carriage Room Inc., owned the Brass Rail at the time of the move in 1973. When she was inspecting the vacated Utopia Hotel building, she found, on the sixth floor, two large stained glass windows. She had the windows installed in the front of her restaurant in Printer's Alley.

Maître d' and room manager James Chambers returned to Nashville in 1983 after eight years with restaurants in New Orleans. Donna Vradenburg, then owner of the Brass Rail Stables, announced Chambers's return. She spoke of him being well known in Nashville, having built a reputation of offering the finest service possible before moving to New Orleans. On April 15, 1984, James H. Jesse reviewed the Brass Rail in his food column in the *Tennessean*. His conclusion was that "the food is pretty good at the Brass Rail, but it really isn't the finest in town."

Mr. and Mrs. Alfredo Katopodis bought the Brass Rail Stables in the spring of 1986. In an article on the restaurant in the *Tennessean* in October 1988, Katopodis, who was also the restaurant's chef, spoke of how well received his Brass Rail White Chocolate Cheesecake had become. He said his customers "just love it." Katopodis also served a China Plate Special that was the Brass Rail version of the Blue Plate Special. It sold for $4.95. By 1991 the Brass Rail Stables had closed.

MRS. BROWN'S COFFEE SHOP was a rustic restaurant located ten miles west of Nashville on State Highway 100. The restaurant featured three private dining rooms and a dance floor. When Nelson Andrews was a student in Vanderbilt in the late 1940s, he suffered a knee injury that ended his football career. To help finance his college education, he started a band called the Dixie Dewdrops that played square dances for fraternity and sorority parties as well as for private groups at Mrs. Brown's Coffee Shop. Mack Gant was a member of the band.

In 1951 Mrs. Brown's Coffee Shop ran an ad in the Vanderbilt *Commodore* which read, "Catering to Vanderbilt Parties." My Vanderbilt class held a tenth reunion party at Mrs. Brown's Coffee Shop in 1966.

Mrs. Brown's Coffee Shop was sold, possibly in the early 1970s, to a group that put a restaurant in the building. The business failed, and the property was auctioned off on the courthouse steps on June 13, 1977. The new owners were Mal and Dell Brown, who opened Trace Tavern Antiques there.

Corsini's Restaurant was owned and operated by Humbert A. Corsini, a native of Italy, who came to Nashville from New York in 1910 to work as one of nine chefs at the Hermitage Hotel. In 1915, he left the Hermitage Hotel to work for Luigart's Café. His next job was as chef for the Chamber of Commerce.

In 1927 Corsini left Nashville to work for hotels in Fort Worth and Birmingham. In 1932, by then a sophisticated and accomplished chef, Corsini returned to Nashville to become chef at the Noel Hotel. Corsini worked there until 1942 when he accepted the position as chef for the Montgomery Hotel in Clarksville. Soldiers from neighboring Camp Campbell flocked to his hotel dining room, often ordering pizzas.

In 1944, Corsini opened his own restaurant, named for himself, at 122 Seventh Avenue North in Nashville. One day, he was embarrassed when a chicken, just butchered in the kitchen, startled his customers by running headless through the dining room. Despite this, Corsini's served good Italian food and, in the late 1950s or early 1960s, introduced frozen pizza to the Nashville Market.

In 1950, Corsini visited Rome, where he stayed at the Excelsior Hotel. He asked the owner if he could work for a week or two in the hotel kitchen to enhance his skills in cooking Italian food. His culinary skills reinforced, Corsini returned to Nashville where he continued in business until about 1965 when Corsini's closed.

Chef Humbert A. Corsini pictured here fourth from the left at the opening of the Hermitage Hotel, September 1910. *Collection of Anita Corsini Monohan.*

CROSS KEYS RESTAURANT was opened by John G. Chiles, who came to Nashville from Louisville, and Ray Iverlett at 221 Sixth Avenue North in 1942. By 1949 the restaurant had locations on Sixth Avenue North and at 237–39 Peachtree Street in Atlanta. By 1955 Cross Keys had a third location in the Green Hills Shopping Center. The Sixth Avenue Cross Keys served lunch and dinner and had a soda fountain. All the food was prepared on-site, including the restaurant's famous yeast rolls and such desserts as apple pie, macaroons, and egg custard. John Chiles served custom cut steaks and butchered premier-grade meat at the store. His most popular meats were roast prime rib, steaks, lamb chops, calves liver, and a fine grade of hamburger. Once, when a customer ordered a filet well done, Chiles refused to serve him. Salads were served with dressings prepared in the kitchen, including a popular oil-based blue cheese dressing. Cross Keys also served Shrimp Arnaud from Arnaud's Restaurant in New Orleans.

After World War II and through the 1950s, Cross Keys was a gathering place for businessmen, shoppers, and local government officials. Until the advent of the shopping malls, Nashville had a bustling retail trade with high-scale men's shops and prestigious jewelry stores lining the 200 block of Sixth Avenue North. The restaurant also catered to families who celebrated birthdays, anniversaries, and other special events at Cross Keys.

Cross Keys was a target for sit-in demonstrators in 1963. One day that spring nine people were arrested after demonstrators, mostly African American college students, scuffled with white hecklers outside Cross Keys. The rowdy white youth had come to town seeking a confrontation.

When liquor-by-the-drink became legal on November 16, 1967, John Chiles Jr. served one of the first legal drinks in Tennessee to Don Dickerson, who had a scotch and soda for which he paid eighty-four cents. He may have been the first customer in the city to take advantage of the new law.

In 1970 Chiles was still working at Cross Keys with his son, John G. Chiles Jr., and Raymond L. Iverlett. In 1972 John Chiles retired and Raymond S. Iverlett closed his Sixth Avenue North Cross Keys, as the retail stores had left downtown. John Chiles Jr. continued to operate Cross Keys in the Green Hills Shopping center until he closed the restaurant in 1978.

Faucon's Restaurant, one of the most famous of the old Nashville restaurants, was located at 419 Union Street. Xavier Faucon emigrated to the United States from France in 1865, first settling in New Orleans, where he entered the restaurant business. He moved to Nashville in 1894, where he established Faucon's Restaurant. It was never pretentious. There was no coat room, no mirrors on the walls, and no flowers on the tables. Guests found their own seats and put their hats and coats on hooks on the walls.

Faucon's Restaurant was immortalized by its famous recipe for Faucon's salad. To make it, a dish was first rubbed with garlic and then the lettuce, eggs, and Roquefort cheese were mixed as only Faucon could mix them, with a dressing composed primarily of oil, mustard, and vinegar.

Faucon also served fish or tender steaks. Rare old French wines added flavor to the meat.

Members of the state legislature were frequently guests at Faucon's. If Faucon knew a guest, he would invariably make a little visit to his table to chat.

Faucon's son, Leon, helped at the restaurant. Each year, Faucon would spend two or three months at his second home in Biloxi, Mississippi. Leon, who grew up working at the restaurant, knew the business as well as his father did and everything ran smoothly when he was in charge. When Leon died prematurely, his father was devastated. By 1926 Faucon closed his restaurant that had served Nashville so well for thirty-two years. For many years, Faucon's salad has been a mainstay of the menu at the Belle Meade Country Club.

HAP TOWNES' RESTAURANT came about when James B. Townes got the idea for serving "meat and three" food from a mobile cart in 1921 when he learned that May Hosiery Mills was serving the same type food in their cafeteria. He opened his restaurant sometime later.

Townes' son, James B. "Hap" Townes, ran the restaurant from about 1945 until he sold it in 1985. Located at 493 Humphreys Street near the Nashville Sounds' Greer Stadium, Hap Townes' Restaurant was a modest affair, having only forty-nine seats. It was, however, excellent, offering typical Southern food—fried chicken or roast beef with turnip greens, stewed tomatoes, mashed potatoes with gravy, corn cakes, and squash casserole. For dessert, Hap's peach cobbler was a favorite. Good food was not the only reason for Hap Townes' success as a restaurateur. Down-to-earth, kind, and considerate, the soft-spoken Townes warmly greeted each guest at the door. His clientele ranged from such Grand Ole Opry stars as Bill Anderson and Chet Atkins to lesser-known musicians, politicians, college students, and laborers. Townes, who gained an appreciation for art from visiting European art galleries while serving in the Air Force during World War II, hung art in his restaurant, including a portrait of Chet Atkins that hung above the seat near the front door where Atkins normally sat. In 2011 Townes donated the portrait to the Country Music Hall of Fame and Museum. The unassuming Townes, who was beloved by his regular clients, died in July 2012 at age eighty-nine.

IRELAND'S, usually called "Butch's," was at 204 Twenty-First Avenue South immediately across from the Vanderbilt campus and next door to the Phi Delta Theta House. When I was an active member of that fraternity in the 1950s, Butch's was the place to be on our side of the campus. Jack "Butch" Jenkins, the Vanderbilt football star of the early 1940s, and his wife, Bernie, who owned the restaurant, were usually there. She was an excellent bridge player, while Jack spent more time playing cards and the pinball machine than he did managing the restaurant.

Ireland's advertised itself as "The home of the Original Steak and Biscuits." In the 1960s, if you went to Ireland's after a Vanderbilt football game, as many Vanderbilt football fans did, you could eat in either the Shamrock Room or the Court Room. You could also see, posted in a prominent place, a list of delinquent customers and how much they owed. Phi Delta Theta members dominated the list.

By 1971, Ireland's had expanded to other SEC football towns—Lexington, Athens, Tuscaloosa, and Memphis. Each Ireland's location offered "Tender morsels of choice steak tucked into hot buttery biscuits and heaped with Irish Skerry fries."

In its later years, Ireland's had a great piano player named Mayfield. One regular at the Nashville Ireland's knew Mayfield well. This patron was a car salesman, who had a special place at the bar. He would begin the mornings at Ireland's with Bloody Marys and biscuits and then return for lunch and two or three more Bloody Marys. Finally, after work, he would stop by for a nightcap. He claimed he sold ten or fifteen cars a month from what he called his "closing corner." Ireland's closed in 1983.

JULIAN'S was a French restaurant at 2412 West End Avenue. It was opened by John Haggard in 1974 and would be, for the next eighteen years, one of Nashville's most expensive restaurants. Its prix fixe Christmas menu in 1988 for $37.50 per person included a choice of two appetizers, three entrées, and two desserts, plus salad, coffee, and Christmas cookies. Julian's was awarded a four-star rating by the Mobil Travel Guide each year from 1978 to 1989.

In 1991 the cost of an entrée at Julian's ranged from $17.50 to $26.50. That year, Julian's hired a new chef when the previous chef resigned to return home to France. The new chef was Boely Boely, a cookbook author and protégé of French chef Roger Verge.

In May 1992 Julian's was one of three Nashville restaurants chosen to receive the Distinguished Restaurant of North America Award given at the National Restaurant Association Show in Chicago. Julian's was also still one of Nashville's three four-star restaurants. Despite this, Julian's was no longer profitable, said its owner, John Haggard, in 1992. Because of the recession in the late 1980s, business entertaining at Julian's dropped off and his regular customers visited less often. When Julian's closed in August 1992, Hoyte Hill, its manager for the previous ten years, left to work at his own restaurants, F. Scott's and Toucan.

KLEEMAN'S was a tea room opened in 1917 by Arthur O. Kleeman and Frank Blair in the Martha Washington Candy Shop on Union Street. Initially, Kleeman and Blair had two or three tables in the candy store where they served sliced chicken and chicken salad sandwiches. Mrs. Martha Gotschall and her sister, Miss Jo Campbell, were always on hand to

Kleeman's, 329 Union Street.
Collection of Ridley Wills II.

greet guests. Campbell also made the delicious candies for which the store was famous. The little business flourished and expanded into the building next door at 329 Union Street.

In the 1930s, the main dining room had tables for two along the walls and a double row of tables for four down the center. To give extra light, there were wall lights and wall fans. There were also several chandeliers hanging from the ceiling.

In 1930, when he started B & W Cafeteria, Fred Webber considered Kleeman's the best restaurant in town with "excellent food and the best apple pie anywhere." He did not worry about Kleeman's as a competitor because "Kleeman's offered a different kind of service in a smaller facility at prices somewhat higher and they did not open for breakfast."

In 1938 Kleeman's moved to Sixth Avenue North, where for more than a decade, it was a favorite spot for Nashvillians. Jean Ewing, who worked at Joy's Flowers in the 1940s, would often have a simple lunch at Kleeman's of cottage cheese, served in a glass ice cream dish, with crackers, for twenty-five cents. The most popular entrée was chicken served on egg bread.

In 1949, after Kleeman died, his daughter, Violet, simply closed the restaurant rather than sell it and have to watch it go downhill under somebody else's management. Martha Gotschall, who supervised Kleeman's kitchen, and her nephew, Richard Campbell, moved to the Allen Hotel at 2004 West End Avenue, where they opened a new restaurant named Miss Martha's. There, they served many of the recipes from Kleeman's famous menus.

LUIGART'S CAFÉ was opened in 1909 by William M. Luigart. Before then, he had run a saloon at 727 Church Street, which he closed when he opened Luigart's Cafe at 411 Church Street. On November 8, 1909, a group of young bachelors met at the new café to organize a literary club that they hoped would catch the flavor of gatherings at the coffee houses of eighteenth-century London. At the meeting, the name "Coffee House Club" was adopted. More than one hundred years later, the Coffee House Club is still active. My son, Ridley III, and I are both members. In 1913 William M. Luigart was proprietor of the café and Carlin Luigart was

Luigart's Café.
Collection of Ridley Wills II.

manager. By 1914 Luigart and Robert P. Horne, the owners, had moved their business to 905 Broadway and converted it into Luigart's Stag Hotel.

MARCHETTI'S RESTAURANT had its beginnings one day in 1946, when Joe Marchetti, who worked at Commerce Union Bank, noticed a "for lease" sign on a small building at 102 Nineteenth Avenue South. Joe recalled thinking, "This would be a good location for a restaurant. It's close to West End and Vanderbilt and there are no restaurants near by." That evening, he drove his brother, Umberto "Bert" Marchetti, who worked for Domenick Petrucelli and Nick Varallo at Domenick's Restaurant at 715 Church Street, by the property, which was grown up in weeds. Bert Marchetti agreed with his brother's assessment, and they decided, on a handshake, to lease the property owned by Sam Garfinkle and open a restaurant there called Marchetti's.

The agreement was that Bert Marchetti would run the restaurant since he had experience in the restaurant business. Joe Marchetti was to continue working at Commerce Union Bank and then help his brother out at Marchetti's every evening. For the next eighteen and one-half years, the brothers ran the restaurant in this fashion. Joe Marchetti recalled in 2012 that, during those years, he and his brother never had a cross word. After a break-even first month, Marchetti's made money every month of its existence. Marchetti's Restaurant served the first pizza in Nashville. Its specialties in 1958 were homemade Italian pizza pie and Italian spaghetti.

In 1965 Joe Marchetti left the restaurant business, leaving it to be run by his brother. When Bert Marchetti died in 1971, his widow, Ruby Marchetti, ran the restaurant with the help of their son-in-law, Dean Click. Marchetti's Restaurant burned in 1982. Today, the Mid-Town Café occupies the site.

Mario's Restaurant, a popular Italian restaurant, was opened by Venice, Italy, native Mario Ferrari on April 15, 1965, at 1815 West End Avenue. Before opening his restaurant with borrowed money, Ferrari spent three years as a bartender and operator of the Executive Club. When he first opened the doors of his restaurant Mario's, a filet mignon cost $9.25 and spaghetti con pomodoro (with tomato sauce) cost $4.50.

The first few years were hard because liquor-by-the-drink was prohibited. Mario said, "If you wanted to serve alcoholic beverages, you had to pay off local officials, and I refused to pay. I didn't believe in greasing anyone's palm. So, I was raided frequently." Passage of the liquor-by-the-drink law in 1967 greatly boosted the restaurant's profitability.

During the 1970s, having made some money, Ferrari attended three different culinary schools in Europe: one in Switzerland, one in Bologna, and the Di Medici Culinary School in Venice. This training must have helped, as Mario's received a four-star award from Mobil Travel Guide from 1978 through 1992.

Mario's remained at 1815 West End Avenue until it closed a few days before Christmas 1985. On the last night it was open, Ferrari's good friend, Walter Thrailkill, lifted his glass and gave a toast "to Nashville's premier restaurateur, Mario Ferrari." Mario sold his property on West End and auctioned his restaurant equipment and all salvageable materials. The building was torn down to make way for a Hampton Inn.

In January 1986 Mario's Restaurant relocated to 2005 Broadway, where, two years earlier, he had purchased the Broadway Bakery & Restaurant.

Mario's general manager was Peter Marti, a Swiss who was assisted by Patrick Hamill, a Scotsman. The executive chef then was Sandro Bozzato, whose most famous salad was "fresh spinach, served cold on a piping hot plate with tiny onion rings and hot bacon and vinegar dressing." Chefs came and went, as it was not easy to work for the demanding Ferrari.

By the late 1980s and early 1990s, Ferrari was the most prominent person in the restaurant business in Nashville. A showman with a fiery temper, he was involved in a lot of controversies over the years. Other restaurateurs were envious and leveled charges against him. For example, rivals claimed that Ferrari often pulled the pork-veal switcheroo and that the quality of the wine he served was suspect. One of his employees coined a jingle that went like this: "There's a squeal in my veal and I'm telling you it is real." Ferrari's reaction was, "When you are number one, a lot of people are envious of you." The maître d' at Mario's in the 1990s was Patrick Hamill.

In 1992 Mario's was owned by Mario Ferrari and Walter Thrailkill. It was one of three local restaurants chosen to receive the distinguished Restaurant of North America Award given by the National Restaurant Association. A year earlier, Mario's Restaurant was named one of the seven top Italian restaurants in America by the magazine *I Restoranti di Veronelli USA*.

Another crowning achievement in Mario Ferrari's restaurant career came in 1993 when his restaurant was honored by the "Best of the Best" and the American Academy of Restaurant Sciences as a Five-Star Diamond "Gold Award" winner, signifying it as one of the ten best restaurants in the country in its category. Ferrari's restaurant joined a select group of seven other restaurants in the southeastern United States to be honored with the award. Ferrari said, "I have worked a long time to see these dreams come true and I am proud to accept the award."

Ironically, that was the year Mario's lost its four-star rating. Instead, Mario's earned a three-star rating in the 1993 Mobil rankings. Mobil officials told Ferrari he lost the four-star distinction because he had neglected his restaurant. Ferrari and the restaurant had received some bad publicity in 1992 that included confusion over the qualifications of a new chef. Ferrari, who fired the chef, explained that he was busy trying to make a go of the Wild Boar, a restaurant he bought in 1991. "I've mistreated Mario's," Ferrari admitted.

In 1994 Mario's won the Readers' Choice for having the best wine list in Nashville. According to his manager Danny Mora, Mario's had an extraordinary array of European wines—640 selections. The list was heavily Italian, but there was a good representation of French wines as well.

In 2007 Mario Ferrari was seventy-five-years-old. It was time to step back from the demanding job of running a first-class restaurant, and so one of the city's highest-profile restaurants closed. Five years later, in December 2012, Ferrari died at age eighty. He had been a legend in the restaurant business.

Satsuma Tea Room, a Nashville institution, was established in 1918 by two independent, strong-willed home economics teachers, Arlene Ziegler and Mabel Ward. They chose as the site of their restaurant a building at 417 Union Street, knowing that it was adjacent to a section of downtown filled with saloons and pool halls. The nearby 200 block of Fourth Avenue North was still known as the "Men's Quarter," and the Hermitage Hotel, two blocks away, still felt it necessary to provide a ladies' entrance on Union Street.

Ziegler and Ward offered a genteel atmosphere that became a sought-after respite for both men and women. They served excellent food in pleasant surroundings. One rule was to never have artificial flowers in the tea room. Instead, they supplied fresh-cut flowers from their own garden in the summer and dried flowers in the winter. Their attractive linen and china, along with the flowers, helped establish an atmosphere where men and women could enjoy fine food and good conversation. From the 1920s through the 1940s, Sgt. Alvin York was a regular customer whenever he was in town. He always stayed at the nearby Hermitage Hotel.

Ziegler's niece, Betty Smith, came to Nashville in 1950 with her husband, Truman Smith, who came to manage the Satsuma. He initiated the Satsuma frozen food line and box lunch catering. The frozen food line became a business of its own, taking up too much time and energy. That line was dropped so Satsuma could focus on its fine food and catering businesses.

The Satsuma Tea Room was known for its Men's Table. Once, in the 1960s, my wife, Irene, stopped in the Satsuma to have lunch with her father, Granbery Jackson Jr. Spotting him sitting with some other men, she sat down, only to quickly discover that she was sitting at the Men's Table. She and her father quietly moved to another table.

Among the delicious entrées served for many years were chicken pot pie, spinach and broccoli casseroles, and gumbo. Desserts served included rhubarb pie and almond ice-box pudding. During the eight years that Lamar Alexander was governor, the Satsuma always had a supply of peanut butter for the occasions when he came in to order his favorite sandwich.

After Mabel Ward died, Arlene Ziegler became the sole owner of the Satsuma. Upon her retirement, Truman Smith bought out her interest. Later, several of his sons became his partners, becoming the third generation of the Ziegler family to operate the tea room.

When Truman Smith retired in 1995, he sold the business to Mary Donahue and her sons, John and Mike Donahue. Mary had twenty years experience as a waitress and manager at the Satsuma before she became owner. Many of the Satsuma waitresses were in their seventies, including Louise Maynard, a lady who still worked there three days a week when she was seventy-eight.

The restaurant closed in 2005, having fed five generations of legislators, mayors, governors, businessmen, and their families.

SHERRIE'S was probably the best-known restaurant in Nashville in 1949. George C. Leffler first established a restaurant in 1928. After sixteen years in one location, he saved enough money to acquire an exclusive site on Harding Road. It was a large two-story brick house, with a tile roof. Leffler named the restaurant for his youngest daughter, Sherrie Ann, who was born in 1942.

With an expansive personality, Leffler made it a point to give a hearty welcome to every guest entering Sherrie's. The restaurant's advertisement in the 1949 Vanderbilt-Arkansas football program read, "Over seventy-five percent of the out-of-town visitors to Nashville prefer Sherrie's." Another Sherrie's slogan's was, "We serve the best because we buy the best."

In the 1950s, Fred Russell, Jimmy Armistead, and "Jimbo" Cooke sometimes stopped for a drink at the bar in Sherrie's after work. The owner, George Leffler, occasionally pulled a prank on the group. To pay him back, they arranged for the McCabe Funeral Home to deliver a casket and fake body to the back entrance of the restaurant.

Sherrie's specialized in serving the finest steaks to its select clientele. Leffler was widely known in the restaurant world and was active in various restaurant associations. Sherrie's closed in about 1956 to make way for the construction of the Belle Meade Plaza Shopping Center.

SURF RESTAURANT, located at 4503 Harding Road, was in front of Royal Oaks Apartments. It was opened by S. Fred Welch and Charles W. Glasgow in about 1948. Nashvillians were excited about having an upscale restaurant serving fresh fish, including sea scallops. The Surf featured a saltwater tank near the entrance. The restaurant was short-lived, closing in about 1956.

ZANINI'S RESTAURANT, an Italian-American restaurant, was located at 223 Capitol Boulevard. Started in about 1927, the restaurant was convenient to the downtown movie theaters. Its motto was: "Where the

Zanini's Restaurant, 1930s.
Collection of Ridley Wills II.

food is different." In the 1930s, Zanini's was considered by some as the best restaurant in town. By 1938, the restaurant was air-conditioned and provided background music for its diners. In the summertime, there were also vases of flowers on each wooden table.

The restaurant, recommended by Duncan Hines, had as its specialties chicken cacciatore, seafood, steaks, spaghetti, and ravioli. During World War II, soldiers on maneuvers near Nashville and from Camp Campbell loved to go to Zanini's to get food they would never have been served in the army.

In 1947 Zanini's advertised itself as "one of the few places in the South serving excellent foods." Joe Zanini was succeed as president by his widow, Marie Zanini. Her general manager in 1951 was Vincent J. Punaro. Zanini's closed on March 2, 1957, to make way for a gift shop that Marie Zanini ran until her retirement a year or so later.

SCHOOLS

DRAUGHON'S BUSINESS COLLEGE was founded by John F. Draughon. The first Draughon School of Business was in East Tennessee in 1879. As a sixteen-year-old, Draughon would haul books from town to town, offering basic business classes. A few years later, he moved to Nashville, where, in 1888, he founded Draughon's Business College, a for-profit school with $300,000 in capital.

In the 1890s, Draughon offered Nashvillians a "lifetime scholarship" that cost fifty dollars for members of their families to attend Draughon's Business College.

By the time Draughon died in 1921, he had established thirty-eight business schools in Southern and Western states. The home office was in Nashville in his four-story building at 131 Eighth Avenue North, behind Hume Fogg High School. Division headquarters were in Atlanta, Dallas, Little Rock, St. Louis, and Washington, DC.

Courses offered included bookkeeping, stenography, typewriting, manifolding, telegraphy, commercial law, and "whatsoever belongs to a thorough and practical business, commercial or technical education." Two of Draughon's earliest teachers were Laura Baird and Professor H. K. Ford, who was the manager of the school.

Professor Draughon's hobby was fox hunting. To carry his hunting dogs to the fox-hunting territory, he designed a wire carriage on four wheels that attached to the back of his automobile. On top of the carriage he stowed his equipment and guns. Draughon was proud that his car and its appendage could go twenty miles an hour and had a postcard made of it in about 1910.

One of the more successful of Draughon's Business Colleges was in Little Rock. It opened in 1900 and operated for more than ninety years. In 1929 an ad in the *Perry County News* touted Draughon's as "Arkansas' Largest Business College." By this time, H. Herbert Coone was president of Draughon's Business College in Nashville.

During the late 1940s, Draughon's Business Colleges, including the one in Nashville, were filled with young men returning from duty in World War II. Rather than spend four years in college, many of them worked during the day and attended Draughon's at night. The schools operated very much like today's vocational and technical schools. The last year the school operated in Nashville may have been 1958. Walter M. Copp was the college's president.

Nashville Business College (NBC), a for-profit business college, was founded by Herman O. Balls soon after World War I. Until about 1932, the school was located at 225 Capitol Boulevard, next to the YMCA. Ball advertised his college "as good as the best for less," offering standard courses at reasonable prices.

Beginning in about 1932, the school moved into the Nashville YMCA building at 301 Seventh Avenue North, where it would ultimately occupy the entire third floor. The school primarily taught young people practical business skills such as shorthand, accounting, human relation skills, secretarial work, and typing. Often these young people, many of whom were young women, were high school graduates from small Middle Tennessee towns.

In about 1939, Ball employed Leo Long, better known as the longtime football and basketball coach at Father Ryan High School, to coach an

NBC women's Amateur Athletic Union (AAU) team. At the time, colleges did not have intercollegiate women's sports teams, and AAU basketball for women was the best in the world, particularly popular in the Southwest and South. One of the early stars was Babe Didrikson, whom M. J. McCombs recruited out of Beaumont High School in Texas, to play for the Employer's Casualty Company (ECC) Golden Cyclones.

NBC's Coach Long was fortunate to have a star of his own in Alline Banks who was the most valuable player in the 1940, 1941, and 1942 AAU national tournaments. The NBC team placed second, second, and third, respectively, in those tournaments.

NBC hired a new coach in 1947. His name was John Head, and he would become a Hall of Fame legend. In 1949 Head recruited the semi-retired Alline Banks, then married and living in Atlanta. Despite being out of shape, Banks led NBC to the finals of the 1949 tournament. NBC won the national AAU title in 1950. After being an also-ran to the Wayland Baptist College team during much of the 1950s, NBC won its second national title in 1958, defeating Wayland College and ending that school's 131-game winning streak.

The two teams traded national championships in 1961 and 1962, when the NBC team established its national supremacy, defeating Wayland in the finals 63–35. This was the first of eight consecutive national championships for NBC. At one time, the school won ninety-six consecutive games. Two NBC stars, Nera White and Joan Crawford, were elected to the women's basketball Hall of Fame, recognized as being among the greatest female basketball players in the world in the mid-twentieth century.

Nashville Business College was still functioning in 1973 in Room 235 of the YMCA building. Otto Byers was then director. Herman Balls was still active, serving as president of the Nashville Auto-Diesel College (which he also founded) and the Economy Printing Company, but he was no longer involved with the Nashville Business College, which closed its Nashville operation in about 1974, when Byers retired.

SIGN COMPANIES

Cummings Signs was founded in 1946 by Thomas L. Cummings Jr. and a college friend, Harold Balton, of Memphis. Each man put up $7,500 to start the business that began in Cummings's parents' garage on Carden Avenue. They called the company Balton & Cummings Inc. The staff initially consisted of Cummings, a service man, and a neon glass tube bender.

Balton & Cummings began by producing signs made of neon tubing and porcelain. In their first year, the company earned profits of $4,500 on sales of $48,000. One of their first clients was H. Brown Furniture company on Broadway. When Balton & Cummings's executive offices moved to 200 Twelfth Avenue South in 1951, their clientele was still primarily local, mainly hotels, motels, and automobile dealers. It would not be long, however, before their clients were nationwide and international. A bank loan from Sam M. Fleming Jr. at Third National Bank helped Cummings make his company a success with accounts with such national firms as Holiday Inn, Chevron, and Chrysler Corporation.

Tom Cummings Jr. bought out his partner in 1954 and changed the company name to Cummings Signs so "people would know what we did." Three years later, Cummings Signs placed the L&C sign, which they manufactured, on top of Life and Casualty's new thirty-one-story tower.

In 1965 the company formed a subsidiary, International Sign Service, so that lighting and sign companies throughout the United States could be licensed by Cummings Signs to install and maintain signs through a partnership agreement.

Their most important client was Holiday Inns of America. Cummings Signs designed and manufactured Holiday Inn signs that took the Cummings product all over the country and into many foreign countries. Cummings Signs owned all the Holiday Inn signs and leased them to Holiday Inn.

Cummings took his company public in 1967. By 1979 Cummings Signs had manufacturing plants in Memphis; Murfreesboro; Nashville; Columbus,

Ohio; Hurst, Texas; and Toronto, Canada. Sales and service facilities were in Detroit; Louisville; and Lachine, Quebec. There were 666 employees. In 1987 Cummings returned his company into private ownership.

When the seventy-five-year-old Cummings stepped aside in 1995 to enable his son, Thomas L. Cummings III, to become chief executive officer of the company, the firm had four hundred employees and was the fourth largest sign company in the United States. The younger Cummings, who had been president and chief operating officer since 1988, had started working for his father during summer vacations at the company's plant in Murfreesboro, where he wired electric signs.

In 1998 Tom Cummings Jr. and Tom Cummings III sold Cummings Signs to two private investors, Steve Lynn and Steve Kerr.

SPORTING GOODS STORES

NASHVILLE SPORTING GOODS COMPANY, owned by Walter Nipper Jr., was the city's largest and oldest sporting goods store in 1977. That year, he had stores in Green Hills at 4105 Hillsboro Road, Hickory Plaza at 5753 Nolensville Road, and downtown at 169 Eighth Avenue North.

Nashville Sporting Goods Company was headquarters for Spanjain Uniforms, Wilson, Rawlings, Spot-Bilt Shoes, Adidas Shoes, Southland Manufacturing Company, MacGregor, Puma Athletic Shoes, Converse Shoes, Dudley, American Cap, New Era Caps, and Bill Kelly Helmets. During the 1990s, Walter Nipper Jr. operated Nashville Sporting Goods at a single location, 4004 Hillsboro Pike. The store closed by 1999.

STONE QUARRIES

SAM WATKINS' QUARRY was between present-day Twelfth and Fourteenth Avenues North and between Pearl Street on the south and Jo Johnston on the north. In 1845 the State of Tennessee needed stone to build the State Capitol. Since Sam Watkins' stone quarry was less than a mile from Campbell's Hill, where the State Capitol would be built, the

State purchased the quarry and used its stone to construct the building. The fact that the state prison was only a few blocks away was also a factor, as prison labor hauled the stone up the hill to the building site. After the massive project was completed, the State of Tennessee sold the property back to Watkins.

Watkins, despite being wealthy and owning property all over town, lived frugally in a small house near the quarry and near his brickyards that were on Charlotte Pike. In 1870 Watkins, who was extremely generous, gave the City of Nashville a rectangular 8.2-acre park near his stone quarry. Originally called Watkins Grove, it became the first park in Nashville's park system. Watkins is best known for having established Watkins Institute with a $100,000 gift in his will.

STUD FARMS

Belle Meade Stud, a world-famous stud farm, began in 1816 when Montgomery Bell's imported stallion, Boaster, stood the season at John Harding's stable on "the Old Natchez Road," six miles southwest of Nashville. The following season, Boaster stood again at Harding's farm. In an advertisement in the *Nashville Whig* on May 12, 1817, Harding wrote that "Boaster will be let to mares at $25 in cash or cotton at cash price delivered at any gin in Davidson County on or before the first day of January next."

Bagdad, a brown Arabian sired in Tripoli, was the next noted stallion known to stand at John Harding's stud. He stood there from 1824 until 1828.

In 1839, the year John Harding turned over to his son, William Giles Harding, responsibility for his Belle Meade Farm and Stud, the younger Harding claimed all the letters of the Greek alphabet from Alpha to Omega for his Thoroughbreds. As his father had been, William Giles was active with the Nashville Jockey Club and raced his Thoroughbreds at the spring and fall races at the Nashville Race Course every year.

By the middle of the 1850s, the Belle Meade Stud had achieved national recognition. By then, Harding, a general in the state militia, had as many as one hundred silver cups, pitchers, and trophies won on the turf and at state and county fairs across the South.

Belle Meade Breeding and Training Farm.
Collection of Ridley Wills II.

The most outstanding race horse bred at Belle Meade before the Civil War was Allendorf, foaled in 1855. In April 1860, the chestnut gelding set an American mile record of 1:44.5 in a race in New Orleans.

The Civil War was hard on Belle Meade. General Harding was incarcerated on Fort Mackinaw Island, Michigan, as a political prisoner for six months in 1862. While he was gone, his plantation felt the wrath of the occupying Union army. There was no racing, breeding came to an abrupt halt, fences were torn down, and crops were taken by Federal troops.

General Harding held his first Thoroughbred yearling sale at Belle Meade in 1867, when Jack Malone and Vandal were his star sires. Horsemen in attendance speculated on that occasion that Belle Meade was on its way to becoming one of the leading studs in the country. Because Vandal died that year, Harding and his son, John Harding Jr., went to Glen Flora Farm, north of Chicago, and purchased Bonnie Scotland, the first American-owned and bred horse to win the English Derby.

Each year, the *Spirit of the Times* covered the annual yearling sales at Belle Meade. For the 1878 season, Belle Meade's old hero, Bonnie Scotland, stood second only to Lexington among American sires in the amount of winnings. Bonnie Scotland's two greatest rivals, Lexington and Leamington, died in 1875 and 1878, respectively. Following their deaths, Bonnie Scotland ranked first among all living American sires in both 1878 and 1879. In 1880 he finally captured the crown as the leading American sire. Bonnie Scotland died at the Belle Meade Stud on February 1 that year. His blood line, established through his illustrious son, Bramble, has been conspicuous in the pedigrees of American Thoroughbreds ever since. Most of the twentieth-century winners of the Kentucky Derby could trace their blood lines back to Bonnie Scotland.

In the spring of 1881, Baron Faverot de Kerbrech and Captain de la Chere of France toured Belle Meade as representatives of the French government inspecting horses and breeding establishments in the United States. In their report, they said that "the best specimen of the Thoroughbred horse was at General Harding's. We saw a crop of Thoroughbred yearlings there that surpassed anything we had ever seen in England or France."

By 1884 the Belle Meade Stud's status as one of the country's premier horse nurseries came from another contingent of Frenchmen who visited. Vicomtes de la Moyne Rouge and DeCoumout, inspectors general of the Ministry of Agriculture of France, stopped at Belle Meade after seeing ten Kentucky studs. Before leaving Nashville, the Frenchmen said, "Nothing we have seen anywhere is comparable to Belle Meade in the number of good horses seen there. Even the mares are of a superior kind. Harding's is indeed the best place we have seen in America."

William Giles Harding died in 1886, but the Belle Meade Stud continued to thrive under the leadership of Gen. William Hicks Jackson, who had helped his father-in-law run Belle Meade since Jackson married Harding's daughter, Selene, in 1867. The plantation finally went under the hammer following Jackson's death in 1903, and the death of his son, William Harding Jackson, later the same year.

In 2012 Belle Meade Plantation, the prize property of the Association for the Preservation of Tennessee Antiquities (APTA) since 1955, had a record-setting paid attendance of 230,000.

HERMITAGE STUD was established in 1887. In the fall of 1886, some members of the Overton family and their neighbor, Van Leer Kirkman, bought about ten Standardbred trotting horses at the dispersal sale of the famous Glenview Stud in Louisville, Kentucky. After returning to Nashville, they decided to put the horses and others they owned on a stud farm they named Hermitage Stud after Andrew Jackson's home. The syndicate consisted of Van Leer Kirkman, president; John Thompson, secretary-treasurer; May Overton, manager; and Jesse M. and Robert L. Overton, members. Robert Overton had taken the place of his brother-in-law, Hugh Craighead. All of the land for the stud, about fourteen hundred acres, was owned by Col. John Overton or his children, Elizabeth Overton, Jesse M. Overton, Mary McConnell "Conn" Thompson, May Overton, and Robert L. Overton. Conn Thompson lived at neighboring Glen Leven Farm with her husband, John Thompson, and their children. Kirkman lived at Oak Hill, property he had bought from Colonel Overton. May, Robert, Jesse, and Elizabeth Overton lived with their father at Travellers Rest.

All but one of the buildings and the training track at the Hermitage Stud were on Overton land west of the Franklin Pike, mostly on the 175 acres Colonel Overton left to his daughter Conn Overton Thompson. Her portion ran from present-day Curtiswood Lane on the north to Oak Hill on the south and to a branch of Brown's creek on the west. The training track ran north and south near the turnpike.

In the 1980s, you could still see the curve of the northern end of the track in the backyard of a home facing Harding Place a few hundred yards from Franklin Pike. A portion of the curve at the southern end is still visible from Franklin Pike.

About one hundred yards from the northern end of the track there was a twenty-four-stall training stable. In the southwest corner, there was a circular colt stable. Most of the brood mares, usually sixty or more, were pastured in a field on the James E. Caldwell Place on the west side of Franklin Pike, about a mile down the turnpike. Their stable was across the pike in the Elysian Fields track then owned by May Overton.

A month after buying the ten trotting horses in Kentucky, May Overton, representing the syndicate, paid John S. Clark $25,000 for the famous Wedgewood, a champion trotter that earned the nickname "The Iron Horse" for running as many as six heats in a single event. His short racing career lasted from 1879 through 1881. In 1880, he won every race in his class in the Grand Circuit.

When the Cumberland Fair and Racing Association's park opened in October 1891, the road connecting the new race course with the Franklin Pike was named Wedgewood in honor of the great horse. Cumberland Driving Park lasted until 1906, when an anti-gambling law killed horse racing in Tennessee. That same year, the track became the State Fair Grounds.

The Hermitage Stud weathered the 1893 Depression, only to close on May 24, 1898, with a dispersal sale of what was advertised as the "Grandest Stud of Trotting Horse Ever in Tennessee." Part of the problem was lack of money and another part was disagreements between the partners. William Gerst, the wealthy Nashville brewer, who was one of the heaviest buyers at the sale, leased the Hermitage Stud for about five years before he either sold his horses or moved them to his own stable.

In about 1908, the Pawnee Bill Circus spent the winter on the Hermitage Stud site. Neighbors remembered that long-legged camels frequently stepped over fences and got on their land. By 1910 Battery Lane had been cut through the old Hermitage Stud property. Soon after that, Conn Thompson donated several acres on the south edge of her property to Robertson Academy.

In 1916–17, the circular colt barn burned after having been used since 1898 primarily as a cow barn. Part of the training stable was used by John and Conn Thompson to stable a saddle horse and a pony or two. The Hermitage Stud office, a square, one-room building, still stood in 2013 in the backyard of a home in the neighborhood.

SURGICAL SUPPLY COMPANIES

Massey Surgical Supply began in the early 1930s. Twenty-four-year-old Jack Carroll Massey came to Nashville from Georgia in 1929 to manage the Atlanta-based Liggett Drugstore chain's new Nashville store at 530 Church Street. A couple of years later, Massey left Liggett, borrowed money from Third National Bank, and purchased the Young and Thompson Drug Store at 718 Church Street.

Because so many doctors and dentists had their offices in the Benni-Dillon Building at 702 Church Street, Massey eventually moved his drugstore there and soon built up a good business selling their customers prescriptions and selling the physicians bandages, sutures, and other medical equipment.

Two friendships Massey made in the tough years of the Depression were with banker Sam Fleming, of Third National, and physician Thomas Frist, whose office was on the second floor of the Doctor's Building next

West End Avenue looking east from Twenty-Second Avenue North, circa 1950. Massey Surgical Supply, 2110 West End Avenue, is on the left. The Cathedral of the Incarnation, 2015 West End Avenue, is on the right.
Metropolitan Nashville Archives.

door. Both would prove to be exceptionally meaningful later in Massey's life.

With the end of World War II, credit became more readily available. Consequently, Massey borrowed heavily from Third National to expand his business and move it to a larger building at 2110 West End Avenue. In 1946, Third National named Massey to its board of directors in appreciation for his banking business but primarily for his obvious financial acumen.

Massey also formed a close relationship with the new Baptist Hospital that took over a floundering Protestant Hospital that owed Massey Surgical Supply $40,000. Had Baptist not paid him, Massey Surgical Supply might have gone out of business. Soon, Massey was on the Baptist Hospital board.

Massey's business operations grew rapidly, and by the mid-1950s, he owned three drugstores, the surgical supply business at 2110 West End Avenue, a laboratory, a florist at 2111 West End Avenue, a brace shop, and a pesticide factory in South Nashville. A few years later, Massey Surgical Supply had branches in Chattanooga, Kingsport, and Knoxville. His salesmen covered an area from Virginia to Alabama.

Jack Massey, at age fifty-six, sold his surgical supply business in 1961 to Brunswick Corporation, of Chicago, a bowling equipment company that had recently gotten into the health-care business.

Too young to retire, Massey went on to be instrumental in taking three companies to listings on the New York Stock Exchange—Kentucky Fried Chicken, Hospital Corporation of America, and Mrs. Winner's. He is the only person in the history of the New York Stock Exchange to accomplish this.

SWEET SHOPPES

CANDYLAND began in December 1921 as a candy counter at 718 Broadway. Angelo Theodoropoulas, who changed his last name to Anderson when he came to America, leased the store with his brother Sam from Henry Sudekum.

Their business partner was Angelo's nephew, Louis Belios. Decades later, Angelo reminisced about the early years. "For the first two or three years, we just sold ice cream and candy, no sandwiches or nothing." They later catered to the lunch crowd. By 1925 Candyland had moved to 631 Church Street on the southeast corner of Seventh and Church. For the next several decades, chocolates and bonbons, homemade candies and ice cream were popular, as were Candyland sandwiches. In 1943 Candyland had a second location at 2916 West End Avenue.

During the 1960s, students from Hume Fogg High School would pile in the downtown Candyland after school for chocolate drifts and other ice cream treats. They sat in darkly finished wooden booths that were described as having character. Uncle Billy Pappas, an outspoken man who loved to argue, owned Candyland from 1966 until 1982, having bought it from Anderson. After Pappas died in 1985, the second Candyland store on West End was renamed Vandyland. Pappas had owned the property for fifty-seven years.

One Candyland employee, Louise Adcock, was a waitress at the store for fifty-three years before she retired in 1980, shortly before her death. Mack was another mainstay at Vandyland. He even had his photograph on the wall.

Michael J. Schoen bought a majority interest in Candyland in 1982. In December 1987 heating problems became so acute that Schoen was forced to close the store and sell the building. To the disappointment of many Nashvillians, Vandyland closed on December 29, 1986.

A Candyland Ice Cream and Candy parlor operated at 2410 Music Valley Drive for several years in the 1980s.

KAY'S OF NASHVILLE INC., opened in 1940, was a popular ice cream shop for young people at 1522 Church Street. It was owned and operated by Glen Caudle, who came to Nashville in 1939 to open an ice cream plant and several retail stores. He had two older partners who ran similar plants and retail stores in Maryland; Washington, DC; and Chattanooga, Tennessee. Caudle named the Church Street store for his wife, Kay.

When World War II began, Caudle, who knew how to fly, was anxious to enlist. However, because his company was supplying ice cream, milk, and fresh fruit to Camp Campbell, it was considered important to the war effort and he was rejected for military service.

In 1946 Caudle had two stores, the original one on Church Street and a branch store at 2405 Franklin Road. Caudle realized that, following the war, there was a demand in Nashville for higher quality ice cream products. Reacting to this, he sold his ownership position in Kay's of Nashville Inc. to his partners and started a new venture called High's Ice Cream. He sold this high-quality product to hotels, restaurants, food markets, and other outlets in Middle Tennessee. In the 1950 city directory, High's Ice Cream, at 2507 Nolensville Road, was owned by Odell and Mamie Callis.

Charles Mitchell, Confectioners and Bakers was owned by Charles Mitchell, a gracious, courtly gentleman, who never seemed perturbed. When Nashville ladies, in the first forty years of the twentieth century, received a distinctive box of Mitchell's candies for Easter, they knew they were getting the best the city had to offer. Located at 323 Union Street on the southwest corner of that street's intersection with Printer's Alley, the store's proprietor, Charles "Charlie" Mitchell, made sure that his delicious candies were made with the purest ingredients, as his discriminating clientele expected such. He also sold distinctive favors and attractive gifts. In 1905 his advertisement in the *Nashville City Directory* focused on "delicious candies and choice bakery products."

When Mitchell died in January 1908, his sons, Charles S. and George G., succeeded him as co-proprietors. George stayed in back where the candies were made, while Charles took care of their clientele.

When my grandfather, Capt. Matt G. Buckner, MD, was stationed at Fort McClelland, Alabama, in August 1918, he wrote to his wife, Elizabeth, in Nashville, asking her to send Captain Brew a box of Mitchell's candy. Brew and his family had been hospitable to Buckner at Fort McClelland, and he wanted to reciprocate with a special Nashville treat.

By 1953 Charles S. Mitchell had died, leaving George Mitchell to run the store, which he did briefly before retiring in 1954.

When my mother moved out of her home at 1201 Belle Meade Boulevard in the early 1990s, cleaning out the house was a chore. In the basement, one room was filled with empty boxes. There were more Mitchell's candy boxes than there were from any other store.

SWEET SHOP, from about 1949 through the 1950s, was one of the most popular places in town for teenagers. Located at 1601 Twenty-First Avenue South, the Sweet Shop catered to Vanderbilt and high school students.

In about 1949, my brother, Matt Wills, and several of his Montgomery Bell Academy classmates, including Bill Bryan and Bill Estes, were driving near Vanderbilt, when something was yelled at some East High School boys in another car. When Matt realized he was being pursued, he pulled our father's Packard into the curb at the Sweet Shop and locked the doors. Two cars quickly blocked Matt's car. After one of the East boys yanked a doorknob off the Packard, Bryan, wearing his MBA football letter jacket, got out of the car and diffused the situation. Matt still had to explain to our father, Jesse Wills, why a doorknob was missing.

Nick L. and William L. Morris were proprietors of the Sweet Shop in the 1950s. They served a hamburger and a milk shake for fifty cents. By 1959 the Sweet Shop had closed, and the building was occupied by a coin wash laundry.

TELEPHONE COMPANIES

CUMBERLAND TELEPHONE & TELEGRAPH COMPANY was an entrepreneural company founded in 1883 and capitalized at $100,000. Incorporators were E. S. Babcock and E. P. Houston, both of Evansville, Indiana; E. M. Barton, of Chicago; Capt. Paul J. Mars, of Henderson, Kentucky; and James E. Caldwell, James Compton, Capt. W. N. Johns, George Knox, Oscar F. Noel, and Isaac T. Rhea, of Nashville. The company served exchanges in Kentucky, Louisiana, Mississippi, Tennessee, and parts of Illinois and Indiana.

Cumberland Telephone & Telegraph Company.
Collection of Ridley Wills II.

By 1884 it had 2,698 subscribers and established the first long-distance lines in the South between Memphis and Nashville. That same year, James E. Caldwell bought the controlling interest in the company. He sold out after a short time, only to reacquire control of the company in 1890.

By 1891 there were two thousand telephones in Nashville. On June 1 of that year, the company's business office moved from Market Street to North College Street.

Cumberland Telephone & Telegraph did so well that its main rival, the American Telephone and Telegraph Company (AT&T), began acquiring large quantities of its stock. In 1912 Caldwell decided to sell out to AT&T. The merger took place on January 1, 1913.

THEATERS

ADELPHI THEATER, designed by Adolphus Heiman, was located at 431 North Cherry Street. The building, completed at a cost of $25,000, exclusive of decorations, was very handsome with a two-story arched entrance, nineteen-by-twenty-three-foot rooms on both sides, and a brick-paved lobby. The theater had a modern ventilation system and, reputedly, the second-largest stage in America.

When the building, 142 feet by 65 feet, was constructed, several unpaid vendors filed claims against the theater company. Consequently, the theater was sold at public auction, and creditors were finally paid.

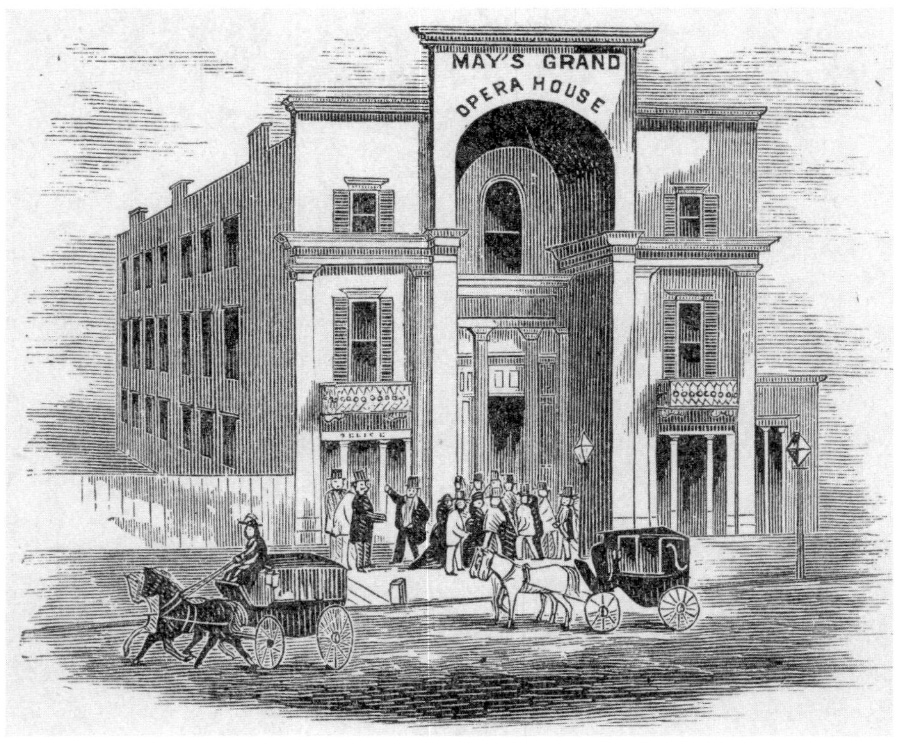

The Adelphi Theater was renamed May's Grand Opera House in 1870.
Metropolitan Nashville Archives.

The property was acquired by the Adelphi Theater Company in 1850 and opened July 1 of that year. The new venture's major stockholders were Anthony Vanleer, J. Walker Percy, and Hugh Kirkman. Its first manager was John Green.

Opening night was a gala affair even though the city was in the throes of a cholera scare. About nine months later, in March 1851, promoter P. T. Barnam brought Jenny Lind, the "Swedish Nightingale," to Nashville to sing. Because the Adelphi Theater was thought to be too small to accommodate the expected crowd, he asked the trustees of the First Presbyterian Church, who had a brand new sanctuary, to allow her performances to be held there in what was the largest meeting place in the city. Not surprisingly, the Calvinists decided not to permit their building to be used for "such an unholy purpose."

Barnam then negotiated with the owners of the Alelphi who agreed to add more seats to accommodate the anticipated crowds at Lind's two performances. A deal was struck, and William Strickland was hired to design the added tier of seats. The new seats were completed barely in time. Dr. Andrew B. Ewing, a prominent Franklin physician, commented on Jenny Lind's visit in an April 1, 1851, letter to his son, Hugh. He wrote, "Jenny Lind is now in Nashville, giving musical concerts at the Adelphi Theater. For the first night's entertainment, $10,000 worth of tickets were sold at auction. The lowest price of a ticket is $5. A goodly number of our people have gone to Nashville to hear her."

Later in the 1850s, Edwin Booth starred in Shakespearean plays to the largest audiences ever assembled in a Nashville theater at the Adelphi. In 1870 new owners changed the name of the theater to May's Grand Opera House.

By 1900 it had been occupied for six years by the Boyle Stock Company, with Tony J. Boyle as the proprietor. The building was devastated by a fire in 1902, but the façade, with its arched entry, survived. The theater was rebuilt and reopened in 1904 as the Bijou Theater.

ALHAMBRA, originally owned by William P. Ready, opened at 216 Fifth Avenue North soon after the Fifth Avenue (also a theater) opened next door in 1909. Both theaters had a music box that blared music the "whole day through." The Alhambra was acquired by the Crescent Amusement Company in about 1913. Crescent ran it for about a decade before it closed in the 1920s.

BELLE MEADE THEATER's construction was announced by Tony Sudekum of the Crescent Amusement Company on November 22, 1938. The theater opened on May 1, 1940. Located immediately to the west of Sudekum's home on Harding Road, the cost of the project, that included four shops in addition to the theater, was $200,000.

The building featured a tower eighty feet tall, with neon tubes and freon, and a new fluorescent-colored light, similar to that being used at the New York World's Fair. The words "Belle Meade Theater" were animated by revolving lights, which flashed as each revolution was completed. At the top of the tower was a polished metal aluminum ball, which picked up colored light and had a sparkling appearance. The exterior finish of the theater was white Georgian marble and red brick, with granite and aluminum trim. Seating capacity was one thousand, and there was a party room on the second floor.

Throughout the 1940s and into the 1950s, E. J. Jordan, the manager of the theater, had a "Happiness Club" every Saturday afternoon, where children could win prizes, including bicycles, and watch a Western. Many a Friday evening in the 1940s, my best friend, Jim Meadows Jr., and I would ride the city bus to the Belle Meade Theater. We then either rode the bus home or, if we had the energy, would walk or run the three miles. At the theater's Happiness Club, patrons could get in for sixteen cents, watch a live stage show and a movie, and sing "Happy Days Are Here Again."

The Sound of Music had the longest run of any movie at the Belle Meade Theater. Jordan held the movie over for six months.

Otus Bentley succeeded Jordan as manager and ran the theater for about ten years during the 1970s and 1980s. By 1988 Phillip Hose was the manager.

After the arrival of multiplex theaters, the Belle Meade Theater closed and in February 1991 was remodeled as the Belle Meade Theater Bookstar, a book superstore that opened October 12, 1991.

BELMONT THEATER located at Twenty-First Avenue South and Blakemore Avenue, was one of a series of Crescent Theaters opened in the 1920s outside the downtown area. It targeted college students in the Hillsboro Village area. W. G. Bush and Company supplied Bush Hollow tile for the exterior. A finish of stucco was applied directly to the tile. The Spanish-style theater was designed by Marr & Holman.

When "talkie" movies arrived in Nashville in 1928, the Belmont quickly switched from silent movies. In 1930 this theater, at an expenditure of $17,000, was newly equipped with the latest and improved Western Electric equipment. Described in an ad that year as a Vitaphone and Movietone theater, it catered to Vanderbilt students. The building was razed in 1962 and was replaced by the Educators Credit Union building.

BIJOU THEATER was built at 431 North Cherry Street (Fourth Avenue North) in about 1902. Earlier, May's Grand Opera House had been

The Beautiful New Belmont Theater

TWENTY-FIRST AVENUE AND BLAKEMORE

Formally Opens Monday, Aug. 31st, at 6:30 P.M.

Exterior View of Belmont Theater and Tony Sudekum, President of the Crescent Amusement Company, Owners of the Theater.

Belmont Theater, August 1925.
Metropolitan Nashville Archives.

on the site. It, however, had been destroyed by fire. The Bijou closed in 1913 due to competition from other theaters, primarily on Fifth Avenue North.

It was resurrected in 1916 when the Bijou Amusement Company, owned by the Milton Starr family, reopened it as the Bijou Theater for Negroes. The theater featured a format that included silent films and live performances and was considered one of the South's leading theaters for African Americans. Ethel Waters, Bessie Smith, and Ma Rainey entertained packed houses there. Special nights were set aside for white audiences to hear such jazz greats as Smith, whose band was named the Jazz Hounds.

The tornado of 1933 lifted the roof of the Bijou and deposited it across the street. Management quickly made temporary repairs and opened the next day.

The Bijou was owned in its later years by Albert Starr, a prominent white businessman. Starr, who became president of the Theater Owners of America, operated other theaters for black Nashvillians, including the Ritz that stood on Jefferson Street near Fisk University.

The Bijou operated until 1957, when it was demolished to make way for the new Municipal Auditorium.

CRESCENT THEATER, located at 233 Fifth Avenue North, was initially called the Twin because two theaters were served by one ticket office. It was one of a number of moving picture theaters that opened on Fifth Avenue in 1907.

Initially owned by W. P. Ready, it was acquired by Tony Sudekum after he formed the Crescent Amusement Company in 1911. He changed the theater's name to the Crescent. The theater later moved to Church Street between Fourth and Fifth Avenues.

In the 1920s, Earle M. Fain was the manager of Loew's Vendome Theater, then one of three hundred theaters operated by Marcus Loew. Fain's motto for Loew's was "Courtesy, Comfort, Cleanliness and, above all, Clean Entertainment." When the Loew's Vendome Theater burned in 1967, the Crescent Theater became the Loew's Crescent Theater.

CRYSTAL THEATER opened in 1906. Its manager in 1915 was W. H. "Bill" Wassman, "The Man Who Made The Nickel Famous." He advertised the Crystal as "Nashville's most popular motion picture theater." This must have been an exaggeration, as the theater closed by 1920.

DIXIE THEATER, housed in a modest building at 222 Fifth Avenue North, opened on April 11, 1907. It was owned by Wiley J. Williams, Henry Sudekum, and Sudekum's son, Anthony "Tony" Sudekum. It was "Mister Tony's" first motion picture theater. The Dixie had a five-cent admission charge that was proudly painted on the ticket window. The theater featured a curved marquee adorned with forty-two electric lights. Inside there were 170 seats, which meant that, if they had a full house, they would pull in $8.50. The projectionist used a small hand-cranked machine to show the first movie, *Montana*, on five reels, each of which lasted seven minutes. The Dixie was called a "nickelodeon" because of the five-cent admission charge. The Dixie closed about 1912.

DONELSON THEATER, a suburban theater, opened on August 8, 1946. It was owned by the Crescent Amusement Company, who purchased it from the original owner. A house formerly stood on the site at 2815 Lebanon Pike.

In 1950 the US Post Office was moved to a room in the rear of the Donelson Theater building. In 1953 Bill Gleaves was the theater manager.

Following him, for about five years beginning later in the 1950s, Lawrence M. Kerrigan, whom the children sometimes called "Meatball," was the manager. At Halloween, Kerrigan once put a casket in front of the theater with a fake body inside that moved. He also played scary music. Of course, this attracted the kids to the horror show inside. Kerrigan later managed a Crescent Theater downtown.

The Donelson Theater closed in the 1970s.

Donelson Theater, Saturday afternoon matinee, 1953. First row, left to right: Phil Gentry, Gary Gentry, Bill Disspaine, L. O. "Buzz" Heidtke, unknown, and unknown. Second row, left to right: unknown, Wanda Jackson, Mike Millspaugh, Joy Harper, and unknowns.
Collection of L. O. "Buzz" Heidtke.

ELITE THEATER was built at 4700 Charlotte Avenue in 1927. Tony Sudekum was its owner and manager. The theater had 824 seats, 663 of which were on the first floor. The remaining 161 were in the balcony. Admission was twenty cents for seats on the main floor and ten cents for balcony seats.

The Elite closed in 1945 and reopened later that year. It closed permanently in 1958. A McDonald's restaurant occupies the site today.

There was an earlier Elite Theater, owned by Crescent Amusement Company. It was at 233 Fifth Avenue North from about 1917 through the early 1920s. Its manager after World War I was James Bradley, who had been in the movie business since 1916. In 1926, an Elite Theater, possibly the same one, was at 813 Monroe Street. It operated there until about 1930.

Fifth Avenue Theater opened in 1909 at 218 Fifth Avenue North. Like all the early moving picture theaters on the street, the Fifth Avenue was acquired by Crescent Amusement Company in 1911.

When Sgt. Alvin C. and Gracie York came to Nashville on their honeymoon in June 1919, they accepted Tony Sudekum's invitation to the Fifth Avenue Theater to attend a Wednesday evening showing of a war movie entitled *The Home Town Girl.* Their pastor, a fundamentalist preacher named Pyle, thought the movie was risqué and convinced the Yorks to cut short their honeymoon and return the next day to their home in Fentress County, Tennessee. They complied and rode the Tennessee Central back to Crossville.

The Fifth Avenue was the longest-lasting theater on Fifth Avenue North. Its last manager was Lee Castleberry, who was there from about 1939 until the thirty-seven-year-old theater closed around 1946.

Green Hills Theater was another Crescent Amusement Company theater. It was located at 4005 Hillsboro Pike, next to the Green Hills Market. The air-conditioned 840-seat theater opened on July 19, 1951, and featured two party rooms, a cry room, concession stand, and spacious parking. The first film shown was *Bedtime for Bonzo*, starring Ronald Reagan. The theater's first manager was Harvey Nokes, the former manager of the Belmont Theater. Ogden Stokes became one of the theater's first ushers. At the end of 1964 and for most of 1965, *My Fair Lady*, the Academy Award–winning movie, was shown.

Martin Theaters bought the Green Hills Theater in 1960. In the late 1970s, multiplex theaters, the electronic explosion, and increasing land values in Green Hills all led to dwindling audiences. Operations at the Green Hills Theater suddenly stopped on June 23, 1978. A sign was put on the ticket office that read "Closed." The building was sold and demolished in 1978 to make way for a new shopping center anchored by a Grace's Shop for Ladies.

Green Hills Theater.
Collection of Grannis Photography.

HILLSBORO THEATER began showing silent pictures at its Hillsboro Road location in 1925. Its proprietor was M. A. Lightman. In the early years of the Depression, the theater closed.

At this time, the Grand Ole Opry was becoming very popular. One day, so many people were pushing and shoving to get in Studio C on the fifth floor of the National Life building that two National Life senior executives were refused admittance to their own building. They suggested that it was time for the Opry to move.

Inglewood Theater, 1950.
Metropolitan Nashville Archives.

A publicity release on October 21, 1934, explained the solution. It read, "The famous Grand Ole Opry has again outdrawn its old clothes ... Saturday night, WSM officials move it to the Hillsboro Theater in Nashville where many will be accommodated. Three different sets of tickets will be issued to admit a person to one hour of the Grand Ole Opry. Already the demand for the first night is taxing the capacity of 2,400 which may now see the Grand Ole Opry weekly. WSM has never charged for admittance to its Opry." Even the Hillsboro Theater space proved inadequate, and in 1936, the Opry moved again, this time to the Dixie Tabernacle on Fatherland Street in East Nashville.

In 1937 the Hillsboro Theater was renamed the Nashville Community Playhouse. Delbert Mann, the director of many cinema and television productions, learned drama at the Nashville Community Playhouse from Fred Coe and Fritz Kleibacker.

After the theater played out, the building's owners moved the theater entrance from 1715 Twenty-First Avenue South to 2104 Belcourt Avenue. The back rows of seats were removed to make a new lobby. The restructured theater took on the new name of Belcourt Cinema in 1966. When the theater closed in 1999, a group called Belcourt YES signed a ten-year lease to save the theater. In 2007 the preservationists purchased the historic theater from Tom Wills for $1.4 million, and now it is venue to cinematic classics, art functions, and film festivals.

INGLEWOOD THEATER was a suburban theater built by Crescent Amusement Company at a cost of $264,000. It opened on April 17, 1950, on Gallatin Pike. Crescent also owned the bowling alley behind the theater. With one thousand seats, the Inglewood Theater quickly became a source of pride to its neighborhood. With the advent of multiplex theaters, the building was closed in December 1977. The site became the home of Joywood Salvage before being torn down and replaced by an Eckerd Drug Store.

KNICKERBOCKER THEATER was a downtown theater that opened in March 1916 with entrances at both 213 Sixth Avenue North and 210 Capitol Boulevard. Its owner was William Henry Wassman. In 1920 the theater was bought by Crescent Amusement Company, owned by Tony Sudekum. The rectangular auditorium had about eleven hundred seats. If one entered from Capitol Boulevard, one would come in facing the screen. If one entered from Sixth Avenue North, one would enter facing the audience.

In 1922 the manager's office was on the Capitol Boulevard side on the mezzanine level. The steps to the mezzanine continued on to the balcony, which had upper and lower sections. The upper balcony had two side sections and a middle section divided by stairs that continued up to the projection booth, which had a door at each end. The first sound movie (containing a musical score and sound effects only) in Tennessee was shown at the Knickerbocker on August 6, 1927. It was *When A Man Loves*, starring John Barrymore. The event was billed as "Tennessee's Sound Premier."

In the early 1920s, Ernest C. Cantrell, the theater manager, used to go to the Knickerbocker every Sunday to hear Dr. William Powell, pastor of First Baptist Church, teach the Allen Fort Memorial Bible Class. Cantrell said this about the theater, "The Knickerbocker is the icicle of the South—keeps the whole town cool." At one point, Porter Woolwine, Tony Sudekum's son-in-law, was manager.

Knickerbocker Theater, 1948, featuring *So Dear to My Heart*, starring Burl Ives and Beulah Bondi. *Collection of Kermit Stengel Jr. Estate.*

During the 1940s and 1950s, the Knickerbocker mostly ran RKO studio pictures. The standard program consisted of a newsreel, a cartoon, sometimes a travelogue, a two-reel comedy, and previews of coming attractions. The Knickerbocker closed on February 4, 1961.

Majestic Theater was opened in 1912 by Andrew N. Johnson, an African American who had arrived in Nashville in 1907 from Alabama with a letter of introduction from Booker T. Washington. His timing was good, as 1907 was the height of a progressive movement in the local African American business community. Johnson, an entrepreneur, became a member of the local Negro Board of Trade and opened the Andrew N. Johnson Funeral Home downtown.

In March 1912 he opened the Majestic Theater in the heart of Nashville's black business district. The *Nashville Globe* described it as a "magnificent playhouse erected at an enormous expense."

The week of June 10, 1912, the Majestic offered five acts of high-class vaudeville, featuring an actor whose nickname was "Chicken Reel." The following March, a debate was held in the theater on the question of whether or not women should be allowed to vote. That same month, Johnson was quoted in the *Nashville Globe* as being perplexed because the black community had not supported his theater as much as he hoped they would. Instead, they continued to patronize the white theaters, paying "as high as $1.00 and sometimes $1.50 to stroll through some side door and make their way to the last story in the house, and strain their eyes and ears to see and hear a performance."

Johnson had built Nashville's first black-owned theater on the expectation that the black community would support it, given the fact that, in white theaters, black patrons were given the "Jim Crow" treatment. Undoubtedly disillusioned, Johnson sold the Majestic Theater to Prof. Dock Liner. As the Bijou Theater for Negroes opened in 1916, it is likely that the Majestic closed by then.

MASONIC THEATER stood at 422 Church Street, separated from the Maxwell House Hotel by an alley. The building had been rebuilt in 1859–60 to include a theater that, over the years, carried various names, including Jenny Wilmore's, the Bijou, the New Masonic, and, finally, toward the close of the nineteenth century, the Masonic. William A. Sheetz managed it until 1900, when he left to manage the Vendome.

He was replaced by T. J. Boyle, who quickly turned the theater over to his wife to manage. She announced that she was booking "shows that have been shut out of the syndicate," referring to a New York company that dominated the dramatic theater business at the time.

The Masonic became the Grand Opera House in 1903, with Mrs. Boyle still its manager. Later in the decade, its name changed to the Grand Theater, which closed in about 1913.

MELROSE THEATER was built by the Crescent Amusement Company in 1942 as a recreational center for AVCO employees and for soldiers at the Classification Center on Thompson Lane. Because building materials were scarce during World War II, the large cooling tower on the roof was purchased from the New York World's Fair that was held in 1939. The theater opened on July 1, 1942, at 2600 Franklin Pike in the Melrose area.

It was leased to the Martin Theater chain in August 1961. The theater shared the same building with the Melrose Bowling Alley and the Melrose Pool Hall that was downstairs in a dark basement.

On August 4, 1983, the Melrose Theater closed its doors, following a showing of the movie *Lovesick*. On December 4, 1983, the *Nashville Banner* announced that the deserted Melrose Theater would be transformed into a studio to produce syndicated television programs of network quality.

ORPHEUM THEATER was built on the west side of Capitol Boulevard after the street was widened from an alley in 1910. The Orpheum was directly across the street from the Knickerbocker and next door to Castner-Knott Department Store. It featured such big traveling shows as Al G. Field's Minstrels and George White's Scandals.

Managed for several years by R. E. Baulch, the Crescent Amusement Company purchased the Orpheum in 1925. During the Depression, the Edward Bellamy Players, who performed there, went broke, so Inez Bassett bought the props and wardrobe for the Hume-Fogg Dramatic Department.

James Nichols was the theater's last manager. The Orpheum closed in about 1938.

PARAMOUNT THEATER was a modern theater built at 721–27 Church Street in 1930. Opening-night festivities attracted twenty-five hundred people who saw *Fast and Loose*, a sophisticated, audacious comedy starring Mirian Hopkins, a gorgeous blonde star of the New York stage.

The theater featured a $50,000 three-manual Wurlitzer organ console that rode on hydraulic lifts up to stage level between shows. The organ was played first by C. Sharp Minor.

In the 1930s, children could ride the streetcar to town for a nickel and get in the Paramount and its Popeye Club for a dime. On Saturday morning, August 14, 1948, American singing star Johnny Desmond performed at a "Teentimers Club" held at the Paramount. He had two big hits in 1946,

Paramount Theater and Zibart's Bookstore, 1960s.
Metropolitan Nashville Archives.

"Don't You Remember Me" (#21) and "Guilty" (#12). The live program was broadcast coast-to-coast on the Mutual Network.

Until integration, the Paramount had a side entrance on the alley for African Americans, who had to sit in the top balcony to see movies. The theater was sold in 1978 to the Martin Theater chain, of Columbus, Georgia, and torn down in the 1980s.

PRINCESS THEATER was at 511 Church Street between the Jackson Building and McKendree Methodist Church. Owned by Tony Sudekum, who considered it his favorite, the theater was a vaudeville house in the 1920s because Sudekum had a fondness for vaudeville. On New Year's Eve 1926, there was a celebration at midnight that featured

Herbert Clifton in his *Travesties of the Weaker Sex*. In the 1920s, Tony's brother, Harry Sudekum, who had graduated from the American School of Osteopathy in 1909, managed the theater. By the 1950s, the movie house, which had a long entrance to the auditorium, was considered second tier. The Princess was torn down and later the Cain-Sloan Department Store was built on the site.

REX THEATER, at 214 Fifth Avenue North, opened in 1914. On the pavement in front of the theater, the contractor laid tiles showing the name of the theater, "Rex," and the words "5 cent motion pictures." It became known for the Western movies it featured.

The Rex's manager in the early 1920s was twenty-two-year-old Theo D. Mousson, who also managed the Rialto Theater. At that time, Mousson had just redecorated the Rex. Kermit Stengel Jr., Tony Sudekum's grandson, remembered that popcorn vendors walked up and down the aisles at the Rex shouting, "Popcorn!" out loud. Kermit added, "It was not a first-class theater." J. M. Lawrence was manager from the late 1920s through the 1940s. The Rex closed in about 1953, when Bruce Hooper was manager.

RIALTO THEATER was yet another Crescent Amusement Company Theater. It was located at 236 Fifth Avenue North. Rialto had a short life span, opening in about 1920 and closing by 1931.

RITZ THEATER, located at 1714 Jefferson Street close to Fisk and Tennessee State Universities, it was the premier African American theater offering first-run movies sometimes before they appeared downtown at the white theaters.

Later owned by Alfred Starr, it had a seating capacity of 644. The Ritz continued to attract movie-goers until the late 1960s, although its Jefferson Street facility closed circa 1970.

In 1973, a new Ritz Theater was built further down Jefferson Street in the direction of Tennessee State University. It remained open until 1980. In June 2001 the theater building was razed.

STRAND movie house advertised itself in the 1915 Vanderbilt *Commodore* yearbook as "Nashville's Leading Moving Picture Theater." Located at 235 Fifth Avenue North, the new theater featured an orchestra, "superior Photo-Plays," and good ventilation. Its owner was W. P. Ready. In 1921 Luther W. Jacobs was president of Strand Theater. He advertised it as "The Little House with the Big Show." Jacobs had an excellent manager, Carson Bradford, "one of the best showmen Nashville ever had." The Strand closed about 1930, when William O'Neil was manager.

TENNESSEE THEATER was the last major theater to open in downtown Nashville. Located in the Sudekum Building at the corner of Sixth Avenue and Church Street and owned by the Crescent Amusement Company, it was called "the Showcase of the South" in 1953.

On April 11, 1957, the Crescent Amusement Company held an anniversary gala at the Tennessee to celebrate fifty years of motion pictures in Nashville. Tony Sudekum did not live to attend the celebration, as he died in 1946.

The Tennessee Theater ceased to exist when the twelve-story Sudekum Building, at 555 Church Street, was demolished by developer Tony Giarrantana in November 1992 to make room for a high-rise condominium.

VENDOME THEATER opened on October 2, 1887, as a first-class playhouse. It stood at 613 Church Street, next to Watkins Institute. One of its early stockholders and managers was J. Oliver Milsom, who also managed the Grand.

W. A. Sheetz was the Vendome manager at the beginning of the twentieth century. He frequently brought New York plays to Nashville with casts that included some of the leading actors and actresses of the day.

Joseph Jefferson appeared often in Nashville. Once, in 1894, he appeared as Rip Van Winkle. On one visit he said, "When I play an engagement in Nashville, I like it to be on Saturday night. The reason is this. On Sunday morning toward noon, I leave my hotel room [in the Maxwell House] and stroll up Church Street to the 'steamboat towers' [referring to the First Presbyterian Church]; the most beautiful women in the world are to be seen leaving that church after services are over."

Ethel Barrymore also appeared there. The Vendome burned in 1902 but reopened before the end of the year with its first attraction: Al G. Field's Minstrels. As early as 1903, the Vendome, which was beautiful but relatively small, began showing moving pictures of automobile races in Europe.

The Vendome became Loew's Vendome in 1920 when Marcus Lowe bought the theater and added it to his three-hundred-theater chain. His Nashville manager was Earle M. Fain. As time went by, the Nashville public increasingly called the theater "Loew's."

Several years later, Loew's management entered an agreement with Tony Sudekum under which his Princess Theater down the street became the only "vaudeville" house in the city and Loew's got the pick of the first-run movies.

On New Year's Eve 1926 Loew's had a big stage show at midnight with Ned Jacobs as master of ceremonies. The show included Rosa Gallagher,

Woodland Street, Five Points, showing the Woodland Theater on the right. *Collection of Grannis Photography.*

The Four Abbott Dancers of the "Moulin Rouge" from Chicago, and Carl Lorriane and his Famous Orchestra.

Loew's had a side entrance for African Americans until the theater was integrated in the early 1960s. Loew's burned again in 1967 and was not rebuilt. The Nashville Public Library occupies the site today.

WOODLAND THEATER, a Spanish-style building on Woodland Street, advertised itself in 1920 as "Nashville's Ace Suburban Theater." It had different feature shows three times a week.

The Woodland Theater closed in 1964 when it was converted into the Woodland Sound Studio, where Johnny Cash, Charlie Daniels, Barbara Mandrell, and others recorded.

TIRE STORES

BLACKWOOD TIRE AND BATTERY COMPANY was a highly successful company founded on August 1, 1912, in a little stall at 1912 Broadway by Herman O. "Hurry On" Blackwood. A North Carolina native, he had moved to Nashville from Winchester, Tennessee, with limited resources. The little space he occupied would hold only one car, so his customers had to "get in line" and take their turn coming in. Blackwood's courteous manner, his straightforward way of doing business, and his good service soon allowed him to enlarge his business.

In 1922 the State of Tennessee opened a landing strip between Shute Lane and The Hermitage called Blackwood Field. It was named for the already successful H. O. Blackwood, who had contributed $1,000 of the $4,000 needed for the air field's construction.

A 1921 cartoon in the *Nashville Tennessean* said this of Blackwood, "There's not a better 'boss' this side of the Mason-Dixon Line, but if you work for him it is understood that you must 'Hurry On.'"

By 1926 "Hurry On" Blackwood had seven stores in Nashville, selling gasoline, tires, and batteries and offering road service. Blackwood Tire and Battery Company was the largest distributor of Goodyear tires in the country and employed over sixty-five people.

Blackwood sold his company in about 1930 to Goodyear Tire and Rubber Company. By 1933 Goodyear had changed the name to Goodyear Service Inc., with D. M. Warren as manager.

Universal Tire Company was founded in October 1944. James R. Pickel had been transferred to Nashville from Columbus, Georgia, to manage B. F. Goodrich's Nashville store. One of his early clients was Super Service Freight Line, owned by Robert M. Crichton. One day, Crichton suggested that they and another friend, Eldridge Doubleday, start an independent tire dealership. After all, they would have at least one solid client, Crichton's freight line.

When the three men founded Universal Tire and Appliance Company, they leased a small Shell Service Station on the southwest corner of Twelfth and Demonbreun as their headquarters. Quickly, Crichton and Pickel bought out Doubleday's interest. On a handshake, Crichton and Pickel then agreed that each of them would own 50 percent of the business that Pickel would manage. There was no written agreement.

Universal Tire and Appliance sold tires to commercial, retail, and wholesale clients. In 1948 Crichton and Pickel decided to go into the tire recapping business and purchased two tire molds. They began the recapping operation in a nearby house they leased. Due to heavy demand, recapping was profitable, encouraging Crichton and Pickel to construct their own recapping facility for what was called "hot cap" retreads.

New tire sales also grew, and by 1953, Universal Tire and Appliance was leasing four warehouses in Nashville in addition to the main warehouse they had built at Twelfth and Demonbreun, where they had or would eventually acquire four acres.

In 1955 two more warehouses came on line. Three years later, Universal Tire and Appliance formed a retread department and became one of the first franchises of Bandag Inc. The company's regional expansion dreams became a reality in 1960, when Universal Tire opened a store in Pickel's hometown of Chattanooga.

In 1966 James R. Pickel's only son, James R. "Jimmy" Pickel Jr., was a lieutenant in the US Army, stationed at Fort Bliss, Texas. When James Pickel died of a heart attack, Jimmy Pickel was given an honorable discharge two months early and came home, realizing that he and his mother owned 50 percent of Universal Tire and that he needed to get in the business to protect his family's interest. Meanwhile, Crichton had named Ira Reese, an employee, president of the company.

Jimmy Pickel asked Reese for a job and was shocked when Reese said he didn't have a position for him. Pickel then went to see Crichton, who intervened on his behalf. Jimmy Pickel went to work for the company in 1966 as a commercial tire salesman. By 1968 Universal had two stores in Nashville and the one in Chattanooga. Sales in 1970 totaled $4 million.

After Crichton's death in 1971, the Pickel family purchased his 50 percent interest in the company, This was accomplished with the help of Andrew Benedict and P. D. Houston Jr., of First American National Bank. At Benedict's suggestion, the Pickel family got an SBA loan of $100,000 that enabled them to gain complete control of the company.

With the purchase complete, twenty-nine-year-old James R. Pickel Jr. became president and chairman of the board in 1971. One of his early changes was to change the name of the company to Universal Tire Company.

The 1970s saw steady growth for Universal Tire Company. Universal signed a franchise agreement with Firestone Tire and Rubber Company in 1971 that included the Nashville, Chattanooga, and new Columbia store. Universal was also representing Dayton and Michelin Tires and was the second-largest Dayton Tire dealer in the world. Universal Tire additionally sold the GE brand of appliances and was GE's largest dealer in Tennessee until the advent of the big-box stores. Universal opened stores in Columbia (1971) and Knoxville (1974) and a truck alignment division in Nashville (1976). In 1979 company sales had grown to $17.5 million.

The accelerated pace continued during the 1980s despite a recession in 1979 and 1980. Universal opened a Murfreesboro Road retail store in 1981 and a new facility in Madisonville, Kentucky, in 1982; commercial sales and service offices in Memphis and Jackson, both in 1983; a sixth Nashville retail store in Green Hills in 1984; and a commercial sales and service facility in Crossville, also in 1984. Growth in the 1980s came partially through the above-named expansions but also through increased store volume.

James R. Pickel Jr.'s conservative business philosophy was to expand out of cash flow, not by borrowing from a bank.

In 1985 Universal Tire was one of seven North American dealers to be named "Classic Dealer" by Bandag Inc. Later in the year, having run out of space at its Twelfth and Demonbreun Warehouse, Universal leased a new forty-eight-thousand-square-foot warehouse on Vulcan Drive. A retreading facility that Universal Tire opened in Trenton, Georgia, in 1986, moved to Chattanooga three years later. Two more retail stores opened in Nashville in 1987, one on Harding Place and the other in the Rivergate area. Rapid growth caused the company to lease an even larger distribution center in 1991, a ninety-thousand-square-foot facility in Space Park South.

Universal Tire's stockholders, all family members, elected Henry Hillenmeyer, Hanley Sayers, David Wood, and Frank Woods as company directors in July 1991. By then, Universal Tire was the largest independent tire dealer in the state and one of the top commercial tire companies in North America. A year later, the company moved its corporate offices to Space Park South.

By 1996 Universal Tire had twenty locations and eight retread plants doing well over one thousand truck retreads a day. The company had locations in nine Tennessee cities; one in Madisonville, Kentucky; three in Alabama at Birmingham, Decatur, and Huntsville; and one in Atlanta, Georgia.

By 1997 James R. Pickel Jr. had talked with his sons, James R. Pickel III and Harold "Hal" Pickel, to gauge their interest in becoming third-generation owners of Universal Tire. As neither son had a strong interest, Pickel negotiated the sale of the company to Bandag Inc. James R. Pickel Jr. had run Universal Tire for twenty-seven years and was ready to turn the reigns over to someone else. He retired from the business with the satisfaction of knowing that he and his associates had grown the company from having sales of $4 million in 1971 to $70 million in 1997.

When Universal Tire was sold in 1998, it was the largest independent tire company in Tennessee and one of the top ten commercial dealerships in North America.

WHOLESALE COMPANIES

McWHORTER-WEAVER & COMPANY, a wholesale hardware company, had as its officers in 1915 J. L. McWhorter, president; William C. "Will" Weaver, vice president; Weaver Harris, treasurer; Felix R. Cheatham, secretary; and C. E. Freeland, sales manager. The business was then located at 306–308 Second Avenue North. The company's motto was "The House That Makes the Price." When McWhorter died, Weaver succeeded him as president.

Weaver's son, William C. "Bill" Weaver Jr., became associated with McWhorter-Weaver & Company in 1933, selling refrigerators door-to-door during the Depression. Bill subsequently became treasurer and president of the company, before accepting a position, in 1940, as loan supervisor in the mortgage loan division of the investment department at National Life and Accident Insurance Company. Even then, Bill would walk down the hill from National Life every afternoon and help out for an hour or so at McWhorter-Weaver & Company, then located at 178–80 Second Avenue North.

With his only son at National Life, Will Weaver knew he needed more management help. In 1940 he employed Lawrence Joseph "Larry" Mulhall as sales manager of the company's appliance division that sold both wholesale hardware and electrical appliances. In June 1942 Mulhall became general sales manager of the company, but six months later left to enter the navy as a lieutenant junior grade.

When Bill Weaver Jr. entered the army and was stationed in Asheville, North Carolina, during World War II, the company had hard times, and Will Weaver must have felt that he had no supporting cast. His focus was to hang on to his dealerships until the war was over and things could return to normal. Will Weaver remained active in the business until a few weeks before his death on June 14, 1943.

When Larry Mulhall was discharged from active duty on September 20, 1945, he returned to McWhorter-Weaver & Company as a partner to fill a leadership vacuum. Will Weaver's nephew, Edmund Weaver, was there to help him. On February 1, 1947, three significant events took place: the company was incorporated, Larry Mulhall was elected president, and Bill Weaver Jr. (who had been president) became board chairman.

In 1949 McWhorter-Weaver & Company advertised their Philco portable radios for $29.95 and up in the Vanderbilt football program. "Why Miss Any of the Games? Carry a Philco Portable With You Wherever You Go," read the ad. A year later, McWhorter-Weaver was also selling Philco television sets.

In the 1950s, McWhorter-Weaver & Company was owned by T. L. Herbert & Sons. Mulhall's management team at McWhorter-Weaver & Company consisted of himself as president, W. B. Herbert Jr. and John S. Herbert as vice presidents, B.L. Bradley as secretary and comptroller, and R. D. Herbert Jr. as treasurer. The company was then selling Youngstown kitchens, Zenith radios, household appliances, and electrical equipment. Later, Mulhall repurchased the company from T. L. Herbert & Sons.

In 1970 Mulhall moved his company from Second Avenue North to 1101 Menzler Drive off Murfreesboro Pike. McWhorter-Weaver & Company was then the dealer for Gibson appliances and Zenith television sets. By 1976 the company retrenched by moving again to 1123 Church Street. By 1978 the company had closed.

NEELY, HARWELL & COMPANY was a wholesale dry goods house located at 324 Public Square in Nashville.

The 1896 *Nashville City Directory* shows Samuel K. Harwell as one of the four principals in Warren, Neely & Company. Sam remained a junior partner at Warren, Neely & Company (which had been founded in 1893) until 1905.

That year, he and John W. Weatherly left Warren, Neely & Company to form Weatherly, Harwell & Company with William E. Park and Beverly R. McKinnie. Located at 116 Public Square, this company was also a wholesale house.

By 1908 Weatherly and McKinnie had dropped out of the firm that was then renamed Harwell, Park & Company. The senior partners were Sam Harwell and William E. Park. Associated with them were Benjamin F. Jones, Charles W. Jones, and Thomas H. Young.

In 1910 or 1911, Harwell, Park & Company closed, and Harwell and his old mentor from Warren, Neely & Company, George M. Neely, formed Neely, Harwell & Company, a wholesale dry goods house located at 324 Public Square. For the next thirty years, Harwell ran the company, which for many years sent drummers (travelling salesmen) fanning out over Middle Tennessee, Northern Alabama, and Southern Kentucky, with trunks of goods for small stores. They traveled either by train or in a rented hack, usually staying in the homes of the merchants they serviced.

By 1921, with automobiles more prevalent, Neely, Harwell & Company's reach had extended to nine states. On Thanksgiving Day that year, the company gave each of its employees a holiday turkey.

When Neely died in 1929, Harwell bought his interest in the company for $50,000 and became the sole proprietor. Harwell died in April 1944, two days after celebrating his eightieth birthday. He had been one of the city's most substantial citizens, and his company was one of the best-known wholesale dry goods houses in Nashville.

Sam K. Harwell's son, Sam K. Harwell Jr., became a member of Neely, Harwell & Company in 1922 after graduating from the University of the South in 1921. He became the company's general manager in 1933 and was a director of the Wholesale Dry Goods Institute in 1939–40. Sam Harwell Jr. died of a heart attack on August 22, 1944, only three months after his father died. He was only forty-three.

After his brother and his father died, Robert Ewing Harwell became president of Neely, Harwell & Company. He was joined by his brother, Coleman A. Harwell, who joined the firm as a vice president upon his discharge from the US Army following World War II. In 1948 Coleman Harwell left to become vice president and editor of the *Nashville Tennessean*, where he had been executive editor from 1937 until 1943.

In 1961, during Robert E. Harwell's presidency, Neely, Harwell & Company built a small three-story building on a parking lot adjacent to their two existing buildings at 324 and 326 Public Square.

The new building's address was 328 Public Square. The next spring, Mayor Ben West announced that the city would build Victory Memorial

Neely, Harwell & Company, Thanksgiving Day 1921.
Morton B. "Mote" Howell is in the first row, fourth from the left.
Sam K. Harwell Jr. is immediately to Howell's right.
Collection of Robert E. Harwell Jr.

Bridge over the Cumberland River. The proposed bridge's right-of-way on the west side of the river would take the company's property on the east side of the Public Square.

After years of waiting for the hammer to drop, Neely, Harwell & Company moved in 1973 across the river to new headquarters at 219 Russell Street. The next year, the city's Urban Renewal program razed all the nineteenth-century buildings on the east side of the Public Square.

By the 1970s, the glory days of wholesale houses had long gone. Nevertheless, Neely, Harwell & Company stayed in business through the

1980s. In 1986 William B. Harwell was president; Robert E. Harwell Jr., vice president; and J. Walton Garrett, secretary-treasurer.

By 1991 a grandson of the founder, Robert E. Harwell Jr., was president. It was his duty to close the business. He did so in 1993, the one hundredth anniversary of the founding of Warren, Neely & Company, the predecessor of Neely, Harwell & Company.

Selected Bibliography

Adams, George Rollie, and Ralph Jerry Christian. *Nashville: A Pictorial History.* Virginia Beach: Donning Company, 1988.

Aiken, Leona Taylor. *Donelson, Tennessee: Its History and Landmarks*. Kingsport, TN: Kingsport Press, 1968.

Battle, Bob. "Apparel Firm Consolidating, Moving." *Nashville Banner*, February 12, 1990.

Batts, William O. *Private Preparatory Schools For Boys in Tennessee Since 1867.* Nashville: Parthenon Press, 1957.

Beasley, Kay. "Moon Drug a Nashville Tradition." *Nashville Banner*, 1991.

———. "Old Transfer Station was Hub of Activity." *Nashville Banner*, 1990s.

———. "Turkey Gifts for the Holidays in 1921." *Nashville Banner*, November 26, 1986.

Booker, George. "100 Years of Bread." *Nashville Banner*, May 7, 1981.

Brandau, Susan. "Shop's Demise Revives Old Memories." *Tennessean*, December 30, 1973.

Bridges, John, and Bruce Dobie. "Where's the Veal?" *Nashville Scene*, October 8, 1992.

Brown, Campbell H., ed. *The Reminiscences of Newton Cannon: First Sergeant, 11th Tennessee Cavalry, C.S.A.* Franklin, TN: Carter House Association, 1963.

Business Week. "Regionals Put It into Narrow Focus." August 7, 1971.

Campanella, Roy. *It's Good to Be Alive.* Lincoln: University of Nebraska Press, 1959.

Carey, Bill. *Fortunes Fiddles & Fried Chicken*. Franklin: Hillsboro Press, 2000.

Cason, Albert. "Equitable Has Part in Third of New Issues." *Nashville Tennessean*, January 8, 1955.

———. "Equitable In 2nd Place." *Nashville Tennessean*, March 26, 1963.

———. "Equitable Plans Spur Purchases." *Nashville Tennessean*, December 5, 1958.
———. "Kusan Inc. Offered for Sale in Quest for Capital." *Tennessean*, March 16, 1988.
———. "Morton & Company To Sell Part of Busness." *Nashville Tennessean*, May 31, 1972.
———. "Store Becomes New Office Building." *Tennessean*, March 23, 1983.
———. "200,000 Spur Share Sales Expected Here." *Nashville Banner*, February 4, 1959.
Center, Linda. "Chancery Court, the Adelphi, and Adolphus Heiman." *Nashville Historical Newsletter*, July–August 1998.
Clayton, W. W. *History of Davidson County, Tennessee*. Philadelphia: J. W. Lewis & Co., 1880.
Coats, Terry L. *Next Stop on Grandpa's Road: History & Architecture of NC&StL Railway & Terminals*. Nashville: Author's Corner LLC, 2009.
Crowe, Jesse Crawford. "The Origin and Development of Tennessee's Prison Problem, 1831–1871." *Tennessee Historical Quarterly*, Vol. XV, No. 2, June 1956.
Crutchfield, James A. and Robert Holladay. *Franklin, Tennessee's Handsomest Town.* Franklin, TN: Hillsboro Press, 1999.
Cunningham, Gary. "The King of Cuisine, Mario Ferrari Dies at 80." *Green Hills News*, December 20, 2012.
Daily American. "The Dummy Railroad." April 22, 1888.
Darnell, Cathy. "What's So Special About Calvert's?—Why, Tradition, Of Course." *Tennessean*, April 13, 1980.
Davis, Louise. "Nashville Had A Zoo!" *Tennessean Magazine*, June 18, 1972.
———. "Mills' Love Affair 90 Years Strong." *Tennessean*, November 7, 1982.
Durham, Walter T., and James W. Thomas. *A Pictorial History of Sumner County, Tennessee, 1786–1986*. Sumner County Historical Society, 1986.
Dyer, Gus W. *Library of American Lives, Tennessee Edition*. Washington, DC: Historical Record Association, 1949.
Egerton, John. *Nashville: The Faces of Two Centuries, 1780–1980*. Nashville: PlusMedia, 1979.
Ferguson, Carrie. "Mario's Loses Its Four-Star Ranking." *Tennessean*, January 14, 1993.
Fitzgerald, Ross. "City Unchallenged Leader in South Financial Circles." *Nashville Banner*, May 30, 1955.
———. "Phillips Buttorff Store Sold." *Nashville Banner*, September 1, 1958.
———. "Spur Oil, Arkansas Firm Merge." *Nashville Banner*, September 8, 1960.

Frank, Fedora. *Beginnings on Market Street*. Nashville: privately printed, 1976.

Garrison, Beverly G. "A Silver Celebration at Mario's Ristorante." *Tennessean*, April 16, 1990.

Hance, Mary. "Elegant Display Saved." *Nashville Banner*, July 10, 1992.

———. "New Herbert Building Reflects Firm's Business." *Nashville Banner*, October 15, 1988.

Harwell, Coleman. *The Centennial History of Westminster Presbyterian Church*. Nashville: Westminster Presbyterian Church, 1979.

Haun, Nicholas F. "Female State Prisoners in Tennessee, 1831–1979." *Tennessee Historical Quarterly*, Vol. XXXIX, No. 4, Winter 1980.

Ikard, Robert W. *Just for Fun: The Story of AAU Women's Basketball*. Fayetteville: University of Arkansas Press, 2005.

J. C. Bradford & Company Timeline. "A Business Built on Relationships." 1998. Collection of Lillian (Mrs. J. C. Jr.) Bradford.

"J. C. Bradford & Company Celebrates 60th Anniversary." Company release, May 22, 1987. Collection of Lillian (Mrs. J. C. Jr.) Bradford.

J. C. Bradford's reminiscences of A. M. Burton. Undated. Collection of Lillian (Mrs. J. C. Jr.) Bradford.

James, Jesse. "Mario's Restaurant Leaves Its Own Mark on Development of Eateries in Nashville." *Tennessean*, January 19, 1986.

———. "Mario's at Top of Totem Pole of Signature Restaurants." *Tennessean*, March 20, 1988.

Jesse French & Sons Piano Company, "Jesse French Piano Company, Nashville, TN," www.frenchfamilyassoc.com.

Jones, Crystal Hill, Naomi C. Manning, and Melanie J. Meadows. *Nashville's Inglewood*. Charleston, SC: Arcadia Publishing, 2009.

Kaplowitz, Craig A. "A Breath of Fresh Air: Segregation, Parks, and Progressivism in Nashville, Tennessee, 1900–1920." *Tennessee Historical Quarterly*, Vol. LVII, No. 2, Fall 1998.

Kelly, Sarah Foster. *West Nashville: Its People and Environs*. Nashville: S. F. Kelley, 1987.

Kenyon, Nellie. "Old Landmark in Bridge Path." *Nashville Tennessean*, March 31, 1962.

Kisber, Matthew. "Vetern Broker Recalls Depression." *Jackson Sun*, July 19, 1981.

Lamon, Lester C. *Black Tennesseans, 1900–1930*. Knoxville: University of Tennessee Press, 1977.

Loggins, Kirk. "Suit Says Bank Cemented Brickmaker's Doom." *Tennessean*, August 10, 1988.

Lovett, Bobby L. *The African-American History of Nashville, Tennessee, 1780–1930*. Fayetteville, AR: Univ. of Arkansas Press, 1999.

———. "Leaders of African-American Nashville." Project of the 1995 Nashville Conference on African-American Culture and History.

"Maitre D' of Brass Rail Returns After Eight Years in New Orleans." *Tennessean*, May 15, 1983.

McCampbell, Candy. "Harrison Flower Shop To Close." *Tennessean*, November 22, 1984.

McPherson, Sam. "Equitable Buys $4 Million County School Bond Issue." *Nashville Banner*, September 27, 1961.

Miller, John. "Bradford's Satisfaction: 'Helping People Create Estates'." *Nashville Tennessean*, January 8, 1967.

Moriarty, Megan. "Generation to Generation: Making Things Happen." *City Paper*, April 29, 2002.

Morrow, Sara. "A Brief History of Theater in Nashville, 1807–1970." *Tennessee Historical Quarterly*, Vol. XXX, No. 2, Summer 1971.

Morton-Young, Tommie. *Black America Series: Nashville, Tennessee*. Charleston, SC: Arcadia Publishing, 2000.

Nashville American. "The President's Coffee." October 20, 1907.

Nashville Banner. "B. O. Curry Jr. Named To Board." March 23, 1961.

———. "Death Claims H. W. Buttorff." September 17, 1915.

———. "Equitable Purchases Trust Building." April 25, 1949.

———. "$50,000 Blaze Destroys Colonial Dinner Club," October 22, 1946.

———. "Fit For A King." October 25, 1907.

———. "Herbert Rodgers Rites Slated For Thursday." February 20, 1963.

———. "Homey Old Faucon's With Its Famous Salad To Close." April 1926.

———. "Investment Giant 'Peck' Owen Dies: Services Monday." November 5, 1983.

———. "Nashville's Welcome to the Nation's Chief." October 21, 1907.

———. "Noted Architect Robert Rodgers Services Friday." July 4, 1994.

———. "Pennington Bend Gets Opryland," October 13, 1969.

———. "President Roosevelt Likes It." October 26, 1907.

———. "Promises to Remember Hermitage in Message." October 22, 1907.

———. "Spur Company Changes Hands." December 16, 1958.

———. "W. J. Anderson Elevated by Investment Firm." April 23, 1952.

Nashville City Schools. "Nashville's Food Heritage." Community Study Series, 1976.

Nashville Globe. "Hon. Napier Register-Treas"; "Baseball All-Stars vs Greenwood Giants, Greenwood Park." August 1, 1913.
Nashville Tennessean. "Brownlee O. Currey Funeral Tomorrow." February 23, 1952.
———. "Bush and Herbert Helped Make History on the Cumberland." January 16, 1972.
———. "Death of Samuel K. Harwell Sr." April 22, 1944.
———. "Harwell Rites At Home Today." April 23, 1944.
———. "Houghland Voted to Oil Hall of Fame." September 6, 1959.
———. "Rich-Schwartz to Relocate in West End Site." October 2, 1955.
———. "S. K. Harwell Jr. Rites Thursday. August 23, 1944.
———. "Saga of City Trams Portrayed; Radnor Makes Last Run." February 2, 1941.
———. "Temco Rose From Ashes." September 4, 1960.
———. "$200,000 Blaze Sweeps Lumber and Stone Firms." April 3, 1928.
Nashvillian. "Mario's Selected to Magnificent Seven." August 22, 1991.
Neal, Richard R. "Mud Tavern." *Nashville Retrospect*, January 2010.
Nichol, Betsy. "Green Hills Market Closing Shop." *Tennessean*, June 1, 1989.
Norvell, William E., II. *Norvell & Wallace: Nashville's 100-Year-Old Lumber Company*. Nashville: privately printed, 1984.
Oliver, Robert. "A Crumbling Fortress: The Tennessee Lunatic Asylum, 1837–1865." *Tennessee Historical Quarterly*, Vol. LIV, No. 2, Summer 1995.
Parish, Sister, Albert Hadley, and Christopher Petkanas. *Parish-Hadley: Sixty Years of American Design*. Boston: Little, Brown and Company, 1995.
Pendergrass, Mark. *Uncommon Grounds: The History of Coffee and How It Transformed Our World*. New York: Perseus Books Group, 2010.
Pettus, Allen. "Equitable On Deal To Buy Insurance Co." *Nashville Tennessean*, March 19, 1953.
Powers, Elvira J. *Hospital Pencillings: Being a Diary While in Jefferson General Hospital, Jeffersonville, Ind., and Others at Nashville, Tennessee, as Matron and Visitor*. Boston: Edward L. Mitchell, 1866.
Preston, Bill, Jr. "Brass Rail Stables Moves A Few Doors Down Alley." *Nashville Tennessean*, December 15, 1972.
Putnam, A. W. *History of Middle Tennessee.* Knoxville: University of Tennessee Press, 1971.
Quigley, Linda. "Cheesecake Satisfies White Chocolate Lovers." *Tennessean*, October 26, 1988.
Randolph, Milton. "Equitable Securities Corp. Buys Missouri Insurance Firm Control." *Nashville Banner*, September 23, 1954.

———. "Quotes & Unquotes." *Nashville Banner*, August 8, 1947.
———. "Quotes & Unquotes." *Nashville Banner*, April 6, 1950.
Roberts, Ken, Jr. "One For the Road." *Nashville Scene*, June 13, 1996.
Rose, Kenneth. "Jenny Lind, Diva." *Tennessee Historical Quarterly*, Vol. VIII, No. 1, March 1949.
Roseman, Jean. *Shalom Nashville: A Jewish History*. Nashville: Eveready Press, 2010.
Scribner, Christopher M. "Nashville Offers Opportunity: The Nashville Globe and Business as a Means of Uplift, 1907–1913." *Tennessee Historical Quarterly*, Vol. LIV, No. 1, Spring 1995.
Shayne, Jonathon A., and Anthony Werthan. *Werthan: A History*. Nashville: Jonathan A. Shayne & Anthony L. Werthan, 2009.
Shield News. Opryland ground breaking issue, vol. 6, no. 30, June 30, 1970.
Stewart, David Marshall. "William T. Berry and His Fabulous Bookstore: An Early Nashville Literary Emporium Without Parallel." *Tennessee Historical Quarterly*, vol. 37, Spring 1978.
Stewart, Elmer. "Kusan Inc. Celebrating 25th Anniversary." *Nashville Tennessean*, December 27, 1971.
Tennessean. "Townes Leaves A Warm Legacy." July 29, 2012.
Thomason, Philip. "The Men's Quarter of Downtown Nashville." *Tennessee Historical Quarterly*, Vol. XLI, No. 1, Spring 1982.
Turf, Field and Farm. "Horse Training Notes." April 9, 1886.
Van West, Carroll. *Tennessee Encyclopedia of History and Culture*. Nashville: Rutledge Hill Press (Tennessee Historical Society), 1998.
Walker, Hugh. "Reupen Wasn't Bookish, But He Founded the Store." *Nashville Tennessean*, 1972.
Wooldridge, John. *History of Nashville, Tenn*. Nashville: Published for H. W. Crew by the Publishing House of the Methodist Episcopal Church, South, 1890.
Wyatt, Gene. "The Last Picture Show." *Tennessean*, February 28, 1991.
Zepp, George. "Hale Hospital Nurtured Thousands of City's Blacks." *Tennessean*, May 21, 2003.
———. "Candyland Stirs Sweet Memories for Many." *Tennessean*, October 29, 2003.
———. "Cross Keys Recalled for Food, Liquor by the Drink, Protests." *Tennessean*, January 7, 2004.
Zuccarello, John, Jr. "Wagon Wheel." *Nashville Retrospect*, November 2010.